Philosophy of the Ancient Maya

D1566285

Studies in Comparative Philosophy and Religion

Series Editor: Douglas Allen, University of Maine

This series explores important intersections within and between the disciplines of religious studies and philosophy. These original studies will emphasize, in particular, aspects of contemporary and classical Asian philosophy and its relationship to Western thought. We welcome a wide variety of manuscript submissions, especially works exhibiting highly focused research and theoretical innovation.

Recent Titles in This Series

Philosophy of the Ancient Maya: Lords of Time, by Alexus McLeod
Making Space for Knowing: A Capacious Approach to Comparative Epistemology, by
    Aaron B. Creller
Postmodern Ethics, Emptiness, Literature: Encounter between East and West, by
    Jae-seong Lee
Metaphor and Metaphilosophy: Philosophy as Combat, Play, and Aesthetic Experience,
    by Sarah A. Mattice
Brahman and Dao: Comparative Studies of Indian and Chinese Philosophy and Religion,
    edited by Ithamar Theodor and Zihua Yao
Nietzsche and Zen: Self Overcoming Without a Self, by André van der Braak
Ethics of Compassion: Bridging Ethical Theory and Religious Moral Discourse, by
    Richard Reilly
Reality, Religion, and Passion: Indian and Western Approaches in Hans-Georg Gadamer
    and Rupa Gosvami, by Jessica Frazier
Pyrrhonism: How the Ancient Greeks Reinvented Buddhism, by Adrian Kuzminski

Philosophy of the Ancient Maya

Lords of Time

Alexus McLeod

LEXINGTON BOOKS
Lanham • Boulder • New York • London

Published by Lexington Books
An imprint of The Rowman & Littlefield Publishing Group, Inc.
4501 Forbes Boulevard, Suite 200, Lanham, Maryland 20706
www.rowman.com

Unit A, Whitacre Mews, 26-34 Stannary Street, London SE11 4AB

British Library Cataloguing in Publication Information Available

The hardback edition of this book was previously catalogued by the Library of Congress as follows:

Library of Congress Cataloging-in-Publication Data Available

ISBN 978-1-4985-3138-2 (cloth : alk. paper)
ISBN 978-1-4985-3140-5 (pbk. : alk. paper)
ISBN 978-1-4985-3139-9 (electronic)

∞™ The paper used in this publication meets the minimum requirements of American National Standard for Information Sciences—Permanence of Paper for Printed Library Materials, ANSI/NISO Z39.48-1992.

Printed in the United States of America

Contents

Preface

In this book my aim is to offer an interpretation of the *philosophical* thought of the ancient Maya in the Classic and Postclassic periods. While much is now known about ancient Maya history, religion, and culture in general, most work done by Mayanists is in anthropology, linguistics, and religious studies. Philosophical methodology has not yet been brought to bear in any robust way on the thought of the ancient Maya. Now that the Maya glyphs have been largely deciphered and our understanding of ancient Maya material culture continues to improve, more abstract features of the ancient Maya world can be revealed. It has become possible to understand ancient Maya history, political thought, economics, and religion. Numerous scholars have applied the tools of various academic fields in order to better understand these aspects of ancient Maya culture. As of yet, however, there has been no effort to understand Maya *philosophy*, as distinct from these other aspects of ancient Maya thought. In this book I argue that the ancient Maya indeed had philosophical thought that we can treat as distinct (in the same way we treat history, religion, etc. as distinct, even though the ancient Maya did not think in terms of these categories). The best way to understand the philosophical thought of the ancient Maya, I propose, is through the adoption of philosophical methodology and the tools of the historian of philosophy. That is, we come to reveal and best understand ancient Maya philosophy by engaging with Maya thought *as* philosophy.

To do this, I look to the texts of the Classic and Postclassic Maya, including the four existing Maya codices and the numerous inscriptions on stelae and architecture at Maya sites. I rely on the interpretation of archaeologists and epigraphers, and also offer my own interpretation of Classic and Postclassic Maya texts involving philosophical methodology, in addition to that used by archaeologists and epigraphers. That is, my interpretations of ancient materials are based on *conceptual* as well as linguistic and material considerations.

I also use the tools of *comparative philosophy* to interpret Maya philosophy. There are numerous parallels between aspects of Maya philosophy and that of early China, and looking to early Chinese philosophy can help us, I argue, to fill out much of what is only implicit in Maya texts, rituals, and traditions. Early China thus serves as the main comparative mirror in this text, through which I develop many aspects of my interpretation of ancient (Classic through Postclassic) Maya philosophy.

Many Mayanists have recognized the complexity and importance of ancient Maya philosophy, and a number of archaeologists, other anthropologists, and linguists have attempted to engage with and offer interpretations of various aspects of Maya philosophy. These studies of Maya philosophy, however, have been mainly piecemeal, in that only particular aspects of Maya philosophical thought are investigated that contribute to non-philosophical aims of the scholars in question. While non-philosophers have been willing to engage with philosophy in their study of the Maya, they of course do not have primarily philosophical goals, and their engagement with Maya philosophy is generally limited and secondary, with another aim in mind. In addition, non-philosophers engage with philosophy in a very different way than philosophers, and the work of non-philosophers in the area, although valuable, can be strengthened and further developed through engagement with ancient Maya thought from a philosophical perspective. This is the first book, or work of any kind, to my knowledge, to engage in such a task. As such, I believe it can make a contribution to Maya studies as well as philosophy.

The book focuses primarily on *metaphysics* in the ancient Maya philosophical tradition, with brief forays into ethics and political philosophy. I focus on first the central concept of time, which is the most fundamental category of ancient Maya metaphysical thought, then continue on to give accounts of the Maya positions on being and worlds, properties and universals, personhood and identity through time, and change, including issues of causation, process, and identity transformation.

I aim with this book to help establish Maya philosophy as an independent area of investigation within both philosophy and Maya studies. Maya thought has not been a concern among professional philosophers, mainly because most philosophers are unfamiliar with issues and developments in Maya studies or Mesoamerican studies in general. Maya thought has been the realm of anthropologists. While a few anthropologists have dealt with particular philosophical issues in their work on the Maya, including David Friedel, Linda Schele, and Joy Parker (*Maya Cosmos*) and Lars Pharo (*The Ritual Practice of Time: Philosophy and Sociopolitics of Mesoamerican* Calendars), few philosophers have dealt with these issues. Perhaps the most notable case is Miguel Leon-Portilla (*Tiempo y realidad en el pensamiento Maya* [*Time and Reality in The Thought of the Maya*]). Recently, there has been increasing focus on Mesoamerican philosophy by philosophers, with Aztec philosophy generating interest among comparative philosophers. A number of articles have appeared in this area, in addition to James Maffie's recent book *Aztec Philosophy* (2014). My contribution on Maya philosophy, while smaller in scope than Maffie's book, aims to bring Maya thought into the philosophical discussion. If this book serves to at least begin the conversation and to bring more scholars to the investigation of Maya and Mesoamerican philosophy (and comparative philosophy), it will have been a success.

Acknowledgments

The writing of this book has been a major task for me. It was the hardest thing I have yet written, for a number of reasons. I have dealt with numerous forms of illness and distress through most of its genesis. I hope that through my struggles I've been able to offer something of value. The vast majority of the writing of this book was done in Colorado, during my all-too-short stay in that magnificent land. I owe an enormous debt to the members of the Department of Philosophy at Colorado State University—they provided me a supportive environment in which to contemplate, experiment, and really stretch out, to engage in this philosophical equivalent of free jazz. This is a strange book—a comparative hybrid that took a great deal of research outside of my field, and it never would have been possible without the truly amazing work of archaeologists, anthropologists, and other Mayanists, on whom I have relied for much here. I thank all of them for teaching me. I also thank earlier scholars who engaged in bold comparative journeys that showed me such a thing was not only possible but vital. A particular influence was Toshihiko Izutsu's *Sufism and Daoism*, another broad comparative work, far more incisive, learned, and penetrating than my own book, that drove home to me the possibility and importance of comparative philosophy outside of the confines of the "West." Thanks also to my CSU colleague Idris Hamid for both introducing me to Izutsu's work and for fruitful discussions about these topics and about comparative philosophy in general. Thanks are due also to a number of other individual people who helped me along the way. Thanks to my current colleagues in philosophy and Asian/Asian American studies at the University of Connecticut, who brought me back to my PhD alma mater despite my restless wanderings through the philosophical traditions of the world. Thanks to members of my fantastic writing group at CSU, Dustin Tucker, Sophie Esch, and Joshua Sbicca, who gave me vital insights and whose careful reading of my work helped shape a number of the chapters included here. Thanks to Jim Maffie at the University of Maryland, who encouraged the project, and whose excellent work in Aztec philosophy was part of the inspiration for it. Thanks to Stephen Walker for some valuable suggestions, and to Asia Guzowska, for tipping me off to the parallel between embedded identity and the Catholic doctrine of transubstantiation. Thanks to a reviewer for Lexington, whose suggestions made the book stronger. Thanks to my student and research assistant, Kristin Culbertson, whose careful eye helped me catch more than a few mistakes. I also thank the Maya people, whose struggle to preserve their proud heritage even in the face of the myriad problems they face can serve as an example of strength and commitment for all of humanity. Finally, special thanks to my wife Shubhalaxmi and my two sons Siddhartha and Francis, for whom I endure it all. *Dios bo'otik.*

West Hartford, CT- 3/2017

Introduction

The World of Maya Thought:
An Experiment in Comparative Philosophy

THE ANCIENT MAYA AND PHILOSOPHICAL THOUGHT

In the tropical rainforest of Guatemala, a collection of pyramid towers reaches from the floor, jutting atop the trees. An ancient and once "lost" city lies in ruin, amid the thick vegetation that must have quickly overtaken it when it was abandoned, sometime around 900–950 CE. The city was once known by its rulers, inhabitants, and people as *Mutul*, center of a once-powerful dynasty that dominated the region. Today we know the remains of this city as *Tikal*. The majestic height of the power of Tikal can still be imagined. And even in its present state of relative disrepair, due to the ravages of time in the inhospitable warm and humid climate, the structures of the ancient city are breathtaking. As in other ancient Maya cities, we can still find massive halls and rooms with inscriptions, stelae raised to commemorate establishments of rulers, dynasties, or important calendric events. The aid of such inscriptions in the ancient Maya glyphic writing system has been invaluable to our coming to understand what went on in ancient cities such as Tikal. They have revealed to us, as they continue to be deciphered, the rich history and ideology of the ancient Maya.

The city of Tikal was one of many urban ritual centers in the Maya region comprising what are today the nations of Guatemala and Belize, as well as southeastern Mexico and the western parts of El Salvador and Honduras. Tikal was one of the most powerful cities in the Maya world during early part of the Classic Period (250–900 CE). The political history of Tikal is recounted in the numerous surviving stelae and monumental inscriptions of the city. They tell the story of dynasties of priest-kings who both controlled human government and had the shamanic ability to communicate with the supramundane aspects of the world that most people could not see. While numerous books documenting ritual were likely written and stored in the buildings of Tikal, all we have left today are the memorials and stelae to tell the story of these people. The texts of stone have proven harder to destroy than books, though it was not for lack of trying. Invading cities often defaced or destroyed stelae as a way of eradicating the essence of a ruler.[1] A portion of the Maya textual material created in the Classic and surrounding periods remains today. Further information about Maya culture and thought has been retrieved by archaeologists from the many artifacts of the ancient Maya left behind, as well as the thought and writings of their descendants in later periods and today.

While Maya people themselves[2] have always understood much of the thought of their ancestors in these ancient periods, certain parts of this knowledge has been lost. The glyphic writing system gave way to the phonetic Latin-based writing system brought to the Americas by the Spanish. The glyphs faded into history, and understanding of their meanings was lost, even while knowledge of the calendars and certain ceremonies endured. Mayan languages survived, and are used down to the current day in the regions where the ancient Maya city-states once thrived. Despite this, much of Maya cultural heritage was destroyed by the Spanish in their attempts to Latinize and Christianize the continent. Missionaries converted many natives to Christianity (although these people often retained elements of their native religions). They rejected and actively suppressed Maya cultural elements as idol worship. They destroyed cultural items, including (and for our purposes most importantly) textual material. The infamous burning of codices[3] at Maní of 1562, carried out by the Spanish Franciscan friar Diego de Landa, resulted in the elimination of a large number of books written by the Maya in the glyphic

Figure 0.1 A solstice celebration at the Great Plaza of Tikal, with the North Acropolis to the left and Temple 1 to the right. Bjørn Christian Tørrissen, bjornfree.com.

script.[4] Maya history, philosophy, religion, and astronomy were consigned to the flames. De Landa could not burn the minds of the Maya people, however. Some of what must have been included in these codices was carried on in cultural memory, and Mayan texts written in Latinized form, such as the *Popol Vuh* of the Kiche Maya, and the various books of *Chilam Balam*, survived in later "post-conquest" versions.[5] While these texts clearly involve syncretism, with adoption of Christian and Spanish imagery and ideas, they also almost certainly preserve some pre-Spanish Maya ideas.[6]

These texts, like some of the inscriptions of Tikal and the other great Maya cities, recount the stories of legendary figures, mythical heroes, the gods, and great men and women.[7] In them, we can find Maya views about all of the major human concerns—life and death, morality and action, the nature of time and space, and even why things exist at all. That is, among the various concerns of the texts of the Maya, *philosophy* is included.

My aim is to make this work accessible to those interested in Maya thought, to give (as much as possible) a coherent account of the philosophy of the ancient Maya, through the lenses of comparative thought, making particular use of early Chinese philosophy. I am not speaking in particular to philosophers or anthropologists alone, although both can benefit from this project. I am writing with those in mind who want to understand the ways of philosophical thought of the ancient Maya world. While most studies of Maya thought use the tools of anthropology or religious studies, in this work, comparative philosophy is the central focus. The tools of philosophy, and in particular comparative philosophy (some of which I develop here and in other works), can help us better understand ancient Maya thought. There may of course be other uses one can make of the conclusions of this work, such as application of these ideas to contemporary philosophical debates, and I suggest some of these in the final chapter. But my primary purpose here is to provide a clearer understanding of how the ancient Maya thought about concepts such as being, time, personhood, identity, and other related concepts that show up in their texts and are suggested by other aspects of their material culture. While I use Chinese philosophical thought as a useful "mirror" to help us understand the much less textually intact philosophical thought of the ancient Maya, in this book it is Maya philosophy that is my main concern, with Chinese philosophy serving as an aid. I should also note here that, despite the many ways in which Chinese philosophy can serve as a useful mirror for Maya philosophy, there is no evidence that the two traditions are historically related in any way. Farfetched speculations about Chinese contact with Mesoamerica in the pre-Columbian period certainly cannot be supported by similarities in the philosophical traditions of China and Mesoamerica.[8] There is also no link between the similarities discussed in this book and the Bering Strait theory of the population of the Americas.[9] Philosophical thought around the world develops in startlingly similar ways, and when certain traditions proceed from similar background assumptions, we often find parallels.

It is important to note here that Maya thought, like the Maya people, is in no way "lost" or "dead." While the primary focus of this book is on the philosophical thought of the Maya from the Classic through early Postclassic Periods (250–1200 CE), which serves as the foundation of subsequent Maya philosophy, the innovation and genius of Maya thought still continues today. It is not true to say that Maya culture flourished during the Classic and Postclassic Periods and died away or disappeared after the arrival and influence of the Spanish in the sixteenth century. One often encounters the claim that Maya culture disappeared or collapsed, and is something relegated to history. This is false. Maya culture and thought, as much as Maya people, are very much alive. Some traditional practices related to those of the early periods discussed in this book still endure in the Maya region, such as the practice of "daykeeping," which I discuss in the following chapters. Thus it is important to know that the philosophical ideas I discuss in this book are not the *whole* of Maya thought and philosophy, but rather they constitute the ancient *foundation*, upon which later Maya people built and continue to build.

There have been many volumes devoted to the material culture of the ancient Maya in the last hundred years or so. We have learned a remarkable amount about the ancient Maya given that before the mid-nineteenth century, Western academics were not even aware of the existence of ancient Maya civilization. It was with the travels and writings of John Lloyd Stephens, appointed ambassador to Central America[10] by U.S. president Martin Van Buren in the 1840s, that the ancient Maya ruins came to the attention of people in the United States and Europe.[11] Stephens' descriptive and effusive *Incidents of Travel in Central America, Chiapas, and Yucatan*, created with the collaboration of illustrator Frederick Catherwood, captured the imaginations of people back home. The volumes offered exotic travel and true mystery—no one in the West at the time knew what these ruins were or who had created them—and Stephens' volumes became among the earliest "bestsellers" in U.S. history.[12] This also kicked off the academic interest in ancient Maya culture. Although Mayanists made progress from this time, it was with the decipherment of Maya glyphs that Maya studies really began to take off. This happened around the middle of the last century, thanks mainly to developments of "outsider" academics like the Russian linguist Yuri Knorosov in the 1950s.[13] With decipherment, more attention was devoted to understanding all aspects of ancient Maya thought.[14]

Renewed interest in the ancient Maya in the United States and Europe came in the 1960s and 1970s with the rise of the "new age" movement, a syncretistic blend of religious, cultural, and invented elements mainly devised by Euro-Americans, and drawing on ancient philosophical and religious systems such as those of early China, India, Africa, and Mesoamerica. It was this movement, and the confusions concerning Maya thought resulting from aspects of it, that led to the insidious view that became popular throughout much of the world of the Maya "end of days" in December 2012, at the end of the thirteenth *baktun* of the Long Count calendar. This erroneous view was brought about mainly through fictionalization. It is true that the current epoch of the Long Count, which began in August of 3114 BCE, was scheduled to— and did—come to an end in December 2012. However, no Maya text, stela, or other source claimed that the end of this period of the Long Count would correspond to the end of time or the destruction of the world. Indeed, as we will see in chapter 1, an idea of an *ending* of time is as incompatible with Maya thought as the idea of eternal time is with Christian thought.

Since the large-scale decipherment of the glyphs, much of the focus of study of the ancient Maya has been on understanding the histories inscribed in the various stelae, codices, and pottery vessels found in the Maya world.[15] There have even been numerous studies devoted to aspects of ancient Maya religion and intellectual culture. But there has not yet been an attempt to systematically give an account of ancient Maya philosophical and religious thought. In order to do this, I look to material evidence, particularly textual evidence from stelae, codices,[16] and other sources, as well as post-contact literature such as the *Popol Vuh* and books of *Chilam Balam*. In addition, I investigate the parallels between ancient Maya and ancient Chinese thought, borrowing concepts and positions from early China to consider possible reconstructions of more detailed ancient Maya views. What we gain through this is one *possible* and plausible reconstruction of ancient Maya thought, but not the only one. We cannot know exactly how close many of the Maya positions I discuss really were to the various Chinese positions I discuss here, simply because the textual evidence is lacking. But, as with any creative interpretation of something of which many parts are missing, the best we can do here is to offer plausible alternatives, to see how they work. I use Chinese thought here to "complete" many of the missing parts of Maya thought because in the known aspects of Maya thought, there are clear parallels with certain aspects of Chinese thought, and the way early Chinese thinkers developed these systems shows us some possible directions the ancient Maya may have taken. This is an example of what I call the "analogical method" of comparative philosophy, which I discuss further below.

Now that much of the glyphic language has been deciphered, and scholars (including anthropologists, astronomers, art historians, and others) have helped us to come to a better understanding of ancient Maya history and culture, new projects are possible. Today, it is possible and valuable for a philosopher like myself, with no archaeological training, to engage with ancient Maya thought in a way that would have been impossible even twenty years ago. Enough has been deciphered, uncovered, and understood about Maya writing and culture that it is now possible to examine Maya philosophy *as* philosophy. Linda Schele and David Friedel wrote (in 1990) that it had recently become possible to discuss Maya *history,* emerging out of the early archaeological and epigraphical work on Maya sites and texts.[17] Since Schele and Friedel wrote this, much more has been uncovered concerning the ancient Maya, and many more works have been written about Maya intellectual culture. No doubt scholars in these fields will continue to advance our understanding of ancient Maya culture. My project here, however, is to use what they have learned and apply philosophical methodology, attempting to understand the ancient Maya systems of thought as representing coherent and systematic worldviews.[18]

Just as the tools of archaeology, sociocultural anthropology, and linguistics can be useful to the study of the ancient Maya, philosophy can play an important role—one that has not yet been realized. As we come to better understand the ancient Maya language and culture, the interpretive methods of the historian of philosophy and speculative philosopher become more useful in application to ancient Maya thought. The fact that philosophy has for the most part failed to play a role in Maya studies up to today is mainly the fault of philosophers. The field of philosophy in general is still struggling with a conservative Western-bias that, in the opinion of an increasing number of philosophers, has held the field back and provincialized it to the extent that it became marginalized and insular. Part of the difficulty within philosophy is that we philosophers were unwilling to engage with non-Western (in the sense of European or American) thought. Another part of the difficulty was our resistance to interdisciplinary work. In areas such as Maya studies, interdisciplinary work is key. No field can use its own methods to completely understand the ancient Maya. We depend on epigraphers to decipher the glyphs, archaeologists to uncover and interpret the material culture, and sociocultural anthropologists to study the practices of the Maya through such tools as ethnography. Any scholar engaged in Maya studies should be familiar with the work and results of these various fields on the ancient Maya. This holds no less for me as a philosopher than for any other scholar working in the area. I must rely on glyphic decipherment and archaeological results as much as any Mayanist. Thus, working on ancient Maya philosophy requires a kind of interdisciplinary focus that philosophers have traditionally shunned. Fortunately, there seem to be increasing signs of change in attitudes among philosophers. Things have been somewhat different in other fields. Anthropologists working on the ancient Maya have tended to be more adventurous in their willingness to engage with philosophical ideas than philosophers have been in engaging with ideas and methodologies outside our field. This is necessary and commendable, and we philosophers should follow the lead of anthropologists. Since I am dealing with an area covered mainly by anthropologists and since most of the Maya scholarship is outside of philosophy and deals with intrinsically different material, I will necessarily engage with anthropology (including archaeology), linguistics, and other fields in this book. In this I hope to facilitate understanding of Maya Philosophy within the discipline of philosophy as well as other fields. I also hope to develop ways to integrate the insights and methodologies of other fields into the discipline of philosophy.

It can be difficult to move from the realm of *material* to the realm of *ideas* in the study of a culture with relatively little remaining textual tradition. In a major sense this is just what this book represents. In most works on the ancient Maya, material and the physical takes center stage. This is because ancient Maya studies until today has been mainly the purview of archaeologists, who study material. Little wonder that almost all of the focus on ancient Maya culture has been focus on material, even where there are suggestions of broader intellectual development. Studies on the person tend to focus on the *body* as material.[19] Studies of the role of time tend to focus on the material aspects of time—Prudence Rice's 2007 discussion of the origins of the Maya calendar has as part of its subtitle "the materialization of time."[20] While these are all valuable studies and investigation of Maya material culture is certainly essential for an understanding of the ancient Maya, the field of Maya studies cannot progress if we focus *only* on material. There is no culture in the world that has been solely concerned with material and has only understood itself and its world in terms of physical images. Every culture has had an intellectual tradition. One of the purposes of this book is to move away from the material, to emphasize, uncover, and interpret the *intellectual* culture of the ancient Maya. This is a work that focuses on ideas rather than materials. Materials are never wholly absent, of course. We learn about Maya ideas through the ideas and the suggestions of ideas they left as signs within materials, whether etchings on memorial stelae and architecture, painting on pottery vessels, or words in codical books. The interest here, however, is in the *intellectual content* of these materials—not in terms of how these ideas related to material lives, but in terms of how the ancient Maya thought about their world, about their philosophical positions concerning what the world is made of, how it works, the meaning of human life, right action, and other timeless questions asked in almost every society in human history.

Maya philosophy as an integrated whole is substantial, unique, interesting, and belongs alongside of other world traditions in philosophical consideration. Pre-Columbian Mesoamerican philosophy in general, like other traditions such as pre-Columbian North American philosophy and African philosophy, has been neglected within the philosophical community. There has been some growth in philosophical consideration of North American indigenous philosophies and African philosophy in recent times, but the work in these areas pales in comparison to work in the much more visible areas of Chinese and Indian philosophy, which themselves are but minor areas in the more robustly studied history of Western philosophy. Mesoamerican thought, however, has been uniquely neglected by philosophers. There are a few possible reasons for this. First—the philosophical community in the Americas, Europe, and Asia has been primarily motivated by concerns arising out of Euro-American philosophical thought of the nineteenth and twentieth centuries (both in the analytic and continental traditions) that sidelined both historical concerns and specifically those of non-Western traditions, which were not seen as related to contemporary issues and debates. The "rise" (if we can call it that) of consideration of Asian philosophies such as those of the Chinese and Indian traditions and to a lesser extent that of the North American indigenous traditions and African traditions were due in large part to the efforts of philosophers with ties to the groups or traditions in question. Thus with more Chinese scholars studying philosophy in the early twentieth century, we begin to see philosophical engagement with Chinese thought.[21]

This has been the case with North American indigenous philosophy and African philosophy as well. The main proponents and scholars of North American indigenous philosophy, such as Anne Waters, Vine Deloria Jr., and others, are members of indigenous communities themselves, and have personal as well as professional interest in furthering understanding of indigenous thought. The same is the case in African philosophy, spearheaded by philosophers such as Kwasi Wiredu, Samuel Imbo, Kwame Gyekye, and others. Perhaps because of the largely Euro-American focus of the field of philosophy, ancient Mesoamerican philosophy has gone almost completely ignored.

This is not the case, of course, with *Latin American* philosophy. But most Latin American philosophy as it is pursued within academic philosophy deals with concepts and ideas drawn from European thought in its engagement with the peoples of "Latin America."[22] Even the name "Latin American" philosophy suggests a post-Columbian tradition, perhaps with some relation to, but also vastly different from, pre-Columbian thought. This situation, however, seems relatively unique to philosophy. In anthropology and other fields, pre-Columbian Mesoamerican thought gets plenty of attention. Perhaps part of the reason for the neglect of Mesoamerican philosophy is the idea that pre-Columbian Mesoamerican peoples did not have philosophical thought. We know now, thanks in part to the work of anthropologists, that this is far from true. Yet philosophical neglect continues.

Like most philosophers, I was almost completely ignorant of Mesoamerican philosophical thought about six years ago. Back then I may have questioned whether there *was* such a thing as Mesoamerican philosophy (as I suspect some philosophers still will today). This skepticism would not have been on the grounds of any doubt that the pre-Columbian Mesoamerican peoples were capable of philosophical thought, or even that they did not produce philosophical texts, but rather simply on the basis of failure to encounter any discussion on Mesoamerican philosophy. From the little I did know of the history of the region, I would have known that much of the material culture, especially textual materials, had been destroyed by Spanish missionaries. My introduction to Maya thought came not through philosophy, but a somewhat different route: astronomy. I have long had an interest in, and also have done academic work on, the history of astronomy.[23] In 2010, I saw a film on ancient Maya astronomy at a local astronomy event at the Boonshoft Museum in Dayton, Ohio, and was fascinated by both the extent of astronomical thought in Classic and Postclassic Maya culture, and by the material evidence that enabled us to understand Maya astronomical thought today. This first kicked off an interest in learning more about Maya astronomy, which soon became an obsessive interest in ancient Maya culture and thought more generally, which became more and more compelling and interesting to me the more I investigated it. Early in my reading, I lamented the fact that there are no extant philosophical texts from the ancient Maya. A people with the kind of magnificent intellectual culture I was discovering through my reading surely must have had philosophy, I thought. But still, I assumed that the early purges of Maya texts effectively destroyed any trace of Maya philosophy. Not long after this, however, I discovered the work of Linda Schele and David Friedel on Maya intellectual culture (and philosophy), masterfully presented in their book *Maya Cosmos* (1993). It was their work that first suggested to me that we can retrieve rich and important ideas on a number of philosophical and religious topics from the ancient Maya—and that contemporary Maya people and their practices can also help us to reconstruct some of these early positions. I began to look for other works in Maya philosophical and religious thought, to which I had been completely blind before. Every one of the works I found was by anthropologists. I marveled at the complexity of Maya ways of thinking about the world as I read the innovative work of scholars such as Miguel Leon-Portilla, David Stuart, Stephen Houston, Schele and Friedel, and others on Maya ideology. I began to understand and piece together not only a coherent worldview, but a coherent *philosophy* in Maya thought, one that had been carefully reconstructed from the extant texts and practices. I had discovered an untapped philosophical gold mine. My surprise shifted from the idea of the existence of Maya philosophy to the fact that philosophers had almost completely neglected Maya philosophy.

Maya philosophy, of course, is not the only interesting Mesoamerican tradition. During my investigations in Maya thought, I discovered the work of philosopher James Maffie, who has for some time worked on Aztec philosophy, and has recently published the first volume of a longer planned work on Aztec thought.[24] The apex of Aztec power coincided with the period of Spanish contact and thus Aztec culture and thought are better preserved than ancient Maya thought, which had reached its intellectual height half a millennium earlier. Still, given the extent of Aztec culture during the period of contact, it is surprising that we do not know much more than we do about their culture and thought. The Spanish attempts to eliminate native culture were persistent,[25] and almost as successful as those of the English and later Americans to suppress North American native cultures, which had the additional disadvantage of having no known textual culture or stone-built permanent sites like those of the Mesoamerican peoples.[26] I owe quite a bit to Maffie's work, for both blazing a trail in Mesoamerican philosophy that I have tried to follow as well as he does (though his experience and knowledge as a Nahuatlist far exceed my own abilities as Mayanist), and for demonstrating the importance of understanding Mesoamerican philosophies *as* philosophy.

Maya thought is often described as different from or even opposed to "Western" thought.[27] A common image in much English scholarship on the Maya is to contrast Maya beliefs and worldviews with "our own," meaning roughly that of the Western academy. As I discovered and learned more about Maya thought, however, I found that the ancient Maya ways of envisioning reality, while certainly unique, are not completely foreign to the ways the world is understood in other traditions, including Western and Asian traditions. The greatest similarity I found in Maya thought, however, was to the indigenous philosophies of North America. From what I know of these traditions, there are quite a few similarities and shared features with Mesoamerican thought. Indeed, some scholars have argued that we can make sense of "indigenous American thought" as a unique system (although I have doubts about this, which I discuss in chapters below).[28] Indeed, it is a very real possibility that there was cultural contact between the Mesoamerican and North American peoples, and so these similarities may be more than coincidental.[29] For whatever reason, however, I found myself increasingly frustrated when reading claims that Maya thought differs from "our own" in essential ways, or is somehow "incommensurable" with Western thought. My difficulties just further illustrate the problems with essentializing cultures—that is, advancing the idea that certain worldviews persist throughout a culture or are universally shared within it.

*

Much of the philosophical thought of the Maya is inaccessible through the most direct means available to us, because a great deal of cultural heritage in the Maya area has been lost. There are a few reasons for this. Many of the texts written by ancient Maya were lost either through the purging of native Maya materials by the Spanish after the conquest, or through decay in the tropical environment of the Maya area, uniquely poorly suited for the survival of the kind of paper texts the ancient Maya created. In areas of the world such as the Middle East and Northern China, texts are sometimes excavated from tombs, ruins, or other sites (the Dead Sea Scrolls in Palestine and the Mawangdui and Guodian texts in China are probably the most famous examples of this). In the fertile forest of the Maya area, however, such excavation of textual materials is unlikely. Any buried texts in the area south of the Yucatan would have decayed centuries ago. The only region in the Maya area in which it might be possible for buried tree-bark paper texts to survive a sufficiently long time is the northern Yucatan. The relatively dry climate of the Yucatan ensures that, unlike the lush tropical rainforest to its south, it remains a low brush covered plain. Although nowhere near as arid as the vicinity of Qumran in Palestine where the Dead Sea Scrolls were found, most of the Yucatan is much more suited for the survival of buried books than the areas in China where texts have been recovered. Perhaps (one can only hope) additional Maya texts will be unearthed in the Yucatan. Indeed, all of the paper texts we have today originated in this region, during the Postclassic Period. Maya culture in the Yucatan did not reach its "height" as far as cultural expression until after the decline of the other lowland states further south in the Terminal Classic Period.[30] During the Preclassic and Classic Periods, the core of Maya civilization was first in the highland cities such as Kaminaljuyu and El Mirador, and later in southern lowland cities such as the majestic Tikal, Calakmul, Palenque, and toward the end of this period, Copan, on the southeastern periphery of the Maya area.[31] Though all four of the Maya books we have today were created in the Yucatan, there are fewer stone monumental texts in this region[32]—the construction in cities like Chichen Itza, Coba, and Tulum (among others) is of a later style, influenced by the (Itza) Maya and possibly central Mexican groups.[33] Texts generally do not figure greatly in this architectural style, as they did in the great Classic Period cities. We also do not see the stelae monuments, including memorial texts that are plentiful in the Classic Period cities. There continued to be a rich textual culture in the Postclassic, however, with numerous codices created and preserved. There were many others beside the four known today, as documented by early Spanish colonists. These texts were stored in ritual centers, which doubled as libraries. Most of these texts, however, due to their concentration in ritually important locations, were easily accessible to over-zealous Spanish missionaries like de Landa.

We are in a difficult position because of the relative dearth of texts. Most of what we have is in the form of the four Postclassic codices and the remaining monumental texts of the southern lowlands. Some of the monumental texts are fairly extensive, such as the monumental history in the temples at Palenque. Monumental texts, however, can be expected to be much different from philosophical and mythological texts. Monuments have a different purpose. The ruler and dates in the life of the ruler feature prominently in the monumental texts, while they are absent from the Maya codices we have. For the most part, mythological, astronomical, and philosophical content was contained in the codical books, and insofar as it was included in the stone monuments, only showed up in bits and pieces. Thus, our task is one of *reconstruction* of ancient Maya philosophical views, on the basis of a limited number of texts, suggestions, and fragments. What can we appeal to?

There are a few other sources we can make use of, some of which have been looked into and others which have not. First, we can make some use of Postconquest texts such as *Popol Vuh* and the books of *Chilam Balam*. Second, we can look into practices and traditions of contemporary Maya people for hints as to the views of their ancient ancestors. Both of these techniques have been taken advantage of by other scholars, in anthropology, history, and literature.[34] These techniques of course are not perfect, and the most we can hope to gain from them are possibilities concerning reconstruction of ancient Maya views. But another resource we have available, and which has not been used by *any* scholars of the ancient Maya to my knowledge, is that of the philosophical texts of other traditions. We certainly have to be careful with how we use these ideas to help reconstruct possible Maya views, but this is no less the case for using any of the other available tools.

For example, many accounts of non-Western philosophy render the traditions in question as holistic as opposed to the supposed inherent dualism of Western philosophical tradition. This seems dubious as a general claim. It is not true that Western philosophy finds discrete boundaries between things and makes a unique distinction between, for example, the immanent and transcendent, while Chinese, Indian, Mesoamerican, Egyptian, sub-Saharan African, North American, and seemingly every other philosophical tradition recognizes a monism in which all things are ultimately one, and the immanent-transcendent distinction is broken down (although I do argue in this book for a monism concerning worlds in ancient Maya thought). I argue that the monistic view is actually much rarer in global philosophical history than a kind of dualistic view. I think much of the reason that non-Western traditions are read as monistic is a general desire to read these traditions as *opposed to* or somehow *alternatives to* Western traditions. Sometimes scholars who work on these traditions are looking for alternatives to the West, things that the West is not, to latch onto or put forward, sometimes as a criticism of the West, sometimes as a complement. We have to remember though, these independent traditions did not develop as reactions to the West, they developed in their own organic and coherent ways that had nothing to do with the West, and in most cases were developed long before there *was* a "West." And they often share more in common with Western tradition than many of us would like to admit. These systems are not simply parallels of those of Western traditions, and there are of course differences. But non-Western traditions also do not tend to fall into a convenient "anti-West" or opposite-from-West distinction. Indeed, it is somewhat unfortunate that we even think of global philosophical traditions as falling into the categories of "Western" and "non-Western," as this has much to do with *why* so-called "non-Western" traditions tend to be interpreted similarly and as contrastive with the West. If some traditions fall within the category of the West, then there must be some substantive difference between these and other philosophical traditions left out of this "West." The problem here, however, is that the idea of the West is not, and never has been, one based on similarity or difference of intellectual culture or tendency. It is mainly a racial, religious, and political distinction, and thus we should expect, as is the case, that the lines will not be clearly drawn concerning intellectual culture.[35] Insofar as philosophical tradition is concerned, then, the West-non-West divide is almost completely arbitrary. It is not something akin to the analytic-continental divide in contemporary philosophy, which, although it may not ultimately be a good or useful distinction, at least *is* based on general intellectual features, styles, and trends. Rather, it would be akin to a distinction between New York City philosophy and Washington DC philosophy. If there are any differences between the two, it is based on coincidences concerning who is working on what in each area—that is, the unique character of each is likely coincidental and artificially maintained. There is no organic and self-contained nature of NYC philosophy as contrasted to DC philosophy. The larger traditions that created regularities in contemporary analytic philosophy, for example, have little or nothing to do with inter-USA civic political distinctions. So using these distinctions to characterize philosophical traditions will necessarily create artificial divides. "Western" and "non-Western" philosophy are largely the same as categories.

A GENERAL ANALOGICAL METHOD

Despite the advances we have made in recent years in understanding ancient Maya thought, the fact remains that we do not have the rich textual resources in the case of the ancient Maya as we do for many other better understood traditions, such as those of ancient Greece, China, and India. Thus, our investigation into Maya philosophy must be different than those into other philosophical traditions. Much of our interpretation must rely on reconstructions based on archaeological evidence and interpretation, on attempting to project backward from postcolonial texts and contemporary Maya thought, and on what I call the "comparative analogical" method, which I see as a uniquely philosophical contribution to the study of ancient Maya thought. This analogical method is essentially comparative, and thus while the main focus throughout this book is on the ancient Maya and their philosophical tradition, I will also engage with other philosophical traditions, particularly those of ancient China, in an attempt to reconstruct the "missing pieces" in ancient Maya thought, or at least to offer plausible possibilities for reconstruction.

Put simply, the analogical method begins with one text about which there are unanswered interpretive questions. One then can find other texts or systems that hold many of the same positions on issues or concepts closely related to the ones intended to be resolved. We might ask the question—what do other texts that express very similar specific views and the same general goals and approach as our target text have to say about the unanswered issue in the target text? It may be that a similar text says *nothing* about the issue, in which case it is passed over. But it may be the case that a text has quite a bit to say about the issue that is left more vague or incomplete in the target text. We might then use what the compared text says about the topic to "fill in the gaps" in the target text, to see if we can make sense of such an overall view. Thus, we are working by *analogy*. One determines that if there is enough similarity concerning a key cluster of views between two thinkers, then they may share another view related to this cluster. It may be the case that the reconstructed view of the target text is inconsistent, in which case we may have to ask the question: Is the compared text inconsistent in the same way? If not, we may have incorrectly drawn the analogy between them. If so, perhaps this inconsistency is shared. Or maybe it's only a flaw of the compared text, regarding which the target text remained silent so as to avoid. This in itself would be an interesting result.

At most, we could only gain the *possibility* that a thinker held some similar view to a different thinker in some other tradition. But this is in general the best we can *ever* do in the history of philosophy. It will be nearly impossible to conclusively demonstrate that a particular interpretation of some historical text is the correct one, because the aspects of texts that require interpretation are just those that are not clear and which admit of multiple interpretive possibilities. Barring the discovery of secret texts by Maya scholars hidden away in a cave that spell out exactly what we want to know and rule out all interpretations but one, we are always in a situation of uncertainty, dealing in nothing stronger than plausibility.

Although this comparative method is not enough to give us a deductive demonstration that a thinker held a given view, it can serve as the basis for perfectly cogent analogical inductions. Theories and systems of thought in general, if we take them as explicable by the same natural laws of the universe as any other phenomenon (or even if they have their own unique rules), can be usefully evaluated in the same way we evaluate other phenomenon, and comparative analogical induction is a time-tested and respected way of discovering new information about entities and phenomena.[36] Of course, such arguments may be of greater or lesser strength, just as any argument, but there is nothing intrinsically outlandish, bizarre, or "pseudoscientific" about analogical reasoning. Indeed, it is one of the most potent tools we have for scientific (and other) reasoning.

The analogical comparative methodology may strike some as artificial or illegitimate. Normally one would assume the usefulness of investigating ancient Maya thinkers through the lenses of contemporary Western concepts, likely because of confidence in the truth or at least reasonableness of these concepts. We tend to privilege contemporary Western approaches and look at everything else with suspicion.[37] In my view, we ought to move away from this insular approach to comparative philosophy and use the resources of other rich philosophical traditions, including those of Mesoamerica, China, India, and elsewhere in the world.

There are at least three possible objections to this method. (1) The historical objection: Given that the traditions in question did not come into contact and developed different concepts, concerns, languages, and texts, to read one in terms of the other is culturally and historically incongruous. Maya thinkers can no more be read as Chinese Zhuangist thinkers, for example, than raga can be understood as big band jazz. The lack of shared concepts and concerns of the traditions makes it impossible to gain much from a consideration of historically unconnected Maya and Indian or Chinese thinkers or texts, and must ultimately then be more misleading and artificial than useful. (2) Even if there are important structural parallels between Maya and other systems, analogical induction is ultimately not a strong method. The clear parallels or similarities between thinkers on a number of issues in some cluster of concepts do not guarantee (or even make likely) that they will agree on some other issue in this cluster. The fact that there are any differences between the thinkers at all shows that it is possible to share certain views while diverging on others. Indeed, even *within* traditions and schools there is disagreement concerning core ideas—so how can we possibly establish the likelihood of interpretations on the basis of analogy with thinkers of radically different traditions? (3) Even if we can somehow show that the reconstructed view of ancient Maya thinkers based on using positions from a Chinese text (for example) as analogy is consistent, this cannot show that the ancient Maya thinkers actually *accepted* such a view. A person's positions can be inconsistent, and one can fail to adopt or hold things that their other positions logically commit them to. One does not have to (and often does not) recognize all of the implications of their philosophical commitments.

In brief, my response to these four objections is as follows:

(1) I of course recognize the disparity between the Maya and other philosophical traditions, and we don't need to make the claim that there was any connection between any of them, direct or indirect. We can simply assume

that the traditions are wholly independent, unaware of one another, and completely isolated one from the other historically. The Maya concept of *baah*
and that of *shen* 身 as used by ancient Chinese thinkers (both of which may
be translated as "self," in the sense of body as well as person more robustly)
are certainly not exactly the same concept, in the sense of a full or "thick"
description, but they certainly track the same "thin" conception of what is
meant by our term "self"—indeed we might say it is this that allows for
translations of the terms to one another. There is enough kinship between
these concepts that it is meaningful and sensible to substitute one for the other
in translations between the languages. To render *shen* into Classic Mayan
as *baah* or into English as "self" is not to arbitrarily select disparate terms
expressing unrelated concepts, but takes the three as compatible or in some
sense expressing the same concept, at least in a thin sense. Any comparative
methodology is to some extent ahistorical. But this ahistoricity is not clearly
any greater or more problematic than that involved in interpreting ancient
Maya thought through Western concepts, which contemporary historians,
philosophers, and scholars of religious study must use in order to do scholarship on the ancient Maya in their own language(s).[38] It must be then just as
useful to speak of ancient Maya philosophy in terms of say Indian Samkhya
or Chinese Daoist philosophy as it is to speak of ancient Maya thought in
terms of Western economic thought or political theory. In general, we can
never completely reconstruct the ideas, arguments, etc. of a tradition, text,
or thinker without simply duplicating what they have said. And even then
we cannot grasp the exact intentions, circumstances, etc. of its authors. No
interpretation is a *pure* interpretation, and the question then becomes what is
our purpose in investigating texts and traditions? Perhaps we can distinguish
between intellectually responsible and irresponsible uses or readings,[39] but
we certainly cannot determine a uniquely privileged reading or methodology
for approaching these texts that will bring us into the minds of the ancients.

   (2) and (3) There is some force to these arguments. The parallels between a
particular Maya concept or theory and that of another tradition certainly cannot show that the traditions must have held the same or even similar positions
concerning things that are not made explicit in one or the other. But this is not
the purpose of the analogical method. The method gives us consistent interpretive possibilities, which is really the most that any interpretive method
can do. This method should be able to generate interpretations of less clear
aspects of a text or tradition consistent with other views more clearly adopted
by the text or tradition. Given that we are never in a position to conclusively
demonstrate that a particular interpretation is the *correct* one, the best we
can do is to show that some interpretations are consistent and justifiable
possibilities (while others are not). In general, we will have to move beyond
the point of simply marshalling textual and linguistic evidence to the stage

of considering coherent interpretive possibilities, their consistency, and their results. The analogical method allows us to do just this.

I use the analogical method throughout this book. The ancient Maya are the centerpiece of the work, but I use the ideas of early Chinese thinkers to offer a rough outline of one possible account of an overall Maya philosophical system. This should be thought of as a *preliminary* investigation of ancient Maya philosophy, offering a rough outline of the contours of Maya philosophical thought that will be filled in with future work on the topic—both my own, and hopefully also that of other philosophers.

THE LANGUAGES OF THE ANCIENT MAYA.

Maya culture and language is diverse, and contains many different elements. There exist many Maya languages and cultures today, and this was likely no different in the periods from the Preclassic to Postclassic.[40]

Most scholars accept the view that the language of most of the inscriptions in the Classic Period lowlands are from an ancestor of the modern Ch'orti' language, directly related to the (now extinct) Ch'olti' language (referred to as "Classic Ch'olti'an").[41] The Ch'orti' language is still spoken in Guatemala and Honduras. Both languages are members of the Cholan branch of Mayan languages, and Classic Ch'olti'an likely influenced a number of other Mayan languages in the region. Distinct non-Ch'olan languages such as Yucatec seem to have borrowed words from this Classic Ch'olti'an language. Even so, there was a large amount of linguistic diversity in the Maya region in ancient times just as there is today. Of the numerous Mayan languages spoken throughout the region, only a few of them are directly related to Classic Ch'olti'an, with the others representing different trees of the Mayan language family. The Mayan languages with the largest number of speakers today, such as the Quichean languages[42] and Yucatec, are from distinct branches of the Mayan language family from the Cholan languages. Their ancestors, then, were spoken in these regions at the same time the Classic Ch'olti'an language was used in the lowlands in the region of Tikal.

Given such rich linguistic diversity in the Maya region, there was inevitably cultural diversity as well. Language is a major component of culture, and even if we reject the extreme positions of linguistic relativists[43] that language determines patterns of thought, distinctness of language is at least a clear indication of distinctness of culture. The ancient Maya glyphs themselves (discussed further below) likely did not represent a *single* language, and I suspect they could have been read in more than one or two languages.[44] The distribution of glyphic writings of the Classic Period seems to have corresponded largely with the Ch'olti'an language area,[45] but there were inevitably other languages such as ancestors of Yucatec also associated with the glyphs, which had a wider distribution than the Ch'olti'an spoken language (especially after the Classic Period).[46]

Not only were there numerous languages used in the ancient Maya world, but there are regional variations in the glyphs as well.[47] The regional variations were mainly stylistic, and the glyphs may have been recognized by Maya from different areas with a distinct glyphic style, but these differences were not trivial and certainly suggest different cultural traits in areas of the Maya region. There are also very different architectural styles represented throughout the Maya region not attributable simply to time differences.[48]

Given all of these local differences within the greater Maya region, we should also expect that there would be differences in intellectual culture. For this reason, it may seem a simply wrongheaded approach to try to understand "Maya thought" as such. While I agree that this is less than ideal, due to the nature of our evidence there is much that we simply have to generalize about. Even though there was almost certainly at least as much intellectual diversity in the ancient Maya world as there was linguistic, artistic, and architectural diversity, there were also unifying features shared across numerous systems of thought, just as the four architectural styles of the Classic Maya Period share a family resemblance, as do of course the Mayan languages, which all trace their ancestry to Proto-Mayan, spoken before 2000 BCE.[49]

The nature of the ancient Maya glyphs can play a role in helping us to understand ancient Maya philosophical thought. The history of the continuing decipherment of the glyphs in the Western academy is well known.[50] Its most important phase took place in the 1950s, with the work of Russian linguist Yuri Knorosov. His work led to our current understanding of the glyphs as neither fully ideographic nor fully phonetic, but rather a combination of both.[51] The most basic glyphs are often representations of objects, such as a fish, the moon, etc. More complex glyphs can be combinations of these ideographs and phonetic glyphs that represent certain sounds. Often times the phonetic components of a glyph are redundant, and supplied to suggest the sound associated with the word written—yet further evidence that there were numerous ways of saying the same glyphic words in the Maya region.[52]

Sometimes a glyph associated with an important concept will give us clues as to the particular ways ancient Maya people understood the concept. Glyphic representation alone, of course, can only tell us so much, but combined with other evidence, including that of the kind of comparative philosophical method I rely on throughout this book, we can construct plausible accounts of key positions in ancient Maya thought.

While I think there is good reason to reject linguistic determinism,[53] features of the language in which a tradition does philosophy is certainly in some

Figure 0.2 **Diego de Landa's Mayan "alphabet," from his Relación de las cosas de Yucatán (1556), constructed using the assistance of Maya informants.** Today we know that de Landa's understanding was inaccurate. He assumed that the Maya language was written phonetically like European languages. While it turns out that ancient Maya script did have phonetic elements, de Landa's attempt to construct an alphabet was misguided. de Landa likely generated this by asking his Maya informant which symbol corresponded to certain sounds in the Spanish alphabet. Some of the above have been discovered to be phonetics, and some simply words pronounced using a certain vowel or syllable. For example u is a word for the third person possessive, "his/her/its," and its glyph is included here under the first "u." Despite its inaccuracy in supplying a Mayan "alphabet" however (no such thing existed), Russian linguist Yuri Knorosov made a major breakthrough in deciphering Maya glyphs in the 1950s by applying the glyph-phonetic connections included in de Landa's "alphabet." Manuscript held by the Tozzer Library.

Figure 0.3 Representation of the development of a few purely logoraphic Chinese characters from prehistoric times to the present. Like ancient Maya written language, Chinese writing uses a combination of phonetic symbols and logographs in compounds. The above are examples of more basic logographs, which are often used as radicals—elements of compound characters, such as 嗎, 魯, or 硨.

way relevant to the shape of philosophy that emerges from the tradition. Even if language does not determine the concepts and theories we develop, it perhaps *suggests* and even *limits* particular approaches. It is relevant then that Classic Mayan and Chinese languages are two of the most unique language groups in the world, and share a strong resemblance with one another in this uniqueness.

Unlike Indo-European, Semitic, and other languages, for example, Classic Mayan and Chinese languages are not completely phonetic in their script. The earliest signs in both languages are logographic—visual representations of words not connected to particular sounds, in many (but not all) cases connected to a visual illustration of the object referred to. As we can see from the image above, the Chinese terms for "horse," "fish," and "carriage" all represent images of the objects referred to by the term. These words are purely logographic in nature. In Chinese languages, generally the earliest and most basic terms are represented by logographic characters alone. These logographic characters are then used as *radicals* to form other characters. In these other characters, the radicals can be used to either signal part of the meaning of the word, or can be used for their phonetic significance, derived from the sound attached to the original word from which the radical is derived.

For example, the character 餌 *êr* (bait) is comprised of two characters. The character on the left is the *radical*, which gives the semantic component of the character. In this case, it is the character 食 *shi* (food/to eat), which one can see is an obvious component of bait. The right half of the character is made up by the *phonetic* component of the character, here the character 耳 *er* (ear). This component of the original character for "bait" is used not for its semantic significance—the term does not mean "food ear," but rather is being used for the *sound* associated with it. The original character 耳 *er* is a logographic character for the ear, but this logograph is borrowed in the case of 餌 to give the character its phonetic pronunciation: *er*. The tones are also different in the two terms 餌 and 耳, so as to further differentiate them in speech. Thus we see that Chinese languages, even though not purely phonetic in terms of symbols directly representing particular sounds as we see in alphabetic languages, have in their script a combination of logographic and syllabic elements. Chinese languages are members of a very small group of languages rendered in this way. The only other members of this group are the ancient Cuneiform script of Persia and surrounding regions, Anatolian hieroglyphs, and Classic Mayan.[54]

Classic Mayan glyphs are constructed very similarly. We can take a basic glyph like that for *tuun* (stone; year) as an example. This glyph (in many of its presentations) includes the logographic representation of a stone, combined with a syllabic element underneath this, representing the sound *ni*. Together, the elements read *tun-ni*, but the syllabic *ni* specifies that the vowel sound of the word represented by the logographic symbol should be extended, and thus the glyph reads *tuun*. The Classic Mayan combinations of logographs and syllables are more complex than that of Chinese languages, and less systematic as well. *Tuun*, for example, could be represented with or without the syllabic *ni* element, or in a different configuration altogether. There was also no standardized position for the logographic and phonetic elements within a glyph. Thus, a phonetic could be a postfix, subfix, or even placed inside of the logograph itself. In Chinese languages, positions for radicals and phonetic elements were fixed, so that the characters would be rendered the same everywhere. There was an element of standardization in this that was never achieved in Classic Mayan. This may have to do with the fact that the Chinese achieved a wide-reaching empire, while the Classic Maya never did, and there remained regional and city-state differences in script rendering throughout the Maya region.

As I show in the chapters below, the linguistic similarities between Mayan and Chinese are just the tip of the iceberg. Chinese thought can be extremely useful in helping us to reconstruct possible ancient Maya philosophical positions, allowing us a plausible path to go farther than we could otherwise using only ancient Maya materials, which are unfortunately scarce. Of course, we must always keep in mind that the ancient Maya were not the ancient Chinese, and that no matter how close the similarity between traditions, there are always divergences. Granting this, however, the suggestive aspects of Maya thought that we gain through the available materials offers us an outline of philosophical positions much like ones we can find in ancient China, and the analogical method becomes a useful way of attempting to fill in the gaps and to put the final touches of color and shade on the Maya views. What we are left with is likely not *exactly* what the ancient Maya held, but it is a vibrant and possible picture that may be more accurate than what we can gain through Maya materials alone. It is in some ways speculative—this much is granted. But it is not wild and imaginative speculation, it is speculation guided by limits, possibilities, similarities, and the terms of the available texts and artifacts of the ancient Maya. Those ultimately dictate the boundaries within which we work. Suggestions of similar views to Chinese schools can be filled out with something like the views of those Chinese schools, modified to fit into a Maya context.

HISTORICAL AND CULTURAL BACKGROUND OF THE MAYA

The robust decipherment of the Mayan glyphs in the last half of the twenty-first century, along with the continual archaeological evidence unearthed and analyzed in that same period, has made it possible to reconstruct a general history of the Maya world through much of the Preclassic, Classic, and Postclassic Periods.[55] Works like this one, of course, are also heavily indebted to the brilliant epigraphic and archaeological work of these scholars of the last century, who in many ways brought ancient Maya culture and history out of the darkness. The role of contemporary Maya people, of course, should not be forgotten in all of this. The advances of scholars would not have yielded very clear conclusions were it not for the sustained traditions and knowledge of the Maya people themselves, which has roots in the views of their ancestors in the ancient period. The beliefs, practices, and texts of contemporary Maya people in many ways reflect the views of the ancient Maya, and while things inevitably change, the vital core of the Maya views of the universe very much remain intact in the thought of the Maya today.[56]

A short account of the general contours of ancient Maya history and thought may be useful as a grounding for understanding some of what comes later in this book—especially for those readers unfamiliar with Maya thought and history. The most I can offer here is a general outline of some major features shared through much of the span of time focused on in this book and through much of the Maya region—although, as with any culture, there is much complexity, there are no universally held elements, and there are always exceptions. Thus, this (and everything in the book, for that matter) should be taken as representing very widely accepted and dispersed patterns of culture that existed among numerous others.

The term "Maya" used for the people of this region originates in Yucatec Mayan, and translates as "calendar cycle."[57] Thus this is not a term non-Yucatec people would have used for themselves. It was a term that came to be applied to the various linguistically related people of the Maya region by the Spanish, whose first contact was with the Yucatec Maya people. Other Maya people called themselves by other names, such as the *K'iche,' Kaqchikel*, etc.

There is some indication that Maya culture may have developed from a relative small number of early groups, as the thirty currently living Mayan languages (there were doubtless others that are closely related, and scholars hypothesize that they likely arose from a "Proto-Mayan" language). Some scholars believe that a Proto-Mayan speaking people originated in the southern highlands of what is today Guatemala,[58] but the postulation of a single ancestral group connected to later Maya communities is difficult to demonstrate, and also implausible.[59]

What we do know is that the highland area in the southwest of the Maya region is where we find the first indication of the features of Maya society which develops into the more complex social structures we begin to see in the middle of the Preclassic Period, and into the most famous periods of Maya history.[60] Maya history is categorized by scholars into three broad periods prior to contact with the Spanish in the mid-sixteenth century: the Preclassic, Classic, and Postclassic Periods. The Preclassic Period, by far the longest of these, comprises the entirety of Maya history prior to the development of stelae erection, including Long Count dates in the Maya city-states. The period spans from the very beginnings of Maya civilization throughout the wider Maya region in the second millennium BCE[61] to the beginning of stelae erection in the southern Maya cities in around 250 CE. The Classic Period, spanning from 250 to 900 CE, is the most well known, and associated with most of the features of ancient Maya culture, society, architecture, and artifacts with which we are familiar today. It was in the Classic Period that the southern lowland cities rose to prominence, and the political structure of the city-state focused on the *ahau* (lord, ruler) reached its peak, including the construction of elaborate glyphic texts with dates in the Long Count calendar throughout the Maya world. The decline of the southern lowland Maya cities around 900 CE and the move of the center of power in the Maya region north into the Yucatan (as well as the final abandonment of once strong southern highland cities such as Kaminaljuyu, at modern day Guatemala City) is where scholars mark the end of the Classic Period and the beginning of the Postclassic, which saw the rise of northern polities like the famous city of Chichen Itza, and the blending of Maya cultures with central Mexican influence from the West. The Postclassic spanned from this time until the Spanish contact and subsequent occupation of most of the Maya region.

All of the printed book texts available to us today come from the Postclassic or Postconquest Periods. The only texts available dating to earlier periods are those carved on stelae, buildings, monuments, or painted on other artifacts like pottery. Most of these date to the Classic and Preclassic Periods. Fortunately, the number of such texts is relatively large, especially texts of the Classic Period. The Maya language(s), expressed in one of the most complex and beautiful scripts in human history, was inscribed everywhere, on buildings, stelae, and general use artifacts. The written language became high art, and also had political, religious, and philosophical significance. Probably the only comparable development of script art on architecture in the world is that of the Islamic world, in which a very different kind of phonetic script (of the Arabic language) was developed into monumental art form. Whole histories are detailed on monuments and stelae in cities during the Classic Period, most often surrounding the lives of the *ahau* (rulers), which are presented in grand terms and connected to important events in the Long Count calendar. Books, of course, fared much worse than stone stelae in the Maya region. The fact that we have only four Maya books today is partly due to the less than ideal environmental conditions of much of the Maya region for storing texts. The central and southern parts of the Maya region are lush and humid rainforest, in which the kinds of bark paper books the Maya produced would not last long. The only part of the Maya region relatively friendly to the preservation of such texts is the far north in the Yucatan, which is much more arid and receives less rainfall. And it is indeed from this area that we have all four of the extant Maya codices. In this region, however, there was a different danger to the preservation of texts—overzealous Spanish missionaries, who sometimes attempted to wipe out what they saw as demonic or pagan elements of Maya culture through the destruction of texts, or Spanish treasure-seekers, who stole or otherwise took the Maya texts as souvenirs to return to Europe. It is through this method that we have access to the extant four codices today.[62] Likely many others were lost or otherwise destroyed.

Some description of the basic history of each of the periods relevant to this study will be useful:

Preclassic (~2000 BCE–250 CE)

I place the beginnings of this period in 2000 BCE rather than 1000 BCE, as seen in some sources, due to the increasingly different kinds of agriculture beginning around this period (at least that we have archaeological evidence for).[63] Interactions between the Maya and the Isthmian peoples, as well as people further inland and north such as the people of the powerful city of Teotihuacan, led to the development of new calendars, mathematical systems, writing systems, and forms of government and political organization. This culminated in the rise of the Preclassic power centers in the southern highlands, such as Izapa, Kaminaljuyu, and El Mirador, among others.[64]

This early period of urban development in the Maya world saw the development of urban centers with the specifically Maya features that would come to rise and dominate the tradition during the Classic Period. The origins of Maya patterns of government and particularly rulership seem to have begun in this period, as well as the centralizing urbanization that would culminate in the great cities of the Classic and Postclassic. The power centers of the Maya region were for the most part in the southern highlands. The cities and culture here were likely influenced by that of the city of Teotihuacan, which was connected to the region through trade and other cultural affiliations. The southern highland sites were important as trade centers between peoples on each side of the Maya to the northwest and southeast, and Preclassic Maya culture developed, as cultures generally do, at the confluence of a number of important influences that likely led to the renaissance we see in the Preclassic Period, with the rise of memorial architecture, elaborate urban design, and urban ritual centers. Each of these became a mainstay of Maya culture for the rest of the pre-Columbian period.

Classic (250–900 CE)

The Classic Period, as its name suggests, has long been taken by Mayanists to represent the pinnacle of the development of Maya culture. In more recent years, scholars have challenged this traditional notion.[65] Yet it is undeniable that we do see a Maya renaissance and the explosion of new forms of expression and life during this period. One of the main developments for our purposes was the beginning of the inclusion of glyphic texts on architecture and the erection of stelae including glyphs and dates in the Long Count calendar throughout the Maya region. New forms of rulership developed, and in particular the concept of the *ahau* (ruler) developed to its height. The *ahau* was seen as a priest-ruler with divine aspects, wholly in charge of a city or region, and expressive of its nature. The *ahau* had contact with the unseen aspects of the world (as I describe and explain in chapter 4), and was identified with the spirit of his realm itself. The "emblem glyphs" of Maya cities during this time (the use of which was a phenomenon that arose during the Classic Period) literally referred to the *ruler* of a particular city, but were used interchangeably as the sign for the city itself. The *ahau* and his polity came to be seen as one.

During the Classic Period, the center of power of the Maya world shifted from the cities of the southern highlands to the more central region of the southern lowlands in current-day Guatemala and Mexico. Cities such as Tikal (in the Petén region of northern Guatemala), Copan (modern day western Honduras), and Palenque (in modern-day Chiapas state, Mexico) became the epicenter of the new developments in Maya culture and thought. Most of the glyphic texts from stelae and monuments of the Classic Period we have today come from these sites, including the amazingly detailed architectural texts of Palenque, from which scholars have been able to reconstruct a detailed history of the ruling dynasty. Memorials and stelae at Classic Period sites document events in the lives of rulers, important battles, conquests, ritual ceremonies, and mythological events. Much of what we might understand of Maya philosophy comes from sources in this period. It is likely that the major focus on time as a central concept of Maya thought solidified during this period, even though there are certainly many indications that time was a major focus of Mesoamerican thought even as far back as the major developments of the Olmec and the people of Teotihuacan.[66]

Postclassic (900–1535 CE)

The Postclassic Period saw the shift of power in form of the central and dominant city-states to the northern lowlands of the Yucatan peninsula, and the rise and dominance of great cities like Chichen Itza, Coba, and other far northern cities along or near the Yucatan coast. It is likely that this continued strength of the northern cities, even while the cities of the central Maya region in the southern lowlands went into decline, was due to the market for salt, which was (and is) abundant in the coastal region of the Yucatan.[67]

In the northern cities of the Postclassic, we see a fascinating fusion of Maya cultural elements and those from further west. There is clear influence from peoples related to the people we know today as the Aztecs. Gods such as Kukulcan (Nahuatl; Quetzalcoatl), the "Plumed Serpent," Itzamna, and the sun god K'inich Ahau came to the fore. All of these deities appear to have Aztec counterparts. The city of Chichen Itza was dominated by a people who called themselves the Itza, of uncertain origin. Some claim they were a Maya group from further south who moved into the region when the southern lowland cities went into decline. Others claim that they were comprised largely of people from the west, Toltec invaders from central Mexico.

Regardless of the origins of the people of Chichen Itza, there are clearly elements of Postclassic Yucatec culture that are closely related to the cultural elements of central Mexican people of the time. It is in northern cities like Chichen Itza that Maya astronomy and astronomical architecture reaches its pinnacle. It is also from the Postclassic Yucatan that we have the only surviving Maya codices. These texts likely contained ritual, history, religious hymns, astronomical data, and other philosophical content. Doubtlessly the more southern areas of the Maya region had scholars producing such works as well, but none of these texts have been found today. There is, of course, the possibility that more texts will be unearthed by archaeologists, but if this is to happen, the strong odds are that it will happen in the northern lowlands of the Yucatan rather than in the southern lowlands or the highlands, for reasons discussed above.

The texts we have from the Postclassic are concerned mainly with divination, astronomy, accounts of creation, and calendrics. There is still a great deal of controversy concerning interpretation of the Postclassic codices (some of which I get into in the chapters below),[68] but they give us a wealth of information about Postclassic Maya society, especially since the decipherment of many of the glyphs included in the codices in relatively recent decades. The culture of northern Yucatan was somewhat different from more southerly Maya culture for a few reasons—the likely influence of groups from central Mexico and the very different climate account for much of the difference. For example, because of the aridity of the northern Yucatan, rain deities and water in general played a much greater religious role than in the southern areas.

The Postclassic period came to an end in the period of Spanish contact in the sixteenth century, which inaugurated the modern period of Maya history, in which the Maya resisted Spanish rule and influence, created vibrant syntheses between Christianity and Maya thought, and struggled to retain their autonomy amid the onslaught of Spanish colonialism. This process created the contemporary Maya world, in which most Maya have adopted Christianity and much of Western culture (albeit heavily influenced by earlier Maya culture). Some Maya still attempt to retain the pre-Spanish Maya ways more fully, however. This is a struggle we see in every culture that has faced colonialism—the attempt to navigate between the ideology and culture of modern life, which is heavily influenced by "foreign" elements, and the native ideology and culture of the people, created and sustained by them alone. The difficult issue of what it means to be Maya in the contemporary world thus echoes so many other issues of colonialized people across the world.

LORDS OF TIME

The chapters of this book cover the metaphysical thought of the Maya—the topics of being, fundamental ontology, personhood, change, and human destiny, among others. For the ancient Maya, one of the fundamental metaphysical categories was that of *time* (as I discuss in chapter 1), although they did not hold that all things *reduce* to time. Time was seen as an animating force of the universe, connecting a variety of essences and things or substances (essences plus material) in a single system of continual creation. For this reason, among others, human life was organized with a close concern with time. It was time, and the control of time, that determined power, spiritual authority, and other aspects of status in the Classic and early Postclassic Periods. The Maya gods and spirits, as I show in chapters below, were understood as aspects and manifestations of time and other important features of the world, related to one another and the world through time. And the rulers of the numerous Maya city-states made their claims to authority and divinity through claimed connection to the deities of time. The ruler in the ancient Maya world not only controlled time, but in a very real sense *represented* or *was* time. Thus, in calling these rulers and the ancient Maya in general "lords of time," I have multiple meanings in mind. They were lords over time, and lords *made* of time, exemplifying time. The title of this book has an additional meaning as well. Perhaps the most unique feature of Maya philosophy, as I argue throughout the book, is its innovative and original conception of time and the role time plays in the operation of the universe as a whole. Even in the close similarities between Maya and early Chinese thought, there is nothing in early China approximating the ancient Maya views concerning time. The Maya people devised and used intricate calendars, formulated complex mathematical and astronomical systems unrivaled anywhere in the world, and developed enduring philosophical systems, all with time at the very center. Anyone who would attempt to understand this most difficult of concepts is at a severe disadvantage without engaging with Maya thought.

NOTES

1. I discuss the Maya conception of essences and physical objects in chapter 3 below.

2. I follow the generally accepted practice here of using the term "Maya" when referring to people, and "Mayan" when referring to language. The *Maya* people speak *Mayan* languages.

3. The Mayan glyphic texts were books written on single folded strips of cloth made from the bark of fig trees. They were thus formed more similarly to modern books than to the scroll texts of other cultures such as that of early China.

4. de Landa's own account in his *Relación de las Cosas de Yucatan* (1562) is the main source for this story. He claims that he destroyed twenty-seven books, while other sources claim he destroyed many more. He writes: "Hallamosles grande número de libros de estas sus letras, y porq no tenían cosa, en que no oviesse superstiçion y falsedades del demonio se los quemamos todos, lo qual a maravilla sentían y les dava pena." ["We found a great number of books in these letters, and since they contained nothing but superstitions and falsehoods of the devil we burned them all, which they took most grievously, and which gave them great pain."]

5. Contemporary translations of these texts include Dennis Tedlock, *Popol Vuh*; Christenson, *Popol Vuh*; Barrera Vásquez *El libro de los libros del Chilam Balam de Chumayel*.

6. Knowlton, *Maya Creation Myths* examines the pre-Columbian content of the books of *Chilam Balam*.

7. As I discuss in later chapters on rulership, one of the most unique and interesting features of Maya thought is the place it accords to women in rulership and religion, a much more egalitarian position than what we find in much of early European or Asian thought (though not perfect, of course).

8. Such speculations have not been limited to non-academics such as Gavin Menzies. Archaeologist Betty Meggers in 1975 made a much more careful argument in that similarities in Shang Chinese and Olmec artifacts and culture give us good reason to consider the *possibility* that there was a link between the two and to do more work to determine whether this was indeed the case. Meggers, "The Transpacific Origin of Mesoamerican Civilization."

9. While the theory has been a mainstay of contemporary archaeology, some have challenged it, including Native American groups. Part of the worry is the political implications of the theory, with the suggestion that it was used by Europeans to delegitimize Native ownership of the land. Vine Deloria Jr. advanced an argument against the theory on these grounds. Deloria, *Spirit and Reason*, 78–100. More recently, a group of scientists raised doubts about it in an article in *Nature* on biological and geological grounds, arguing that the region of the strait would have been uninhabitable at the time the earliest groups were said to have moved through the area. Pedersen et al., "Postglacial Viability and Colonization in North America's Ice-Free Corridor." I remain neutral here on the question of the theory's acceptability.

10. At the time, the states of Central America were unified in the short-lived Federal Republic of Central America, which dissolved during Stephens' time there, as the result of civil war, which ultimately ended with the establishment of the five states that had comprised the Republic (Nicaragua, Honduras, Costa Rica, El Salvador, and Guatemala) as independent republics. The remaining part of the Republic, a segment of the state of Los Altos, was annexed by Mexico, becoming the state of Chiapas.

11. Though Stephens is sometimes credited as the modern "discoverer" of the Maya cities, he did no such thing. Stephens and Catherwood's native guides knew very well where these cities were, which is why they were able to lead Stephens to these sites, as did presumably everyone else living in the region.

12. William Carlsen tells the story of the travels of Stephens and Catherwood in Carlsen, *Jungle of Stone*.

13. Michael Coe offers a dramatic and detailed account of the events and discoveries that contributed to decipherment in his 1992 *Breaking the Maya Code*.

14. Our understanding of the ancient Maya script is still far from complete, however, despite wide use of the term "decipherment" to explain the leap forward in understanding in the later twentieth century.

15. Attempts at offering systematic histories based on the available evidence seem to have peaked in the 1930s and 1990s. Good examples include Linda Schele and David Friedel's 1990 *A Forest of Kings* and Tatiana Proskouriakoff's *Maya History*, which she worked on in the years just before her death in 1985, but which appeared in print in 1993.

16. Only four precolonial codices, or books, in ancient Maya script are known to still exist, though many more were written and did not survive, either due to the climate of the Maya area, inhospitable to preservation of texts, or the deliberate destruction of codices by the Spanish in the sixteenth century.

17. Schele and Friedel, *Forest of Kings*, 19.

18. Note that here I suggest that there are likely *numerous* systems of thought created by ancient Maya thinkers, rather than a single monolithic "ancient Maya thought." Although I argue below that the evidence supports this, I suggest that we should always assume that any intellectual culture includes a diversity of views and arguments, just as do the ones we have a fuller understanding of. Sinologists have recently learned this lesson. Better understanding of the Chinese philosophical tradition in the last fifty years or so has led to the drastic decline of claims about the "Chinese view."

19. Houston, Stuart, and Taube, *The Memory of Bones*; Joyce and Meskell, *Embodied Lives*.

20. Rice, *Maya Political Science*.

21. In particular the work of Western-trained Chinese philosophers such as Feng Youlan and Hu Shi in the early to mid-twentieth century. In the decades since their work, non-Chinese scholars have also done a great deal of work in the area. But the philosophical investigation of China began largely with Chinese scholars.

22. Gracia and Vargas, "Latin American Philosophy."

23. See McLeod, *Astronomy in the Ancient World*, which includes an explanation of and reflection on ancient Maya astronomy.

24. Maffie, *Aztec Philosophy.*

25. Not all of the Spanish in Mesoamerica, of course, can be saddled with this. Not even every *missionary* took it as a duty to eliminate native Maya culture. The efforts of Bartolomé de las Casas famously advocated for the rights of native people of Mesoamerica in Spain, at the same time he tried to convert them to Christianity. Bernardino de Sahagún, also a missionary, aided in the preservation of knowledge in the west of Aztec and Maya cultures through his ethnographic work.

26. This is not to say that North American people did not build cities on massive scales akin to those of the Mesoamericans. The Mississippian city of Cahokia, the remains of which stand to this day along the Mississippi River east of St. Louis, MO, was among the largest cities in the world during its peak. See Pauketat, *Cahokia*. North American cities—dwellings and other structures—were not built with stone and more permanent materials, however, as they were in Mesoamerica, and so we do not find the preserved structures and stelae of Mesoamerica in North America. Nor do we have evidence of written language among the North American peoples (although this does not rule out the possibility that they did have writing).

27. For example, Mercedes de la Garza, "Time and World in Maya and Nahuatl Thought," 105: "It would be true to say that the ideas that the Nahuas and Mayas hold about their gods, the world and man show the originality of their worldview, where there is little room for the logical classifications of Western thought." I will deal with the issue of the purported "cyclical" nature of time for the Maya in opposition to a "linear" conception of time in the West in chapter 1.

28. Miguel Angel Astor-Aguilera argues for the existence of something like an "indigenous thought" common to North American and Mesoamerican groups in Astor-Aguilera, *Communicating Objects.*

29. Timothy Pauketat and Steven Lekson are advocates of the "robust connection" view.

30. Demarest, "The Collapse of the Classic Maya Kingdoms of the Southwest Petén"; Culbert, *The Classic Maya Collapse.*

31. These aspects of the Postclassic are discussed in Sharer, *The Ancient Maya*, Coe, *The Maya.*

32. Foster, *Handbook to Life in the Ancient Maya World*, 223.

33. It was generally considered that the "Toltec" influenced the Yucatan region, but it is argued (Kristan-Graham, "Structuring Identity at Tula," 533) that there were multiple important sites associated with the name "Tula" or "Tollan," including within the Maya region. It may be possible that the Toltec of the "Tula" of central Mexico were actually influenced by the peoples of Maya cities such as Chichen Itza, rather than the other way around.

34. A few examples are Astor-Aguilera, *The Maya World of Communicating Objects*, Tedlock, *Time and the Highland Maya*, and Friedel, Schele, and Parker's classic *Maya Cosmos.*

35. Alastair Bonnett's book *The Idea of the West* argues that non-Western people were as responsible for its construction as westerners.

36. See Bartha, Paul. "Analogy and Analogical Reasoning." *Stanford Encyclopedia of Philosophy.*

37. The kind of "whig history" underlying this assumption presupposes that the theories and concepts popular today are somehow more advanced, more likely to be true, or otherwise better than their historical counterparts. The idea that we know more today and are closer to the truth than our intellectual predecessors is an assumption without argument to support it. Some scholars, such as Alasdair MacIntyre for example, hold that we are today in a relatively ignorant and unenlightened age as compared with a number of points in the past. MacIntyre speaks of today as a "new dark age" in his *After Virtue*, 263. We cannot simply assume that he is wrong about this.

38. Indeed, the way the concepts of *history*, *economy*, *religion*, etc. are understood in the Western academy are far different from ancient Maya concepts, yet we unhesitatingly use these concepts to describe ancient Maya realities.

39. Although I am wary of making such a distinction, as a general bar to creativity and a bludgeon with which to ensure methodological conformity within certain fields—to assume that we need "ground rules" is to accept that we're playing a competitive game. And why think we should be doing that?

40. Despite this clear diversity, the development of a "Pan-Maya" ethnic identity has been taking place in recent years in the Maya region of Central America, in part to empower the greater Maya community, which has struggled with racism and oppression by hostile groups and regimes in the last few centuries. Victor Montejo discusses this "Pan-Maya" movement in his *Maya Intellectual Renaissance*, 16–36.

41. Houston, Robertson, and Stuart, "The Language of Classic Maya Inscriptions."

42. Including the most widely spoken Mayan language, K'iche', the language of the *Popol Vuh.*

43. Often associated with the so-called "Sapir-Whorf hypothesis."

44. Just as identical Chinese characters can be read in a number of different dialects and languages.

45. Schele, *Maya Glyphs,* Introduction #2.

46. Perhaps this was even part of the reason for creating a glyphic written language—it would be recognized more widely than a particular spoken language. Speakers of Cholan and Yucatecan languages may have been unable to understand each other's speech, but both recognize terms and statements in glyphic representation, just as would be the case for a Mandarin and Cantonese speaker with regard to Chinese script.

47. Kelley, *Deciphering the Maya Script,* 15.

48. Parmington, *Space and Sculpture in the Classic Maya City,* 7 ("While acknowledging similarities in architectural traditions throughout the ancient Maya world, there are some regional difference that should be outlined here briefly. There are four principle styles that characterize Classic Maya architecture; these are the Petén architectural style, the Usumacinta architectural style, the Southeastern Lowland architectural style, and the Puuc architectural style.").

49. Foster, *Handbook to Life in the Ancient Maya World,* 274.

50. See, in particular, Michael Coe, *Breaking the Maya Code.*

51. The academic "consensus" prior to Knorosov's breakthrough had been fixed by the agenda set by British archaeologist and epigrapher Eric Thompson, who saw the glyphs as purely ideographic, with no phonetic components.

52. McKillop, *The Ancient Maya,* 296.

53. Among the problems for a strong form of the Sapir-Whorf hypothesis is that it would make translation impossible, and thus also make it impossible to learn new languages using translation. We would have to learn each new language as infants do, and even with facility in multiple languages, would be unable to translate them to one another.

54. Other combination logograph-phonetic systems, such as Egyptian hieroglyphs, have consonants rather than syllables as the phonetic element.

55. Schele and Friedel (*A Forest of Kings*) offered just such an account.

56. Examples of contemporary or modern Maya thought offering us windows onto the ancient Maya, as well as interpretation or corroboration of the results of scholars, include Barbara Tedlock's *Time and the Highland Maya,* the fifteenth-century play *Rabinal Achi,* Alfonso Villa Rojas, *Estudios etnológicos: los mayas.*

57. Herring, *Art and Writing in the Maya Cities,* 34.

58. Sharer, *The Ancient Maya,* 28.

59. There is a similar situation for the so-called "Proto-Indo-Europeans," or speakers of the Proto-Indo-European language that was the ancestor of most of the languages of Europe, West-Central Asia, and North India. The PIE language was likely spoken by a cluster of different peoples in the region around the Caspian Sea, who moved out of the region in different waves, and integrated with different peoples. A similar situation is likely for Proto-Mayan-speaking groups.

60. Foster, *Handbook*, 35. The earliest erection of memorial stelae, including texts in glyphs, is associated with this development.

61. One traditional (but somewhat arbitrary) categorization has the Preclassic Period begin in 2000 BCE.

62. Witschey, *Encyclopedia of the Ancient Maya*, 100.

63. Domesticated maize was introduced in 3000 BCE, and the earliest Mesoamerican pottery appeared around 2000 BCE along the Pacific coast. Foster, *Handbook*, 21–22.

64. López Austin and López Luján, *El pasado indígena*, ch. 2.

65. Demarest, Rice, and Rice, *The Terminal Classic in the Maya Lowlands*, Introduction.

66. Olmec or Isthmian origins of the Long Count, the alignments of Teotihuacan. Malmstrom, *Cycles of the Sun, Mysteries of the Moon*.

67. Sharer, *Daily Life in Maya Civilization*, 100.

68. Vail and Hernandez, in *Re-Creating Primordial Time,* read the codices as containing calendric rituals as well as creation myths and cosmogony. Pharo, in *The Ritual Practice of Time*, on the other hand, rejects the view that the codices refer specifically to creation accounts.

Chapter 1

Calendrics, Ritual, and Organization

AVOIDING EXOTICISM OF NON-WESTERN THOUGHT, AND MAYA THOUGHT AS PHILOSOPHY

There can be a temptation when we read non-Western philosophy to see it as necessarily opposed to Western philosophy.[1] Thus we see a tendency to interpret many non-Western philosophical traditions (including that of the Maya) as fundamentally monistic concerning aspects of metaphysics in which much of the Western philosophical tradition is dualist. Scholars often read the Western tradition as dualistic concerning issues such as the distinction between mind and body (at least from Plato to the modern period). We also tend to claim that views of transcendence are prevalent in the West (Plato's dual realms, God and human souls as transcendent or outside the natural order, etc.).

Scholars often read the history of non-Western philosophical traditions as rejecting dualistic understandings of the world, and instead endorsing monistic views.[2] Much of this interpretation of non-Western traditions is guided by the desire to present these traditions as alternatives to the West. Well intentioned though this approach may be, many problematic claims have been made through its use. This one, from Sarvepalli Radhakrishnan's classic *Sourcebook in Indian Philosophy*, is a good example:

> The tendency of Indian philosophy, especially Hinduism, has been in the direction of monistic idealism. Almost all Indian philosophy believes that reality is ultimately one and ultimately spiritual. Some systems have seemed to espouse dualism or pluralism, but even these have been deeply permeated by a strong monistic character.[3]

This claim is demonstrably false. The Indian tradition, more than any other "Non-Western" tradition, shares most of the dualistic views of its Western

1

cousins concerning mind and body, human and divine worlds, etc. It is especially similar to the traditions of ancient Greece. And it is no accident that this is the case—the Indian and Greek philosophical traditions are related to one another, just as the Sanskrit and Greek languages are related.[4] Schools such as the Vedanta schools, present dominance notwithstanding, were the exception rather than the rule just as in the Western tradition. For some reason, however, we tend to overestimate the influence and centrality of such schools and texts in non-Western traditions, presenting them as representative of entire traditions in ways they never were. This is an ever-present danger of looking for difference when approaching non-Western traditions. If discovering difference is our goal, then when we find it we will tend to focus on it exclusively, which then colors our general understanding of an overall tradition.

It is not the case that Western philosophy finds discrete boundaries between things and makes a unique distinction between, for example, the immanent and transcendent, while Chinese, Indian, Mesoamerican, Egyptian, Sub-Saharan African, North American, and seemingly every other philosophical tradition recognizes a monism in which all things are ultimately one and the immanent-transcendent distinction is broken down. Indeed, I think there is little reason, when we explore these philosophical traditions, to see this going on almost *anywhere*. I argue that the "holistic" or monistic view is actually much rarer than dualistic views on the above-mentioned topics in global philosophical history. In addition, the numerous Western views that are taken as the paradigm cases of "dualism" aren't as dualistic as they are made out to be.

We have to remember that these independent traditions did not develop as reactions to the West, they developed in their own ways that had nothing to do with the West, and in most cases were developed long before there *was* any conception of the "West" as a distinct entity, in Europe or anywhere else in the world. And they often share more in common with Western tradition than we recognize. These systems are not simply parallels of those of Western traditions, and we can always find robust differences. But non-Western traditions also do not tend to fall into a convenient "anti-West" or opposite-from-West distinction. Indeed, it is somewhat unfortunate that we even think of global philosophical traditions as falling into the categories of "Western" and "Non-Western," as this may in part explain *why* so-called "Non-Western" traditions tend to be interpreted similarly and as contrastive with the West. If some traditions fall within the category of the West, then there must be some substantive difference between these and other philosophical traditions left out of this "West."

One problem here is that the idea of the West is not, and never has been, one based on similarity or difference of intellectual culture or tendency. It is mainly a racial, religious, and political idea,[5] and thus we should expect, as is the case, that the lines will not be clearly drawn concerning intellectual culture. Insofar as *philosophical* tradition is concerned, then, the West/non-West divide is almost completely arbitrary. It is not akin to the analytic-continental divide in contemporary philosophy, which, although it may not ultimately be a useful distinction, at least *is* based on general differences in intellectual features, styles, and trends. Rather, making a distinction between Western and non-Western philosophy is closer to making a distinction between New York City philosophy and Washington DC philosophy (though the analogy is not perfect). If there are any differences between the two, it is based on coincidences concerning who is working on what in each area—that is, the unique character of each is likely coincidental and artificially maintained. There is no organic and self-contained nature of NYC philosophy as contrasted to DC philosophy. The larger traditions that created regularities in contemporary analytic philosophy, for example, have little or nothing to do with inter-USA civic political distinctions. So using these distinctions to characterize philosophical traditions will necessarily create artificial divides. "Western" and "Non-Western" philosophy are largely the same as philosophical categories, however well they might work in other areas.

Another interpretation one tends to see of non-Western traditions, albeit one more often found in anthropological rather than philosophical circles, is that non-Western traditions focus on the *material* as opposed to the *ideal*. This seems to me to be based in the same tendency seen in philosophy to focus on the "otherness" of non-Western thought. This trend in anthropology, however, seems to me even more dangerous and fraught with difficulty than that of philosophy that tends to read non-Western traditions as metaphysically monistic. Numerous recent studies focus on the physical body as central and exclusive in the Maya concept of the person.[6] In the realm of time as well, Mayanist scholars tend to advance interpretations of ancient Maya as understanding time primarily through reflecting on the physicality of its expression.[7]

There are numerous problems with this. Perhaps the biggest problem is that the available textual data simply does not support the idea that the ancient Maya were essentially physicalist in the way some anthropologists interpret them.[8] Meskell and Joyce, for example, present the Maya conception of the person as one opposed to what they call a "Cartesian" conception of the person as primarily a thinking thing only contingently embodied.[9] They argue that the ancient Maya saw personhood as primarily physical, and rejected the dualistic view of a distinction between physical and mental aspects of persons. This position, however, is difficult to maintain in the face of textual evidence. As discussed in chapter 4, there are a number of elements of personhood for the ancient Maya that cannot be explained as physical, including the concepts of the *pix* (spirit), and the *way*—an animal spirit-companion or

representative, similar to the concept of the *totem* in North American thought
(from the Ojibwe work *dodaem*). Miguel Astor-Aguilera says of the Maya
concept of spirit:

> the Mayan word *pixan*, apparently from the root of *piix*, as sheath, has often
> been glossed into the Christian concept of spirit or soul. Piix, however, is bet-
> ter understood as representing bound and fixed personhood that makes humans
> or other things and objects kux'an, that is, alive. The pixan is what becomes
> untethered from the body of a human, or other thing or object, at death. If the
> pixan strays too long or leaves the body vessel permanently, it renders that
> object devoid of volition and personhood, that is, lifeless. The human body, in
> this sense, is no different from other sorts of material objects. A person within
> my Maya consultants' world view is simply an object that has sentient agency
> attached to it. Persons can be and are attached to things other than human. My
> j'meen consultants can, if they know how, communicate with cross persons, tree
> persons, plant persons, animal persons, rock persons, and so on down the line.
> These persons, as linked to regeneration, are very different from the animism
> that is often attributed to the Maya and many Native Americans.[10]

One might argue that Astor-Aguilera's explanation here is of *contemporary*
Maya concepts, particularly in the Yucatan. These very ideas, however, can
be found in ancient Maya sources as well, and should be taken as representative of earlier Maya thought, rather than as due to Christian or other Western
influence. While the ancient Maya *did*, I argue below, accept monism about
worlds, the single world did not, according to their view, contain only material objects. No immaterial world was seen as necessary to explain the existence of immaterial entities.

A number of other concepts that Meskell and Joyce set aside also refer to
mental or spiritual aspects of the person with no apparent physical manifestation. It is hard to make sense of these aspects of the Maya conception of
personhood if the Maya are taken as physicalist.

In the case of anthropology, I suspect one of the reasons there is so much
focus on the physical is the nature of the field. Most Mayanists are archaeologists, and it is the nature of archaeology to be concerned with physical
materials. For much of Maya culture, such study of the physical can be
enormously useful. However, it fares less well in the realm of ideas, in which
the intellectual historian and philosopher work. In philosophy, though we
can (and must!) be concerned with materials, primarily textual material, we
proceed from there independently of materials, considering the coherence of
ideas drawn from those texts with one another. In addition, the significance
of these ideas does not, for the philosopher, have to be connected to or
grounded in other nonphilosophical aspects of the original thinker's life. That
is, ideas can be entertained and advanced because they are *philosophically*

edifying—because a thinker believes that they offer an explanation of the world. Philosophical justifications for ideas can then be distinct from political or economic justifications, and the former do not always simply reduce to the latter. For the philosopher, the question of why the ancient Maya held the views they did about time does not ground out in the political or economic efficacy of the view, or in the ability of the view to fulfill desires, but in its coherence and its ability to genuinely make sense of the phenomenon of time. In this way, the ultimate test of views for the philosopher is their plausibility and coherence, as well as their ability to elegantly and adequately make sense of the world and other views held in a system. While other fields tend to be reductionist about philosophy and ideology, such that philosophical views are held primarily as political or economic expedients, the philosopher will insist that philosophical reasons can be legitimate reasons that do not reduce. Among human concerns are *philosophical* concerns. We have a basic desire to answer fundamental questions concerning the world and our lives. Thus engagement in philosophical thought need not be understood as grounded in a desire for something else, such as political control or economic success.[11]

There has been little attention paid by Mayanists to Maya philosophical thought concerning the concept of time.[12] Many scholars recognize the importance of the concept of time in Maya thought, as well as its various representations in texts, memorial architecture, and cultural practices. But few have attempted to offer interpretations of Maya conceptions of time and the role they play in the broader metaphysical systems of the Maya.

Prudence Rice remarks on this hesitancy on the part of Mayanists:

> scholars commonly pay lip service to the concept of Maya kings as "lords of time," but they have not examined what this might mean in an evidentiary or hypothetico-deductive sense: *if* Maya kings were indeed lords of time, *then* how does that structure our expectations about how this role might be manifest in the material record?[13]

Indeed, I think we can and should go beyond even this. I agree with Rice that scholars have not paid enough attention to just what the role of time in ancient Maya thought was, but even more than this, some have failed to pay attention to how the role of the Maya kings as "lords of time" manifests *intellectual* culture and ties into Maya religious and philosophical beliefs and perhaps argument considered distinct from the material record.

Many scholars who have recently come to investigate Maya intellectual culture have taken it as representative of "pan-Mesoamerican" intellectual tendencies, described by some of the great interpreters of Aztec intellectual tradition, particularly Miguel Leon-Portilla.[14] At the same time, it is almost universal among scholars to see the Maya as having *time* as either the fundamental aspect or a fundamental aspect of ontology, and this is something very different than what we see in the Aztec context. What is going on here? As Timothy Knowlton points out, Mayanist concern with intellectual culture is much more recent than that of Nahuatlists.[15] I would argue that Mayanists *still* have not engaged in the kind of investigation of Maya intellectual culture akin to what scholars have done with the Aztecs. Thus, Mayanists who discuss Maya intellectual culture inevitably rely on well-worked-out theories of Aztec thought. While studies of Aztec thought can certainly be helpful in our attempt to interpret ancient Maya philosophy, we can make headway in understanding the ancient Maya material in its own context as well.

THE CONCEPT OF K'IN AND THE MAYA CALENDARS

The term for "day" in Classic Mayan is *k'in*, written with the glyph above. Some scholars, most famously Eric Thompson and Miguel Leon-Portilla,[16] argued that *k'in* played a central role in Maya thought surrounding time, the calendars, and the organization of the cosmos. Some of this may be due to the fact that *k'in* is used as an element of the names of important deities and rulers.[17] There is concentration on *k'in* as a time element beyond what we find for other time elements, such as *winals*, *katuns*, or other units. All of this is perhaps what we should expect—the day is the most obvious visible expression of time in human experience, around which we pattern our regular activities. While the day may be a fundamental component of human experience, however, we cannot conclude just on the basis of this that it held a key role in Maya ontology of time, that it was a basic unit of time, or that it had a particular philosophical significance. *K'in*, I contend, is a more complex concept than simply that of the "day," and we have reason to reject a kind of "atomism" about time that takes *k'in* to be the basic unit of time on which others are constructed.

The various Maya calendars represent different combinations and parsings of the *k'in*. In the Long Count, all of the major time units are based on the day. The *tuun*, or "stone" is initially a count number for days—360 days, roughly equivalent to a year. While the Maya were quite aware of the length of the tropical year as between 365 and 366 days,[18] the official year was only 360, and an additional 5 days falling outside of the calendar were added to the end of each year.[19] One way to think of the *haab* is as a *tuun* with the addition of 5 days.

On the surface, *k'in* refers to the sun, and also in this sense signifies a *day* (a usage for which the term for "sun" stands in many languages). It also forms part of the compound term *k'inich*, which stands for the Sun God (*k'inich ahau*).[20] The term *k'inich* is also commonly appropriated by Classic Period rulers as part of their own names—presumably reign names, though its conceivable members of a court may have taken it as a given name as well in grooming for rulership and claim to future legitimacy.[21] It was adopted in

Figure 1.1　The k'in glyph is composed of a main sign [K'IN] on the top, the phonetic [-ni] as subfix. The glyph as a whole is read k'in (following the Yucatec pronunciation ascribed to the Classic glyphs by Mayanists). Drawing by Shubhalaxmi McLeod.

part to reinforce their authority as central priests and primary controllers of the cosmos.

Miguel Leon-Portilla sees in the concept of *k'in* something even more foundational to Classic Period Maya thought, linking the concept of being with that of time.[22] According to Leon-Portilla, *k'in* as time represents the background on which being is possible, and thus is linked with (even identified with) being. It is for this reason, according to Leon-Portilla and others,[23] that the various Maya gods are identified with particular times, with portions of the calendars. The Classic Maya ontology then, if this is right, is primarily one constructed of units of *time*. All other categories in ancient Maya thought reduce to time, according to this position. While I argue against that view in this section, I argue that we can make sense of the central position of time in Maya metaphysics without accepting a reductionism of the type Leon-Portilla endorses.

This reliance on identification with the sun as a symbol of rulership does not in itself show that *k'in*, as the sun and representation of time, has the kind of unifying metaphysical role that Leon-Portilla attributes to it. The sun was a common image adopted by rulers worldwide, adopted by the pharaoh Akhenaten of the eighteenth Dynasty of Egypt, who associated himself with the sun, the Roman emperor Constantine, whose sun king imagery (adoption of the character of the deity *Sol Invictus*, the "Unconquered Sun") became associated with Christianity, the religion he patronized and brought to ascendancy in Europe, and the French "Sun King" Louis XIV, among many others. In none of these cultures was there a correlative cosmology with the sun as representative of time at the center as claimed for the ancient Maya. So we need more than just this fact to rely on. Leon-Portilla argues for the centrality of *k'in* by making a move from the meaning of *k'in* as the sun (or *a* solar cycle) to the sum of all solar cycles—the sun taken in the sense of the entirety of its motion and existence.[24]

Figures 1.2   K'inich Ahau, as Solar Deity, from a Ceramic Vase, and as Symbol of Rulership. Photo by Justin Kerr.

Figure 1.3 K'inich Ahau Glyph, Found in the Dresden Codex. Drawing by the author.

There is little doubt that the Maya calendar plays a large role in thinking about the cosmos in general, and also about being as a general category. The details of the origin and operation of the various calendars in use in and around the Classic Period in the Maya area are still not completely understood, but we are well aware of some of the basics. We also have access to the practices of contemporary daykeepers, which can further illuminate ancient practices. The unit *k'in* is used in all of the calendars, the "Long Count" as well as the 360-day solar year (*haab*) calendar and the 260-day *tzolk'in*.[25] The most well-known of the Maya calendars, which we refer to as the "Long Count" calendar, had its origins not in the Maya region but further to the West, with Mixe-Zoque people, perhaps the Olmec.[26] The calendar has become most closely associated with the Maya, however, in part because they seem to have used it in a more robust way, possibly even to organize political hierarchies.[27] Although the calendar was not created by the Maya, the Maya did *perfect* the calendar that they adopted from other peoples. In addition to their extension and development of the calendar, they invented a mathematical system used for the count, based in a *vigesimal* numeral system, rather than the more familiar *decimal* system used in the majority of societies today.

This requires some explanation. A *decimal* system of numbers is one in Base 10, that is, in which the basic collection is ten numbers, after which a new unit is begun. So, for example, we count one through ten, and then after ten we begin to count the *next* group of tens, eleven through twenty, and so on. The decimal system of numbers counts based on powers of ten. So we have 10, 20, 30, 40, and so on, beginning a new count of 10s for every ten. Although we are so familiar with this system as to completely take it for granted, there is no particular reason we *need* to count in a decimal system. It is believed that the reason many societies adopted a decimal system is the rather obvious one—we have ten fingers, and thus grouping numbers into units of tens is very intuitive when one is using fingers to count. But say we had eight fingers, or we just decided to adopt a different system. We could perfectly well adopt a Base Eight system of numerals, or any other base for that matter. Base Eight would take each unit or place to have eight numerals, such that our counts would look like this:

1, 2, 3, 4, 5, 6, 7, 10, 11, 12, 13, 14, 15, 16, 17, 20, ... and so on.

In the Maya vigesimal system, or Base-20, there are 19 numerals before a new numeral place is reached. The numeral writing system allowed this with much more ease than does our own decimal system (since we have fewer basic numerals than the Maya). The Maya system used a dot to represent one, and a dash to represent five. Thus, three dashes and four dots would be the final numeral in the initial series before movement to a different place, with 20. The way this worked was similar to how our own place system works, but the Maya numbers were written vertically from top to bottom (similar to the classical Chinese), rather than left to right as in our own system, or right to left as in Semitic languages such as Arabic and Hebrew.

The bottom line is the 20s place, representing 1 to 19. The next line up represents the second 20s place (or 400th place), containing numbers 20 to 399. The next line up from there is the third 20s place (or 8,000th place), containing numbers 400 (twenty 20s) to 7,999 (where 8,000 is twenty 400s). And so on, each place being a new multiplicand of 20. Thus, the numeral

….

———

———

is equivalent to our numeral 1,705, reading from the top line down thus: 1,600 (four 400s) +100 (five 20s)+ 5. One possibility is that there may be numbers with *zero* units in any given place, and for this the Maya needed a conception of zero in order to make sense of this. Thus, we see the development in Maya (and earlier) mathematics of the concept of zero, which some scholars believed developed even before the discovery of the concept of zero in India, a region which is commonly accorded the credit for discovery of the concept. Our number 1,605, for example, is rendered in the Maya system thus:

.... (four 400s= 1,600)

0 (zero twenties)

___ (five)

These numbers were used in the Long Count calendar to keep track of days, months, and years, in a sequence beginning in what we know as 3113 BCE and continuing to 2012 CE. The previous *baktun* sequence of the Maya Long Count calendar, in use during the Maya Classic Period, came to an end on a winter solstice day—December 21, 2012.

The Maya maintained two other calendars as well—the 260-day ritual calendar, "short count," or *tzolk'in*, and the 365-day solar year "vague" calendar, or *haab* (just as with the Long Count, the Maya did not invent these calendars, but adapted them). While it may at first seem strange to us to have multiple calendars, when we think about what this really amounts to, as well as our own practices, we will see that it makes sense. Academic calendars are a good example, familiar to most of us—those who work in academia, as well as those of us who have gone to the university at some point. The academic calendar runs alongside the Gregorian calendar we use to determine years, but is not the same as this calendar, and has different beginning and ending dates, different holidays, etc. The academic calendar generally (for an institution running on semesters) has nine months rather than twelve (as any academic who is paid on a nine-month contract is acutely aware), has years which begin not in January as do the Gregorian's, but instead in late August, and end not in December but in early or mid-May. For those of us who live and move in academia, the academic calendar has as much, if not more, significance than the Gregorian calendar, which we also use. In my own life, then, I have two significant calendars, the academic and the Gregorian. It is easier for me to organize years of my own life in terms of the academic calendar than the Gregorian. When I think of 2008 in the Gregorian calendar, for example, this is usually somewhat vague for me until I consider it in terms of two distinct academic years, the 2007–2008 academic year, and the 2008–2009 academic year. My memory of something that happened in 2008 can sometimes turn out to be something that happened in 2007, but was fixed in my mind to the

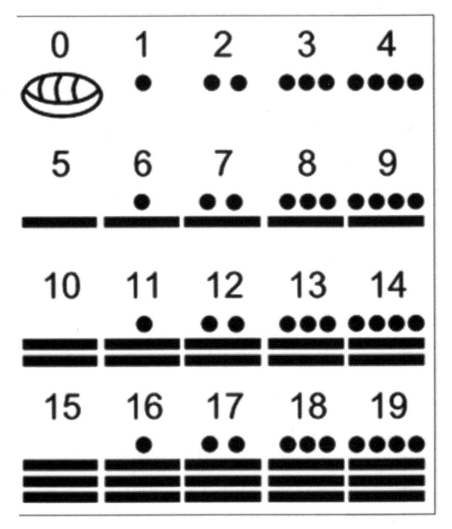

Figure 1.4   The Maya numeral system was a Base-20, or vigesimal system, in comparison to our Base-10 (decimal) system. The system contained nineteen distinct numerals, based on a dot signifying one to the dash signifying five, and a glyph of a shell, representing zero. The concept of zero was necessary for the ability to shift places, as we do in our own decimal system. Without it, one has a clunky numerical system that is difficult to use for calculation, like that of the Romans. Image by Bryan Derksen—free use under Creative Commons, accessed https://en.wikipedia.org/wiki/Maya_numerals#/media/File:Maya.svg.

2007–2008 academic year, which I associate with 2008. Most people who have at one time been students (which is just about all of us) thought in the same way while students. So we see that having multiple calendars is not so strange after all.

The Maya calendars, like our academic, Gregorian, and other calendars, played different roles in the community. The *haab* and *tzolk'in* calendars were often linked to one another (just as our academic and Gregorian calendars are linked), and in the famous Aztec calendar stone, the two are represented together, such that on any given date one can tell the day in both calendars. The operation of the 365-day *haab* calendar will be simple to anyone reading this, as our own calendar is a version of such a solar calendar. The Mesoamerican version, however, did not include the conception of the "leap year" to calibrate the calendar every four years. The need for a leap-year day, of course, arises from the fact that the full sidereal year, the time it takes for the earth to make one complete orbit around the sun, such that the sun will at the end point to be in the same position against the background stars as at the beginning point, is not exactly 365 days, but 365.25636 days. This means that every four years, a 365-day calendar will be a day behind the sidereal year. With enough years passing without calibration, the calendar will slowly creep backward, and the seasons will diverge from the calendar. If we begin with December 23 marking the winter solstice, after 120 years, the calendar will be off by a full month, with November 23 marking the solstice (Notice also that since the discrepancy between the sidereal year and solar calendar is not exactly .25, occasionally leap *seconds* have to be added to our calendar as well). In temperate regions in the northern and southern hemisphere, this is critical. In tropical regions, however, such as that of the Mesoamerican civilizations, this may be less of a concern, and thus we see that the 365-day calendar did not contain a calibration leap-year day or any other such device, even though the Maya were aware of the one-fourth day divergence between the sidereal year and the solar calendar.[28]

The 260-day *tzolk'in* ritual calendar is one of the most unique calendars of the Mesoamerican world, and an interesting and complex one. This was the calendar (along with the *haab*) used by the Aztecs, who did not adopt the Long Count so prized and perfected by the Maya. The 260-day calendar was broken into twenty named days (following the Maya vigesimal series of 20), starting with *Imix*, continuing through the series of 20, then starting with the next set. Along with each day, one of a set of 13 numerals was attached. Thus, each day of the calendar would be fixed with a day sign and a numeral, beginning with 1 *Imix*. The following day would be 2 *Ik* ("Ik" being the second day sign), and so forth, until the set of twenty days completed and returned to *Imix*, the twenty-first day. Because each day gets 1 of 13 numerals, however, the second appearance of *Imix* would not be 2 *Imix*, but 8 *Imix*. The next appearance of *Imix* after that would be 2 *Imix*, then 9 *Imix*, and so on, until every day sign had thirteen rounds, after which the calendar would be completed, until the inauguration of the next ritual year.

The centrality of *k'in* in Maya thought, according to Leon-Portilla, is shown by its use in defining all other components of time. The most basic sense of the term *k'in* is "day," but *k'in* as central metaphysical concept of the Maya conception of time includes more than this, according to Leon-Portilla. He explains how the concept of the day became the concept of time itself:

> If in [Maya] thought the day was a solar presence, time was the limitless succession of all solar cycles. Thus *k'in* spontaneously acquired its most ample meaning: duration that cannot be expressed because it has no limits, time, the sum of all possible solar cycles.[29]

While I disagree with Leon-Portilla that *k'in* itself represented the fundamental component of time, we have good reason to think that he was right that the Maya took time as being without limit and marked by regular processes. To talk about the Maya conception of time in terms of *cycles* is somewhat problematic. The reason for this is that much of the discussion of "cyclical time" misses what is truly unique about Maya philosophy of time, and mistakes much of it as well. Time, for the ancient Maya, certainly has cyclic aspects, but the fundamentally important feature of time is that it is linked to the experience of persons, whether human or otherwise.[30] What ultimately characterizes time is its ability to be understood in terms of the connectivity of experiences of different persons and entities, and the *patterns* in which those entities are connected. This is not altogether different from a very contemporary understanding of time, as connected to motions in space and events. This is why we have the contemporary conception of "spacetime." For the Maya, likewise, time can be understood only in terms of the processive events of continual creation and the link between different entities in this creative process. It is this processive motion that *defines* time, and commemorations of ritual celebrations of time can thus be seen as commemorations and celebrations of particular events in the process of continual creation.

A key ritual in ancient Maya practice was the marking of "period ending" Long Count calendar dates in memorials and stelae.[31] Many of the stelae in Maya cities were erected by rulers on days that ended (and simultaneously began) on certain *katuns* or other units of the Long Count. The rulers of the city of Pusilha, for example, erected stelae at the endings of period 9.12.0.0.0 (Stela K, erected by Ruler D,[32]) 9.14.0.0.0 (Stela M, erected by Ruler E).[33] These markings of time privileged not only *k'in*, but also larger time units, aligning in the endings of particular *katuns*. The *katun* seems to have had a more central significance than the *k'in*. Another interesting feature of the Maya Long Count units is the term for the twenty-day period, *uinal*. This term is related to the term *uinic*, which means "person,"[34] suggesting a more intimate connection to human life than units such as the *katun* or *k'in*. All of

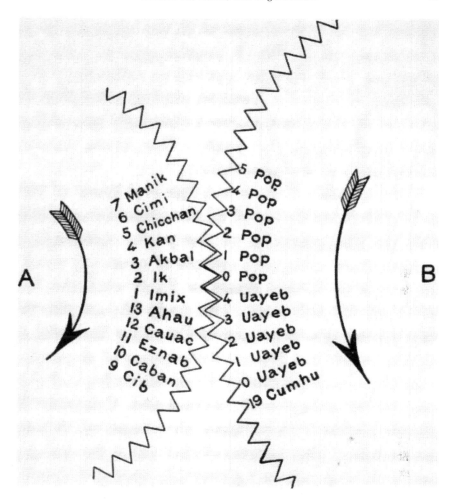

Figure 1.5 The *tzolk'in* 260-day calendar (left), combined with the *haab* 360-day calendar (right) yields fifty-two years of uniquely named and numbered days. Sylvanus Morley, An Introduction to the Study of Maya Hieroglyphs, 1915.

this suggests that the primary significance of time is in its *ritual* significance, which I will argue below consists in the human construction of the cosmos in cooperation with the rest of nature.

THE SIGNIFICANCE OF TIME AND "SEATING" (CHUM)

There is a danger of misunderstanding the role of time in ancient Maya thought due to the nature of the materials available to us from the Classic and surrounding periods. Much of what survives is concerned with ritual presentations of time. We must be careful to remember, however, that such textual information is simply what we have available to us, not necessarily representative of the general concerns found in ancient Maya texts. The four Postclassic Period Maya books we have today show less concern with dates than do the engravings found in Maya cities, and these four books likely represent a tiny fragment of what was available before the destruction of books by the Spanish.

The fact that much of the textual information that remains is concerned with dates has a perfectly good explanation with nothing to do with philosophy or religion. The vast majority of texts we have access to are from inscriptions on stelae and architecture. Many of these from the Classic Period and before were already buried in layers of jungle or soil by the time the Spanish arrived in the Maya realm. Even those that were exposed, however, would have been much more difficult for Spanish missionaries to destroy than were palm bark codices, which easily succumbed to flames. The inscription texts were carved into massive buildings, or on enormous stone stelae that would have been extremely difficult if not impossible to destroy without access to explosives. Indeed, even earlier conflicts between Maya groups proved the durability of these monuments. A common practice on defeating the ruler of a city-state was to break the objects memorializing him and his accomplishments. As I argue in chapter 4, the ancient Maya saw objects associated with an individual ruler as participating in, rather than representing, the personhood of the ruler. The carved memorial in an important sense was part of the ruler. Thus, destroying it was to destroy a part of the ruler himself. Even given this, however, we find a number of stelae and other memorials intact even after evidence of the defeat and sack of a city. Smaller memorials were often broken, but the larger and more durable of the monuments proved hard to eliminate. Sometimes the easiest answer was simply to cover them over with new development—and thanks to this practice, we are able to recover them today.

It is no accident that these memorials proved so difficult to destroy. Maya rulers built their memorials to last. They had plenty of reason to construct these memorials so as to be enduring and indestructible. This was in part a statement of the ruler's power and essential nature. When we reflect on the subject matter of the memorials, it is also clear why dates and time would play such a central role. The monuments memorialized important accomplishments of rulers and linked them to sacred events and entities. Time would have played an important role in this. None of this is to say that time was *not* central in Maya thought in general, but its centrality in the largest collection of texts we have from the ancient Maya, that of the inscriptions, is not enough in itself to determine its centrality in Maya thought. Time may simply play a larger role in memorial texts than it would have in other kinds of text, and there is plenty of reason to think this would be the case. The relative lack of concern with ritual and rulership dates in the codices and the Postconquest texts such as *Popol Vuh* and the books of *Chilam Balam* demonstrates this.

It is clear from Classic Period stelae that there were ceremonial celebrations surrounding the beginnings and endings of time periods such as the *katun* and the *baktun*. Many of the stelae themselves were erected on commemorative holidays coinciding with the ending of a particular period. These dates can be supposed to have had a central significance and power for the Maya. Rulers, as representatives of the deities and thus also time itself, had an important role as themselves tied into the maintenance and celebration of time. Erecting a stela commemorating important events in the timeline of a ruler, including birth, conquest, enthronement (seating, *chum-*), would generally itself correspond to an important calendar point.

The concept of "seating" (*chum*) itself was used in connection with both the ascendance of rulers and the beginning of time periods.[35] A ruler is seated (*chumaj*) at his accession, in the same way a certain period of time is seated at its beginning. The same term is used to describe the beginning of a year, for example (*chum tuun*), or the beginning of a new *katun* (*chum katun*). The last day of one of the twenty-day months (*uinal*) of the calendar was called the seating day of the following month. Thus, for example, the last day of the month *Yax* was referred to as the "seating of *Sak*" (*Sak* being the following month), or 0 *Sak*. The following day would be 1 *Sak*.[36]

Other evidence from the memorial stelae supports the association of rulers with time periods. A commonly seen glyph in stelae is that for *katun ajaw* (Lord of the Katun), associated with rulers as well as deities representative of the *katuns*. Each *katun ajaw* presided over a current *katun*, and the deities (if not necessarily the rulers) would cycle with each new *katun*.[37]

According to a number of Mayanist scholars, the "seating" days in the *tzolk'in* calendar were considered part of *both* the successive and the succeeding month, creating a bridge between the two.[38] The word (and glyph) *chum* is used to signify seating in the temporal sense mentioned above—the nesting of one time period within another which becomes that other—as well as seating in the sense of accession to a position, most often rulership or a position of authority. The sense of *chum* remains the same in this context. On the accession of a new ruler, the new ruler is "seated" in the place of, and within the identity of, the previous ruler. For the ancient Maya (from what evidence we have, at least), there is no discrete ontological distinction between successive time periods or between successive rulers, when there is seating involved. I argue further below that the same thing holds for persons in general. The purpose of this section is to try to make sense of this Maya view based around "seating," in its connection to time in particular, by considering possible

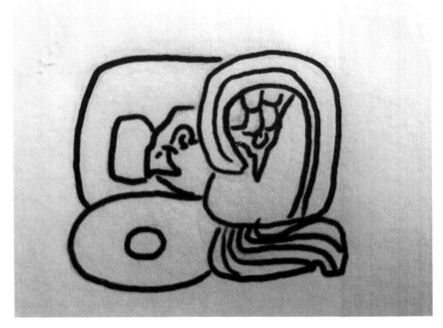

Figure 1.6   In this glyph, the year (*tuun*) is seated. It reads *chum (mu) tuun (ni)> chum tuun* ("seating of the year [*tuun*]"). The right side of the glyph represents a stone (*tuun,* literally "stone," used as a count of 360 k'in, "days"). The left side is the seating glyph. Drawing by the author.

interpretations, looking at how contemporary Maya people envision similar concepts, and comparing it to relevantly similar positions in other traditions.[39]

The Maya conception of *chum* goes beyond merely the notion of accession or beginning. The new entity is not just seated in a particular position that some other entity previously occupied, but it is *fused* with that other entity itself. That is, a new month is not only seated into the "present-place-in-the-calendar," it is seated *within* the previous (or current) month. This is why the "seating" day of one month is not the beginning day of that month, but the final day of the previous month. In the seating, the new month begins its reign within the old.

How can we understand how seemingly distinct entities can have an internal effect on one other, such that one thing can be seen as the *bearer* of the other, in the sense of containing the other? And what does it mean for one entity to contain another? One plausible view is that this simply refers to *identity*. For a month or ruler to be seated in another entity, or for the latter entity to come to bear the former, may simply mean to say that the entities have become identical. Of course, this entails that there are originally multiple (two or more) nonidentical entities that become identical. This is a particular unique and interesting view of Maya philosophy that I refer to as "embedded identity," discussed in greater detail in chapters 2 and 4.

Leon-Portilla speaks of the Gods as the "bearers" of time,[40] and we might likewise see the relationship between particular individuals and the ruler (representative of deity) as similar. The particular gods are thus identified with time—we see figure representations of numbers, time periods, and deities. Is identity being claimed here? Or is there something else going on? Is *time period* simply a *role description*, like "president of the United States" or "the Pope"? If so, then numerous individuals can play the role, and be associated with the role, without being identical to it. Currently, we will answer the question "who is the Pope?" by pointing out Francis (or Jorge Bergoglio), and answer questions such as "what does the Pope look like?" with a description of that individual. But Francis and the Pope are not identical—Francis does not provide us with a definition of the Pope, is not essentially the Pope. Before he was Pope, someone else was, and after his time, someone else will be Pope. At that time we will answer those questions differently. "Pope" is a role description rather than a proper name. Likewise, perhaps we should treat time period names like 5 Ahau or the 13th *katun* as descriptions that can have numerous bearers, each time the cycles repeat. Notice that the Gregorian calendar is not this way—although we have multiple iterations of July 13, for example, we only have a single July 13, 1998, which picks out a particular day. The Aztecs used the *tonalpohualli* calendar (effectively identical to the Maya *tzolk'in* calendar) without using the Long Count.[41] In this system, there was no way to distinguish days meeting a certain description outside of a fifty-two-year period. Thus a particular month and day name did not uniquely pick out a particular day, but could refer to such a named day in any given fifty-two-year cycle.[42]

It is in the Classic Period, with the rise of the concept of individual hereditary rulership, that we begin to see proliferation of commemorative stelae and the concern with time. Surely we can say that time was seen as central to rulership, as rulers strived to identify themselves with important periods and associated deities. But it turns out that this is not unique to the Maya at all. Rulers in all times and places have attempted to identify themselves with and control key aspects of time, most crucially represented in the calendar. There are likely many good reasons for this. To control and dictate time is very much to control and dictate the everyday lives of one's people. We organize our lives, our plans and activities, using time. If the ruler controls time, or even better, *is* time in some important sense, then the ruler comes to fill a necessary and central position in our lives. We cannot function without the ruler—we become directionless, and in a complete chaos. Or at least this is the idea the ruler desires to create.

This goes for the supernatural "ruler" as well. Plato has time created and organized by the Demiurge, the god-like figure of his *Timaeus*. The Demiurge organizes the preexisting chaos to create the world and the timeline as we know it. In a very real sense, time itself is created by the demiurge, through this organizational power, through the act of constraining and focusing what was a primordial and unordered jumble, where there was no time. Time, according to Plato, is fundamentally an organizational principle, rather than a fundamental constituent of the world. The demiurge did *not* create the universe—things existed in their chaotic state before the demiurge's organizational activity. These features of the universe were able to exist of themselves, without being brought into existence by an agent. Organized time, however, required an agent in order to come into existence.[43]

This seems to represent a suspicion about the anthropocentricity of time, or at least agent-relativity of time, that humans have shared across many cultural contexts. Time is fundamental to our experience, but the way we measure time and integrate it into our lives and institutions varies dramatically between cultures. And a widely shared intuition concerning time seems to be that it is at least in part dependent on human consciousness—that we don't just experience time, but that time in part *is* our experience of the world, that it is constituted by our experience in the world and is thus variable and relative based on features of the individual or community experiencing the world. Perhaps this explains the phenomena of memory, of our subjective feeling of the slowing or speeding of time depending on preoccupations of our minds, and of our seeming differential perception of the speed of its passage as we age. There are many examples of the seeming subjective qualities of time, both individually and communally, from philosophical and nonphilosophical sources alike. It is well known that people report traumatic events such as earthquakes or car crashes as lasting longer than they actually did—a ten-second quake will often be reported by those who experienced it as lasting for a minute or more.[44]

John Mbiti generalizes about time for African philosophical traditions that "time is simply a composition of events which have occurred, those which are taking place now and those which are immediately to occur."[45] Somewhat similarly, in the view of many Buddhist schools, time is not a fundamental constituent of the world but is instead a feature of human perception. Ultimate reality is the unconditioned, available only in the state of Nirvana, and time is not included in the unconditioned, so is ultimately without essence, and a mental formation connected with suffering.[46] The enlightened person is in a real sense *outside* of time, because this person recognizes the unreality of time and has thus in some sense transcended it.

TIME AS A CONSTRUCT OF
HUMAN-NATURE COOPERATION

In the Maya context, even though ritual specialists must *enact* the calendar and keep the days, time appears to be a more fundamental component of nature, at least mostly independent from human experience. It is in part this that accounts for the identification of time by some as *the* fundamental or basic component of Maya ontology. I argue here that although time is a mind-independent and basic constituent of reality according to the Maya, time is not the basis on which the entirety of Maya metaphysics is constructed. That is, the ancient Maya were neither reductionists with time as the sole basic entity, nor temporal "monists," seeing everything as emerging from and ultimately identifiable with time. Instead, they held a metaphysics with what I call "embedded identity" at its center, in which both time and other features of the world are contingent features of an ultimately ineffable ground of being (similar to the Warring States and Han period Daoist conceptions of *dao* 道), and which are defined by the regularities that determine types of transformations between objects and events. The ritual experts and rulers did not *create* time, but rather *completed* time. There is a relationship between humanity and nature at the core of Maya thought, in which humanity completes the raw material provided by nature, following the patterns given by this same nature. This picture is very similar to one found in late Warring States and Early Han Dynasty Chinese philosophy, which I outline below, in order to give substance to what I take to be the Maya view concerning time. In the Chinese case, the discussion concerns *ritual* rather than time, but the structure of the system offers us a way of thinking about the cooperation between humanity and nature in constructing time in the Maya case.

There are powerful arguments from a number of scholars that seem to show that time stood at the very center of the Maya intellectual tradition, in the political as well as religious and philosophical realm. Prudence Rice argues that the Maya calendar was a major component in the shifting of centers of power and legitimacy of particular cities to rule. She argues in *Maya Political Science* that a new urban center would take up the mantle of regional rule and focus of religious ritual each 256-year period (*may*).[47] While there is some evidence in Classic Period and Postconquest texts that different time periods could be associated with different regions and cities, the evidence Rice puts forward seems not much different from that which we might offer concerning the connection between persons and the characteristic qualities of their day of birth according to the 260-day *tzolk'in* calendar. That is, association of different regions and cities with divine as well as secular power in texts like the books of the *Chilam Balam* and Classic Period memorials seems reminiscent of the association of *tzolk'in* days with character types, prognos-tications, and medicinal remedies, also found in similar texts. The *may* cycle as understood in the Postclassic Period, which Rice relies on, may also have had a similar structure. There may have been, as there often is, a disconnect between political authority and religious or intellectual preeminence. Oxford is not the capital of England, nor Cambridge or New Haven the capital of the United States. The accounted practices of Postclassic Maya and the divina-tory texts such as the *Chilam Balam* books are of ambiguous significance when it comes to the issue of political power.

Near the beginning of the *Popol Vuh*, when Heart-of-Sky and Plumed Serpent are in the process of their attempts to create humanity (the *idea* of which preexists its creation), they lament the fact that the wooden people they have created do not keep the days. Daykeeping is an essential task of the beings they are creating. The text already refers to them as humans,[48] just as the world is already suggested to exist when the two gods appear on the scene. I argue here that this is not just dramatic effect or carelessness on part of the author(s) of the text. All of this points to the preexistence of all of these features of the cosmos—world, gods, humans, and the construction of these. As the enaction of the *Popol Vuh* through its performance is intended not simply *reenact*, but also to *represent* the activities described in it, the performance offers us a window on a process that is not one of the distant past at some origin point of the world, something like what we see in the origin stories of the Abrahamic religions, for example. Rather, the creation story of the *Popol Vuh* is one being enacted at each time, in each moment. It is a *continual creation*, normally invisible to us, that the performance of the *Popol Vuh* allows us to see. It is not that the Maya view the creation process as *cyclical*, in the sense of the Nietzschean eternal return, and thus the gods, humans, and cosmos are all being re-formed at the beginning of the *Popol Vuh*. Rather, it is that this act of creation is continually unfolding, having no beginning point and no ending point, other than where we choose to (or are able to) pay attention to the process.

It is this unfolding that is described by the *Popol Vuh* itself. The connection of daykeeping to humans as a central function is of particular importance. Humans play a pivotal role in the ordering of the cosmos and its continual creation. The ordering of the days does not happen without humans, and this, the *Popol Vuh* argues, is one of the most important features of humanity. It is for their inability to keep the days that the gods declared their early attempts to create humans to be failures, and went back to the drawing board. Time as ordering principle is central to the Maya conception of the world. The world is structured in and through time. As this is the case, the keeping of the cal-endar, which itself plays the role of *tz'ak* (ordering) the days,[49] is a critical part of ordering the (preexistent) chaos of the universe.[50] When we say that this chaos is preexistent, however, this does not suggest a beginning at an earlier point in time. Rather, it is a *conceptual* priority rather than a temporal one. The existence of the primordial "world-stuff," the ground of being (akin to the Chinese Daoist conception of *dao*), is necessary for the keeping of the days. Like Chinese correlative cosmology, with the *wu xing* (five phases) as part of its basis, the days are linked, by the skilled daykeeper, to the patterns of other aspects of the world. The days not only *keep track*, but manifest and express these unseen aspects of the cosmos.[51]

The daykeeping, however, is not arbitrary. That is, one cannot simply establish the calendar starting wherever one pleases. There are certain features of the world that the calendar must be responsive to that are not created by the establishment of days, but expressed by them. This is a difficulty we see concerning realism about human-created expressions rooted in the world in numerous traditions. Humans *play a role* in the continual creation of things through their daykeeping and other rituals, but these rituals are not completely conventional, arbitrarily set by humans. Keeping the days properly and performing rituals properly is a matter of understanding the patterns inherent in the world. We see a very similar view in ancient China. The similarities of these positions, I argue, show us why there is an emphasis in both ancient Maya and Chinese culture on similar elements of the natural world, such as astronomy. The astronomical realm—that is, the skies—could be used as a (relatively) unchanging template with which to understand humanity and other aspects of the world. We see a correlativity in Maya thought not altogether different from Chinese correlative metaphysics, with the daykeeper tying the strands together. This is perhaps the reason for the continued significance of the daykeeper as primary bearer of Maya cultural rituals in the Yucatan.[52] Kaylee Spencer-Ahrens and Linnea Wren write:

> To the ancient Maya, the measured cycles of the calendars and the planets were seen as a cosmic pattern that pervaded all aspects of existence. Within this pattern, cycles of smaller networks overlapped and were interwoven with textile-like intricacy where the threads of one cycle become dependent on the looping of another. These patterns shaped the Maya universe within which all things had to fit. The Maya recognized these patterns and actively sought to define their space within the cosmos and the supernatural realm. Knowledge of time and its efficacy allowed the Maya to replicate the sacred networks in their daily life.[53]

Humans and human ritual are necessary to do part of the work of continual creation that simultaneously constructs and maintains the cosmos. In the *Popol Vuh*, we see suggestions of a preexisting chaotic and disorganized structure that is given shape by the gods and later completed by humans, in their keeping of the days. As pointed out above, this should not be seen as a temporal succession, but rather as an explanation of conceptual priority. The ritual completion of humans responds to and organizes patterns inherent in the world but unexpressed or unusable on their own.

Lars Pharo has recently argued that there was no specific date of creation offered in Maya texts, and that we should read the references to August 3114 BCE not as a creation point but rather as a specific ritual origin of the current cycle of the Long Count calendar.[54] I agree with Pharo that there is nothing like a specific creation point found in Maya thought, in contrast to what we see in Abrahamic religions. There is certainly creation mythology connected to a particular linear story of creation, which is likely the reason that numerous interpreters have read the 3114 BCE date as a point of creation. There are many reasons, however, to reject the idea of a creation point in Maya thought. Linda Schele recognized that certain dates in the year coincide with astronomical alignments that follow the traditional story of creation, particularly the date of August 13.[55] Although Schele held the 3114 point-of-creation view, she noted that the proper astronomical alignments lined up not with the night sky on August 13 3114 BCE, but the sky as it appeared much later, during the Classic Period. She concluded from this that "the Maya, or perhaps their predecessors the Olmecs, would have wanted the astronomy to work with the myth when they could see it, rather than in a mythological past."[56] I think the best explanation for this is that the ancient Maya did not view creation as a single event that happened in some distant past, but as an ongoing process that sometimes revealed itself to humans (through astronomical alignments) and could be seen through windows into these fundamental processes via ritual. This was a view held by later K'iche' Maya people in their thought about the *Popol Vuh*—performance of the *Popol Vuh* allowed a window onto the process of continual creation, through the substitution of ritual performers with characters of the *Popol Vuh*, who themselves represent vital forces active in the cosmos.

There are a number of non-Maya views similar to what we see here. Numerous traditions have struggled with the question of how to understand the ways in which human ritual, language, or other artifacts might be understood to express or mirror patterns inherent to nature not otherwise accessible to us, or accessible but inexpressible in themselves. The question of the conventionality of human linguistic and ritual constructions is one that has arisen in many philosophical traditions. There are also parallels between the Maya view on creation and ones we see in other traditions, particularly in Chinese philosophy. Looking to other traditions on both of these issues may help us to understand what is going on in the Maya case. The questions of 1) the conventionality of ritual, and 2) the operation of continual creation, though they arise in the Maya case, are not explicitly dealt with in the Maya tradition, even though what we do find suggests certain positions on these issues.

Looking to these other traditions for parallels, we might consider whether key aspects of the Maya position that we find in the Maya texts and practices make it plausible that they shared views similar to these.

CALENDARS AND ORDERING (TZ'AK)

One function of a calendar for any society is to organize and order the experience of the people, generally political or religious institutions that control the calendar. This calendric control can come in different forms, depending on the nature of the calendar. Our own calendars are kept with an aim at consistency with the most accurate (atomic) clocks and the most precise possible measurement of the earth's motion. Scientists working for the national government are responsible for making changes to the calendar, in concert with the authority of that government. The National Institute of Standards and Technology in the United States is the federal organization that oversees such. The situation is similar in other contemporary nations.

In the ancient world, it was generally also governments who held the power to modify calendric standards, and the power of the ruler was accorded sometimes to changes made by astronomical or calendric experts in the employ of the ruler or rulers. In the case of early China, court astronomers were involved in the process. For the Maya as well, in both the ancient periods and today, calendric experts hold and transmit calendric knowledge. Today, this concerns mainly the *tzolk'in* calendar, but we might imagine that in the Classic Period, experts would have been responsible for additional calendric knowledge concerning the Long Count as well as the other significant calendric elements such as the Lords of the Night series and lunation information, all of which was generally included on memorials and stelae. Of course, while there was certainly a class of distinct ritual experts, the priestly and scholarly class of the *sahalob*,[57] the ruler, as himself from the *sahal* class, and as the head representative of this class, was understood as the priest of priests, the high priest with the highest religious authority.[58] The ruler played a central role in the creation of order through the definition of time in the ancient Maya world.

For the ruler to play a central role in the organization of time is not in itself unique. How human experience is structured by time—that is, how people understand their lives within certain orderings of time—is often guided by rulers. The ruler, or the state in general, will certainly have a major interest in controlling the reins of the systems people use to think about time, as controlling a people's experience of time is to have a central control over their lives. We can think of this in terms of the way that companies, for example, define their "calendric" systems. In making Monday to Friday 9am–5pm, with a

12–1pm lunch break, for example, the standard business schedule, companies we work for order our experiences and create the boundaries within which we live and must think of our own lives and experience. 9 to 5 on the weekdays becomes "work time," distinct from the "rest time" after 5, or the "enjoyment time" on the weekend. The patterns of action we engage in can be explained in large part by situational features of our environment, and the way our activities are distributed according to time affects how we engage in these activities, *what* activities we engage in, and what role we see them as playing in our lives and the life of the community. Structuring of time is much more than simply organization. This is why rulers, governments (and more recently corporations) throughout history have been so keen on controlling this structuring.

The reforms made in Rome under the rule of Julius Caesar that resulted in the Julian calendar were in part political. The association of the distribution of units of time with the concerns and identity of a particular ruler, entity, or ideology can have a powerful effect on the minds of people. The leaders of the French Revolution in the late eighteenth century were certainly aware of this, when they abolished the old calendar in exchange for the new time distribution they referred to as the *calendrier républicain français* (French Republican Calendar, also known as the "revolutionary calendar"). With this new calendar, they began the year count with the epoch beginning September 22, 1792 on the establishment of the French Republic. In addition to new year counts, the revolutionary calendar also had new names for its twelve months completely different from those of the Gregorian calendar in use previously, as well as a reorganization of weeks. Each month in the revolutionary calendar contained three weeks, called *decades,* comprised of ten days. Each of the months was given a name connected with the weather (in France, of course) associated with that time of year. So, instead of months named for emperors, such as August and July, the revolutionary calendar opted for names such as *Thermidor* and *Fructidor* for summer months and *Nivose* ("snowy") and *Ventose* ("windy") for winter months. This followed with revolutionary ideology, to eliminate the influence of nobility and religious authority and instead recast the organization of society in terms of "nature" and "reason"—ideas that gained traction during the Enlightenment, to which the revolutionary French were committed. The ten-day week as well was thought to be a more "natural" distribution, given our Base-10, or *decimal* system—this was also the idea behind the metric system.

Part of the idea behind all of these calendric reforms was that control of both the names and other organizational features of time constituted an important aspect of control over the lives of people. And this should be understood not only in terms of a kind of external compelling. Organizing calendars certain ways eventually changes the ways we think about ourselves and about the world.

Markus Eberl argues that the Classic Maya term *tz'ak* represents the concept of ordering in general. It can be applied to the ordering of rulers, the people, or the ordering of time. Considering it in terms of time, the ordering can be understood as the distinguishing of different time units, but also, similar to the points I made above, the ordering of the experience of time of people.[59] A unique feature of the term *tz'ak* is that it not only can refer backward to the ordering of events or time periods in the past, but also project forward to ordering of future events. Eberl argues that the ancient Maya used this concept to tie together privileged and particular orderings of known events with the present and future, in order to form a particular conception of an extended present period—to combine the significance and meaning of past figures and events with those of present and future, into what he calls "framing of a now moment," based on the phenomenological understandings of time of figures such as Husserl and Merleau-Ponty.[60]

Phenomenological technicalities aside, the idea of the construction of a notion of the "present" or relevant "human time" from association with key moments and events in the past, including the reign of important rulers and mythological events, is an important part of the process of the construction and manifestation of power by rulers in the ancient Maya world. In addition, grounding experience in *tz'ak*, or construction, allows humans to make sense of their own lives as connected to those of the historical past and the future both in the sense of shared significance as well, as we will see, in the sense of ontology.

This is part of the reason we see a focus on completions of Long Count time cycles in the memorials and stelae. Eberl argues that this focus shows the ancient Maya concern with ordering both space and time around the person of the *ajaw* (ruler). He writes:

> Classic Maya rulers saw themselves as the *axis mundi* in the center of the cosmogram, with time and space revolving around them. To celebrate the period ending, Yik'in Chan K'awiil connected earth and otherworld and conjured Akhan on earth and onto his back rack. His ritual performance completed a circular logic in which he created an interpretation of time and space while also portraying it as already existing. The yax-shaped portal recalls Yik'in Chan K'awiil's position in the center of the universe. Tikal's divine king materialized space and time in concrete places and actions.[61]

One of the keys to understanding this conception of time is that the ordering of time around the ruler is an attempt both to direct the attention of the people toward the ruler and the patterns the ruler endorses as key components of time, but also to identify the ruler himself with time. The concept of the *baah* (image, self), which I explain further in chapter 4 is, according to Eberl, meant to represent an image of a time period embodied in the ruler himself.[62]

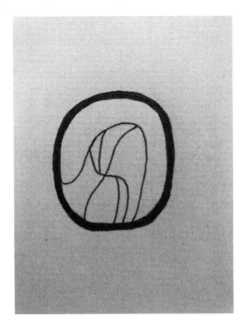

Figure 1.7   The *tz'ak* glyph. Drawing by Shubhalaxmi McLeod.

He discusses an example of a text from Stela 9 at Calakmul, in which a lady presents herself as the image (*baah*) of the *tzolk'in* date 11 Ajaw 18 Ch'en.[63] Eberl presents other cases in which there seem to be claims to identity with time, and argues that the spatial elements of structures built to commemorate rulers also signify temporal elements. The staircases documenting histories of the ruler(s) at Copan serve, according to this view, to associate movement up and down the staircase with movement in time, through the history recounted by the glyphic text.[64] In this way, time and space both become fused together, with the figure of the ruler the *tz'ak*, the ordering that holds them together. In this way the Maya rulers were truly "lords of time"—though perhaps we should go beyond this and claim that more correctly they should be considered lords of time, space, and being.

The idea of the "now moment" discussed by Eberl and the role of temporal ordering expressed by *tz'ak* to create a coherent historical experience embedded in the present experience in the people is a useful construct for understanding how the ancient Maya understood the role of time in their overall metaphysics. While Eberl argues that the "now moment" should be understood in terms of Husserl's phenomenology, I think that there are deep problems with that view, and also that the ancient Maya themselves did not have the same concerns as the phenomenologists. The concerns of the ancient Maya were not with how to make sense of an extended sense of "now" constructed from discrete individual (and presumably point-like or infinitesi-mally small) moments. This assumes a particular metaphysics of time that privileges these moments as foundational or atomic, with larger components of time as simply aggregates of these moments. While this view of time is, I think, faulty, it is also a view of time foreign to the ancient Maya. The basic "units" of time for the ancient Maya should not be thought of as uniform and discrete atoms to which every other length of time reduces. Rather, there are manifestations of time associated with different entities and which have a natural length of their own as based on their positions in a cycle or their overall significance in a cosmic system. While there are certainly useful features of the "now moment" apparatus, application of this to the ancient Maya context requires a rethinking of just what is being fused into the "now moment"—what is being made present, made the object of historical and present experience.

The descriptions of time in ancient Maya texts, from the Classic Period through Postconquest text, are never couched in terms of fragments of time forming larger components. While the Long Count certainly has cycles *within* other cycles (so 20 *kin* for example is one *winal*), there is no conception here that a *winal* is simply an aggregation of *kin*, and that there is some basic unit that adds up to the others. Instead, what we see are coexisting series that interact with one another and gain their meaningfulness and interpretation in connection with one another. In "aggregative" views of time, we do not see such a position. The *tzolk'in* calendar shows us one clear kind of relational sig-nificance—the ordering of the days is not in a sequence of numbers attached to day signs, such as 1 September, 2 September, etc., but the numbers are attached to consecutive day names, such as 1 *Ahau*, 2 *Imix*, etc. This may be intended to stress the individual significance of each day sign and day, independent of a series in which days are collected within a certain day sign. Each day has its own nature and relationship to the others, rather than being a unit added up to gain a longer segment of time to which we can then accord meaning.

This is also one of the reasons it is ultimately a mistake to see *k'in* (sun, day) as the fundamental atomic component of time (as does Miguel Leon-Portilla). While *k'in* is the smallest unit of time that we see is given sig-nificance in Classic Maya texts, this should not be understood as a statement of its atomic nature, as the ancient Maya did not, I argue, have an atomic conception of time.

First, there is the issue of the differing calendars. The Long Count and the *tzolk'in* were used alongside one another, but days were treated differently in each. *K'in* counts were included in the Long Count, while days had alterna-tive day names in the *tzolk'in*, and days were not counted as collections in this calendar. The two calendars give us very different ways of understand-ing days, in the Long Count perhaps as basic units built into larger units, but in the *tzolk'in* as placeholders for the day name in a non-additive calendar. Second—the focus of the Classic Period texts discussing the calendars is hardly ever on the *k'in*. The focus tended to be on completions of larger periods, especially *katun* periods. Stelae were erected on such occasions, and the importance of them was based on the end of a *katun* series, rather than a much smaller *k'in* series. Thus, perhaps we should take *katuns* to be the central focus of Maya thought on time, and understand the day as simply an abstraction from this, rather than vice versa. The Maya texts simply do not give us enough information to know.

As an example of this, the "Tablet of the 96 Glyphs" at Palenque marks *katuns* and *tuns* as important endings, but mentions *k'in* only in connection to distances and in reference to the endings of *katuns*.[65] The ruler is described as erecting monuments at the end of his first *katun* as ruler, and *katuns* endings are flagged throughout the text. This suggests that if any Long Count unit is to be taken as central in Classic Period Maya thought, it should be the *katun*. The final collection of glyphs in the texts reads:

> 7 days earlier, 13 Ahau 13 Muan was the 13th tun, and then he completed his first katun as *ahau*; he erected a monument; he sacrificed (?), under the auspices of Pacal and then he finished his first katun as *ahau*.[66]

K'in become important in ritual celebrations, for example *tzolk'in* New Year celebrations, in a different way. Of the twenty *tzol'kin* day names, only four of them could fall on a New Year day. A particular day had its significance in connection with the larger event, in this case the New Year day of the 260-day calendar. The larger processes, rather than the day units, were the focus and more fundamental element of Maya thought concerning time. The *k'in* can then be seen as a way of *focusing* on one aspect of the larger continuum of time, rather than as a basic unit of time. Even if we agree with Leon-Portilla that *k'in* ultimately represents the entirety of time, this should cast a doubt on the idea that it is a basic unit out of which larger time units are constructed.

In the *Popol Vuh*, there is discussion by the gods in the first book of "keeping the days" as a necessary act, and the "Master of Days" is a figure of importance early in the text. In his commentary, Allen Christenson explains:

> *Aj q'ij* is still the title used by Quiché priests who divine the will of deity through a ritual counting of the days in the sacred calendar. The title means literally "he/she of days" or "master of days," although modern ethnographers often refer to them as "daykeepers." Because Xmucane and Xpiyacoc assisted in the creation of the universe at the beginning of time, thus setting in motion the endless cycles of day and night, birth and death, sowing and harvest, they stand as the ideal interpreters through divination of these cycles.[67]

The keeping of days or creation of days, we can see, *focuses* or makes manifest something that is preexistent. It makes tangible to humans an aspect of the world that we would otherwise be unable to access. Keeping of the calendar then does not *create* time, it focuses and makes manifest time. The same is the case with other rituals, as I argue below. Other passages from the *Popol Vuh* suggest such a view with respect to other aspects of the world. The gods mention the need for humans to express or *speak* in order to manifest the activity and objects of the gods in the world. In the first part of the *Popol Vuh*, the gods undertake various attempts to create beings who can properly speak, perform the rituals, and keep the days. Their early attempts end in failure, as one or the other feature of the created being does not allow it to fulfill the proper function. Prior to one of the attempts, the creation of the wooden people, the gods say:

> It shall be found; it shall be discovered how we are to create shaped and framed people who will be our providers and sustainers. May we be called upon, and may we be remembered. For it is with words that we are sustained, O Midwife and Patriarch, our Grandmother and Grandfather, Xpiyacoc and Xmucane. Thus may it be spoken. May it be sown. May it dawn so that we are called upon and supported, so that we are remembered by framed and shaped people, by effigies and forms of people. Hearken and let it be so.[68]

The gods say here that they are *sustained* with words. The ritual actions of humans play a role in the continual creation of the cosmos. The gods create the patterns and the original stuff of the world, which is then molded, manifested, and sustained by humanity. *K'in* then is a human concept based in the patterns of the world that is used to manifest or focus on the larger process of time created by the gods. Time in itself should be seen as an undifferentiated process including within it certain patterns that humans can understand and with which we can create concepts such as *k'in* and all of the others that we use connected with time and other elements of the world. We will see that the conception of ritual in early China is a very close parallel to this conception, and it can help us understand the Maya view. The Chinese comparison is more apt here than that between the Maya and Western views, because the Maya view falls uncomfortably between two different kinds of metaphysical views current in Western philosophy. Metaphysical conventionalist views come somewhat close to capturing the Maya position. According to the conventionalist, objects have their essential properties as a matter of semantic convention, and thus are in this sense constructs of semantic convention.[69] What exists independently of our semantic conventions is a kind of undifferentiated "world-stuff."[70] This world-stuff is undifferentiated—that is, does not contain objects with essential properties, and does not individuate objects on its own. It can perhaps be thought of as a single object with a number of accidental or contingent properties which we, through *conceptualization*, carve into objects.[71] That is, it is our concepts that allow us to pick out certain features of the world as essential properties associated with objects. Philosopher Alan Sidelle writes:

> while there are trees, sweaters, and other ordinary objects, our substance terms are not, in fact, substance terms, but pick out these objects according to accidental properties, much as we ordinarily think that "redhead" is an accidental way of picking out a person who happens to have red hair. Being a tree, or a sweater, is an accidental property of something more basic, and standardly, at least, when something ceases to be a tree or a sweater, it continues to exist."[72]

This position is not quite the same as the Maya view, as it holds that conceptualization is responsible for the construction of objects, while on the Maya view, objects seem to be taken for granted as part of the world independent of human conceptualization. Something close to Sidelle's conceptualization, the "speaking" or ritual manifestation of the Maya, plays a role in *completing* or making manifest objects in the world, including discrete periods of time, but does not *create* these objects. The completion or ritual manifestation of objects in the human realm is based on a grasp of the intrinsic patterns of the world independent of ritual and human speech (perhaps we can liken this to concepts), and these patterns, though hidden from most people, are discernible to certain savants, who can through their understanding construct concepts that help the rest of society to access these underlying patterns. There is *some* similarity between the Maya view and conventionalism, but there is far more similarity between the Maya view and the early Chinese view of the relationship between the patterns inherent in nature (*tian li* 天理) and objects or things (*wu* 物). Thus, the early Chinese view, as I lay out below, is a better lens through which to understand the ancient Maya view.

While daykeeping is perhaps the most important and central ritual in numerous Maya texts, especially when we get into the Postclassic and Postconquest periods,[73] there are numerous other rituals which have cosmic significance as well. Some of the possible responsibilities of a daykeeper mentioned by Prudence Rice suggest the numerous ritual roles:

> such individuals—whether they were identified as diviners, shamans, shaman-priests, calendar priests, skywatchers, or daykeepers—probably consulted written books to aid them in their prognostications.[74]

We can see from these features that the Maya position seems to have been one in which ritual and texts were seen as *organizing* a preexistent world based on patterns themselves contained in that world. That is, the role of humans is to use ritual, which shows us the patterns inherent in the world, to help enact these patterns properly. The world cannot complete its harmonious patterns on its own, but requires the intermediation of humans and its structuring through the enactment of ritual. This position, as I show below, is not unique to the ancient Maya (though their specific version of it may be)—rather, this is a position that can be found, explicitly or implicitly, in most human systems of thought. Without going so far as to say that it can be found in *every* global philosophical tradition, it can be found so widely that perhaps we could say that it comes close to being part of a "perennial philosophy," the search for which has today become outmoded.

There are a number of features of Maya ritual, and as suggested by Rice's quote above we can look for support of the existence of such a view among the ancient Maya.

Printed texts specifically held an important role in the ritual functions of the daykeepers and other important figures (if there was a distinction). The textual culture in the Classic Period attests to this, with texts carved on monuments and stelae throughout the Maya area from the beginning of the Classic Period through the period of Spanish contact[75] (although the recording of dates in Long Count seems to have declined in the Yucatan during the Postclassic, perhaps due to central Mexican influence.[76])

The glyphs themselves, whether on stelae, architecture, or codices, had a significance beyond simply the expression or storage of ideas. The glyphs were often defaced on the conquest or sack of one city-state by another, with the idea that in defacing the glyphs associated with a particular ruler, one was eliminating part of the *essence* of that ruler.[77] The glyphic text on stelae and other material were also sometimes destroyed as part of the renewal of ritual sites for the establishment of new ones.[78] In the glyphs themselves, given the nature of the Maya script, we see presentations of the images of the represented object. The ancient Maya were concerned, as we have seen, with *imagery* and its unique ability to contain the essence of an object. It is through envisioning an object that we seem to gain a grasp on what it *truly is*.[79] If we think of the way we generally react to the information of our senses as it concerns other persons, we may find the same to be the case. Hearing someone does not seem to give us as much a sense of who and what they are as *seeing* them. And seeing the *face* is particularly important in this revelation of essence.

The ancient Maya too accorded particular significance to the face (or head) as revealer of essence. Indeed, the term *baah*, used to refer to the self, also has the connotation of "face" or "head." Houston, Stuart, and Taube discuss the connection between the conception of face/head and that of the self overall, arguing that *baah* represents the "visage" of an individual that then can be used in the sense of self-reflexivity. This understanding helps to show us how the link can be made between the self and the glyphic image. Houston, Stuart, and Taube write:

Tzotzil and Yucatek Mayan define *baah* and its various forms as aspects of appearance, a recognizable "visage" or overall mien, if always in a corporeal, embodied sense. That visage is transferable to an "image" or "portrait," a "thing similar to another thing," as in *bail*. A deeper notion operates as well. The body extends visibly to other representations, yet essence transfers along with resemblance; the surface, the "face," does not so much mimic aspects of identity as realize them. In terms of being, an image embodies more than a clever artifice that simulates identity; it both resembles and *is* the entity it reproduces.[80]

And this expression of essence is much more *direct* than what we find in other languages. It is not that the *meaning* expressed through the glyph contains part of the essence of the thing represented—rather there is a more direct connection between sign and signified, which is made more visible and obvious through the resemblance of the sign to the signified. The word "fish" is not an image of a fish, and a person without knowledge of English would have no way of knowing what the word referred to. Even without knowledge of Classic Mayan, however, one might correctly guess what the word expresses in Mayan.

The connection between glyphic representation and the world for the ancient Maya is then closer than that allowed by most theories of meaning in contemporary philosophy. The glyphs do more than *refer* to particular entities, but rather include part of the essence of those entities. Of course, one could always simply make this claim for a theory of meaning using English or any other language, and it is still relatively vague here just what "containing part of the essence" of a thing amounts to. The general view of language most of us in the contemporary West hold is that words are signs that have meaning and refer, but do not in themselves (either as type or token) have any essential connection to the things to which they refer. They so refer because we have coined them to do such. Even for onomatopoeic words—they refer not on the basis of their resemblance or a feature of the word itself, but on how we use it and intend it to refer. We might call this is a *conventionalist* view of language.

An alternative view, not often found among scholars today, is focused on sounds (rather than images) as having a more direct connection with things through built-in meanings. Notice that this focus on *sound* bypasses the issue of possible built-in meaning in the written components of languages like the Chinese or (pre-Columbian) Mayan languages, in which there are elements unconnected to phonemes. In Indo-European languages, everything written in the script signifies a sound, while this is not the case in either Chinese languages or pre-Columbian Maya languages. There are logographic elements that sometimes directly illustrate the object referred to. This is especially the case in Classic Mayan, which has perhaps the richest and most complex logographic scripts of any known language. Even the various different

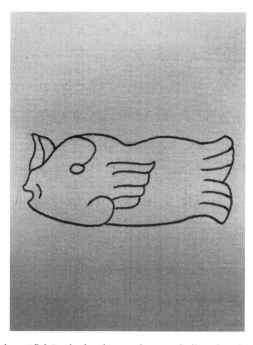

Figure 1.8 The *chay* ("fish") glyph, also used to symbolize the phonetic ka. Drawing by Shubhalaxmi McLeod.

stylizations and flourishes on the script and its combinations are unbelievably complex for someone coming from a linear language like English or other Indo-European languages. Glyph element combinations can be made from any direction and integrated in numerous ways, unlike Chinese characters, which can be stylized, but would become unreadable if the radicals and elements of the characters were moved within the character. Also, there are numerous ways of rendering the same glyph, with the same pronunciation. This was also a feature of Chinese in its older forms, but it has become much less common today, as standardization of the characters happened through time.

The logographic elements of very many Mayan glyphs are illustrations of the object the word refers to. Phonetic glyphs also can derive their sound from the word or part of a word associated with the thing signified by a logographic meaning of the glyph. For example, "ka" in Classic Mayan and its corresponding glyph can be translated as "fish." But this glyph and its variants (all depicting parts of a fish—the head or fin) can also be used (and was more commonly used in the extant texts) as a phonetic sign independently of its meaning as "fish." It signified in these contexts the sound *ka*. Thus, the word *kakao* (cacao, chocolate) is often rendered phonetically as *ka-ka-wa*, with the fish head (or fin) glyph playing the phonetic rather than logographic role.[81] It appears here then that even sounds are *secondary* to visual meanings. The fundamental and basic way of expressing meaning in Classic Mayan seems to have been through visual representation of a thing—through illustration. This illustration may have been thought of as an alternative kind of *substitution*. Just as the performers of the Hero Twins story can through their dance and recitation enact and become the Hero Twins, the glyphs can enact and this become the entities they refer to. Indeed, this system *bypasses* reference altogether. Words have their meaning not through *referring* to things in the world, but through *substituting* and *enacting* those things in the world. Substitution as explaining meaning has interesting implications for a theory of truth—and while the extant ancient Maya texts never offer anything approaching explicit theory of truth, a few concepts used in Maya text *do* seem to offer us some clear hints as to what such a theory may have looked like, connected to this idea of meaning as substitution.

Notice that if meaning is based on substitution, then meaning as such can belong to anything that substituted, including humans or other objects that substitute or impersonate the gods or other aspects of the world. When a ruler-priest impersonates Hunahpu and in that *becomes* Hunahpu, we can also say that the ruler-priests actions *mean* Hunahpu. As I show below, the concept of *itz* (truth, substance, vital essence) may be connected to this conception of meaning and identity. There are, as pointed out above, different levels of detail in the glyphic or pictorial representation of objects. At one end, we have the full-figure glyphs representing the Long Count time periods and numbers, or the full-figure image of Waxaklajuun Ubaah Kawil in the stelae at Copan, while on the other end, we have the minimalist representations of numbers as dots, or the fish as a single fin. In both cases, however, what is represented is being represented in that its essence is expressed by and in the glyph itself. That is, the glyph contains part of the essence of the object expressed, rather than representing it. It is not something *separate from* but referring to an object, but something in which the object in part inheres. We can see why such a view would have radical implications for any theory of truth the Maya may have constructed, and why such a theory of truth would look very different from "traditional" theories familiar in the West. Not only is this view significant for its implications for truth, but it is also significant for its implications concerning objects, the world, and language. It implies that the Maya have a deep realism concerning objects and language, rather than a conventionalism. There is something distinct in the world expressible and expressed by a glyphic representation, as the glyph contains the essence of this thing, which would not be possible if language were purely conventional, or if objects were determined via convention.

RITUAL AND THE ROLE OF THE SAGE IN
COMPLETING NATURE'S WORK

We can gain a great deal from looking at conceptions of time in other traditions. Certain traditions share essential features with the Maya understanding of time, and using the analogical method I outlined in the Introduction above, we can draw out some possibilities concerning what the Maya view may have been, in areas where there is too little (or no) information to adequately fill out the view. Two interesting views of time and how time fits into an overall metaphysical system that seems most relevant for our purposes here are ones that arise in the early Chinese philosophical tradition and the West African philosophical tradition.

How a culture thinks about time explains much about its view of metaphysics in general—its understanding of change, causation, identity, and substance. Looking at African, Chinese, and Indian conceptions of time can give us different accounts. The accounts I look at here are very similar to the Maya account on certain levels and strikingly different on others. They share features we might expect as due to their similar climates and latitudes. But the particular time focus shows us the important points of divergence that can help us learn about the unique features of Maya philosophy of time and what these unique features may signify for Maya metaphysics in general.

In the metaphysics of time of the Akan of West Africa (today mainly located in current-day Ghana), there are a number of very similar elements to Maya conceptions of time.[82] Some of the similarities are so striking as to suggest the possibility of some kind of natural similarity in the Maya and Akan areas that made certain conceptions of time more useful. The Akan area is and has traditionally been around the region just above the equator in West Africa, around the southern part of Ghana. This region, although a bit further south in latitude than the Maya area, is subject to a similar climate—little temperature and sunlight hour variability throughout the year, due to its position in the tropical zone, and rainy and dry seasons that determine agricultural schedules (rather than the solar seasonal schedule more familiar in temperate regions). As in the Maya area (and everywhere else), one of the most important features of a calendar was to regulate social activities, such as agriculture. In the absence of robust social coordination, no calendar is necessary. Agriculture is one of the most basic human activities to require such coordination, and we generally find the development of various kinds of calendars in societies connected with likely agricultural purposes. Different kinds of organization are possible as well, such as governments and other associations (universities, for example). And we see the development of new calendars for such purposes (usually coinciding with the use of other calendars). But the agricultural basis for some of the most widely used calendars in some societies is central. John Monaghan describes the Balinese *pawukon* calendar, which was used for coordination of irrigation systems in rice growing. The *tzolk'in* calendar may have had a similar purpose.[83]

In the Akan system, there are seven- (or eight-) day week counts, the *nnawotwe*. The week fits into a forty-day month, *obosom*, which may be based on lunar cycles.[84] The months, like the weeks, are not fixed to particular points in a solar year, but are based on natural changes, which may happen in longer or shorter spans. Thus, the calendar is a *variable* calendar. Time, at least measured calendric time, for the Akan, is based strictly on important events and changes. Indeed, even the way people fix important or personally significant events in time is not in connection with an impersonal calendar independent of events, but with the events as themselves primary.[85]

Adjaye writes:

> Two events are used in direct association with each other as time indicators. A number of events or occurrences of two types, either natural phenomena (for example, earthquakes, solar eclipses, droughts) or memorable human events (for example the death of a great kind, a major war, the visit of a world dignitary, a major political change), may be employed as time indicators. Thus, one might hear a statement to this effect: "My first child was born after King X died," the death of King X being used as a time referent. At the national level, examples of such events that are commonly used for time reference include *eso kese* (the big war, that is, World War II). ... At the ethnic level, local histories abound with many appropriate examples. The common feature of all these events is that they are considered so extraordinary or unusual that they remain indelible in people's minds, and therefore, easy reference can be made to them as time indicators.[86]

We see such referencing in Maya conceptions of time as well, but this is in addition to the placement of such events (in the Classic Period at least) in the Long Count and *tzolk'in* calendars. This in itself is not something that happens only within the Maya tradition. In Western cultures, people also think of events in terms of their relationship to other major events that fix a sense of being in time, independently from the Gregorian calendar. We may not remember May 18, 1986, for example, but we will remember major life events or political events that happened that day. People often struggle to remember Gregorian calendar dates (this is one of the most common complaints about grade school history courses, which used to be geared primarily toward memorization of the Gregorian dates of important events), but they do not struggle to remember the events themselves. Thus, it is fairly easy to remember the Battle of Hastings or the assassination of Abraham Lincoln, but fewer people will know the Gregorian associations of these events with October 14, 1066 CE and April 14, 1865 (indeed, while I know the year dates, even I had to look up the month and day). This is perhaps an exception for events that have come to be crucially associated with Gregorian dates, such as the bombings of the World Trade Center and the Pentagon in the United States, which has become better known as simply September 11, 2001, or in common usage "9/11." Presumably part of the reason for this is that *multiple* historical events happened as part of the violence on that day, so that it became easier to refer to them by the Gregorian date itself. This is still the exception, however, rather than the rule.

We see something similar in the ancient Maya world. Accessions, births, and deaths of rulers, along with important battles, conquests, and other central events are memorialized in stelae and other memorial constructions, and associated with Long Count, *tzolk'in*, and other calendric data. But one of the things this data does, distinctly from what we see in the Gregorian calendar, but very similar to the Akan date system, is to fix events with respect to other historical events. The Maya calendars are abstract constructions, but they also are used to create a *numerical* connection of events to one another. Both in the Maya and the Akan calendars, what we see is not *cyclical* time (in the sense described by earlier scholars), but rather *correlative* time (which I argue we also see in the ancient Chinese context). In the Akan context, day names are seen as containing aspects of elements of personhood, as well as characterizing people and events from other times associated with that name. Adjaye writes:

> Day names, praise names, appellations, and by-names must be seen as part of the cultural apparatus by which the Akan perceive and define personhood and personality. Further, aspects of Akan names, such as appellations, go beyond person definition to characterize perception of time, because in seeking to transfer attributes and historic accomplishments of someone who lived long ago to the current bearer of that name, those characteristics are transposed from the past to the present, and, in a sense, detemporized.[87]

This is largely the same in the Maya system of day names based on the *tzolk'in* calendar, as well as presumably the associations with Lords of the Night and other calendric elements in the Classic Period. Day names in the *tzolk'in* are accorded with certain characteristics that, while not completely determinative, suggest associations with past persons and events, and general characteristics of a day that one who is born on it will be associated with. These features are associated with calendar days through a complex history. It is not that there is a fully formed explanation of the characteristics associated with each period that rigidly determines what a person will be like. Rather, the actual lives of individuals associated with certain dates, as well as important events taking place on those dates, shape the way we understand the properties associated with the days. The element of renewal and transformation of characteristics associated with periods cannot be forgotten here. In a correlative system such as that of the Maya, time characterizes human beings and events, but human beings and events also characterize time. There is a mutual effect between them. This is one of the reasons I reject time as the fundamental metaphysical entity. If this were the case, time and its features would determine everything, and it could not itself be transformed by other elements of the world.

One way to understand the correlativity involved here is through the case of association of important events in the individual and communal life to the objective or impersonal calendar. This is part of what the Classic Period *ahauob* attempted to do in their erection of stelae and memorials, which focused on events in their lives and rule in the context of the numerous Maya calendars. There were even careful changes often made from what must have been the correct dates of certain events to different ones in order to create the proper associations. This may not have been seen as simply disingenuous fiction making to support regimes. The *ahau*, as controller of time and ordering, was seen as responsible in important ways for the orderings and also necessarily having certain features of other rulers, ancestors, and important figures. Given this fact, time itself could respond to the properties of the ruler as much as the other way around. Just as discussed above, the relationship between the ruler and time was as much a reciprocal relationship, in which each held power (in some sense) relative to the other as time and events. This correlative system of time mirrors, I argue, a general correlative metaphysics very similar to what we see developed in the early Chinese tradition in the Han Dynasty. The correlative relationship between the ruler and *time* is echoed in the correlative relationship between one ruler and his successors and forebears. Identity is ultimately even fixed by the correlative relationships between a present entity—human or otherwise, and corresponding entities in different times or places.

While the specific terminology most associated with Chinese correlative thought, including *ganying* 感應(resonance) and *tianren heyi* 天人合一(nature and humanity form one unity) are not coined in the *Huainanzi*, we see the main apparatus behind correlative thought first developed in this text. In the *Huainanzi*, the structure of *ben-mo* 本末(root and branches) is used to explain the relationship of all individual components in the world to the *dao* 道 (way) and ultimately to one another as well. Because all things ultimately share the same *ben*, they can be in this sense understood as co-originating and sharing certain essential features. The key to both understanding and making use of objects, according to the *Huainanzi*, is to discover the *ben* unifying things and how it is manifest in terms of the particularities attributable to the *mo* (branches). *Ben* is associated with *dao*, which is a notoriously difficult concept discussed in earlier "Daoist" schools, associated with something like a "ground of being." Part of the problem is that *dao* in itself is ineffable and impossible to fully grasp.

In Chinese philosophy of the Han Dynasty, we find the development of a robust explanation of how humans participate, via ritual, in completing the raw stuff provided by nature into a cosmos intelligible to humanity, including moral and social norms, and even physical things (*wu* 物). We can look to this account for an example of how humans can play a necessary intermediating role between nature and the products of culture in a way that avoids relativism. This is exactly what we see in ancient Maya thought. While humans play a necessary role in completion of the cosmos, in "keeping the days," the proper organization of the cosmos (through the symbol of the calendar) is not a matter of convention or decision on the part of humans. Rather, it is a matter of the human ability to understand the patterns inherent in the world, and to construct rituals that manifest these patterns through human society, in a way that humans can clearly understand and access. Thus, there is necessarily a kind of creativity involved, but this creativity is not an inventive creativity in terms of its innovation in ritual construction—rather it is a creativity based in properly expressing an intrinsic (but hidden) principle of nature. It is more akin to a certain kind of creativity in theoretical and practical science than it is to creativity in the arts (though it shares some family resemblances with both).[88]

The Maya conception of construction and organization of human life through completion of the patterns of nature focuses mainly on time and rulership (or at least this is what we know of the ancient Maya conception through the texts we have access to). The Chinese conception, on the other hand, tends to focus not on time but on social and political norms for the governance of individual and collective action. Where time is a philosophical focus-point of Maya thought, society is the major philosophical focus-point of early Chinese thought (though there are of course exceptions to this).[89] Despite this difference, early Chinese accounts of how humans institute ritual and how it then plays a role in the completion of the cosmos are consistent with and can possibly illuminate the Maya view here. That is, if we take the ancient Maya to have held views similar to the late Warring States and early Han Chinese philosophers on ritual and completion of natural patterns, we are left with an elegant solution to the problem of philosophical lacunae in the Maya account. Below, I present an overview of these Chinese accounts, before returning to tie them in to the Maya account as I've presented it thus far, in order to offer a plausible fleshed-out ancient Maya account of temporal ritual.

In the early Confucian text *Xunzi*, we find a discussion of ritual and its connection to the world and humanity that is one of the most robust and developed of its time. The philosopher Xun Kuang (also known as Xunzi, or "Master Xun," after whom the text is named) took ritual (*li* 禮) as one of his central concerns. He developed an account of ritual included in a number of chapters in the *Xunzi*, most prominently the *Lilun* 禮論("Discussion of Ritual") and *Xing'e* 性惡("Human Nature is Evil") chapters. According to Xunzi and other early Confucian philosophers, ritual is a necessary aspect of human culture, as it is used to shape behavior in such a way as to achieve overall social harmony. One aspect of ritual is thus ritual as behavioral norms. Ritual, according to early Confucians, is shared by members of society and used by each individual person both to tie them to the community and to regulate their own mental states. Xunzi argues that there are two central functions of ritual, which we can call the *intrapersonal* and *interpersonal* functions. It is this aspect of Xunzi's explanation of ritual that goes beyond what we find in earlier Confucian work. The interpersonal function of ritual is to create social harmony, while the intrapersonal function is to satisfy the individual's desires. Both of these functions are enacted by the single performance of ritual as social norm. While the social and personal functions of ritual are most important for Xunzi and other early Confucians, there is also a sense in which they see ritual as manifesting something contained in the world, independently of humans. Ritual helps us to pattern human conduct after the inherent patterns in the world. This latter point has led to competing readings of the Xunzi on ritual, with some advocating a "conventionalist" reading in which ritual is the construct of humans, and others advocating a "realist" reading in which ritual is inherent in the world and independent of human construction. I have argued in other work for something close to the latter interpretation,[90] but I will not repeat these arguments here. For my purposes here, it will be enough to say that a realist reading of Xunzi offers us something approaching the Maya view of ritual, which is uncontroversially realist. Thus, in order for the parallel with Xunzi to be comparatively fruitful, I assume here a realist interpretation of Xunzi on ritual. The most important consideration here is that such an account offers us a plausible way of thinking about how we may reconstruct a realist ritual system, and apply this to the Maya case.[91]

Paul Goldin offers a succinct and powerful statement of Xunzian realism about ritual. He writes:

> The rituals of the Sage Kings identify the natural order, and augment it, by confirming the distinctions that people are bound to make by nature. This is why there is only one set of legitimate rituals. There is only one Way. The Sage Kings apprehended it, and their rituals embody it. There is no other way, and no other constellation of rituals that conforms to the Way."[92]

In this, we see a mirror of the opening of the *Popol Vuh*, in which the gods continually destroy their creation due to the failure of each being to "keep the days," to engage in the kind of ritual necessary to complete the organization of the cosmos. The daykeeping ritual itself is independent of humans—part of the pattern or structure of the world, which humans must discover and use, rather than create. Surely there must be *some* creative element involved in the structuring and following of ritual, because we do not see ritual happening "of itself" in the world, but both Xunzi and the *Popol Vuh* insist that the essence of ritual itself is inherent in the cosmos, rather than the result of human convention or creative construction. Xunzi offers some explanation for why this is in the *Lilun* chapter, explaining that rituals are fixed and perfect expressions of certain human emotions or other states. He writes:

三年之喪,何也?曰:稱情而立文,因以飾群,別親疏貴賤之節,而不可益損也。故曰:無適不易之術也。

Why must the mourning period be three years? My response is this: it is capturing the emotions and establishing the outward sign, in order to adorn the community. One does not neglect relatives whether rich or poor, and (likewise the mourning period) cannot be augmented or decreased. Therefore I say: it is without match and this method (of ritual) is not to be changed.[93]

The sages, according to Xunzi, are perfected moral exemplars, usually rulers or nobles, who are responsible for the discovery and expression of ritual. Ritual is *enacted* by the society collectively, but it is established by the sages alone. Notice, however, that ritual is necessary for the proper expression of human life. Without the funerary rituals, the emotion of grief cannot be properly expressed, with the implication that the community will break down. Ritual is something that is uniquely fixed by facts about the world, but it not expressed or enacted until humans enact it through "deliberate effort" (*wei*).

This "deliberate effort" is an important element of Xunzi's explanation of how humans (in particular, the sages) play a role in the establishment of the ritual inherent in the world. Since ritual is not practiced in the absence of humans, it requires humans for its expression, and its expression has certain effects on human community. The first stage in the establishment of ritual is for the sages to discover and make manifest ritual based on the inherent patterns of the world. In the *Xing'e* ("Human Nature is Evil") chapter, Xunzi writes:

凡禮義者,是生於聖人之偽

In each case ritual and appropriateness are derived from the deliberate effort (*wei*) of the sages.[94]

The deliberate effort Xunzi describes here is not a *creative* effort in terms of construction of something new. For such an effort, the term *zuo* 作(creation) would be used. This term is carefully avoided in discussions of the establishment of ritual. In the opening passage of the *Lilun* chapter, Xunzi describes the establishment of ritual by the sages in terms of "mandating" or instituting (*zhi* 制). The passage reads:

先王惡其亂也,故制禮義以分之,以養人之欲,給人之求

The former kings hated disorder, therefore they instituted (*zhi*) ritual and righteousness (*yi*) in order to (properly) make distinctions, in order to nourish the desires of the people, in order to provide what the people sought.[95]

Xunzi's words suggest that the role of the sages in instituting ritual is one of establishment or making manifest. There may be a creative element in this establishment, but ritual is not a human convention and is not constructed by humans alone. It is a feature of the cosmos itself, and humans discover and give voice to ritual. This parallels the Maya position on ritual as found in the *Popol Vuh* and the Classic Period stelae. There is a problem here, however. If ritual does not manifest by itself without human activity, in what sense can it be said to be contained in nature? And if human activity somehow makes it manifest, then in what sense can it be said to be *not* the creation of humans?

Part of the answer to this question is given not in the *Xunzi* itself, but in the later Confucian text *Chunqiu Fanlu*, dating to the early Han Dynasty. Here, we find a more developed account of *tian* 天 (heaven; nature) and its operation—what it contains, and how the sage establishes ritual on the basis of natural patterns. The *Chunqiu Fanlu* explains that humans *complete* what *tian* provides. *Tian* provides the raw stuff and the patterns which humans shape into ritual (and other elements of the world) along the lines consistent with the patterns inherent in things. This conception of pattern, or *li* 理, is a feature of early Chinese thought most thoroughly developed in Daoist texts such as the *Zhuangzi*, and picked up by early Han texts to explain the connection between human activity and expression of ritual and other basic elements of the world and society.

Li is understood in terms of basic patterns inherent in the world, which determine how things develop and unfold. The generation of things as well as the activity of these things follows the patterns inherent in them, which is a matter of nature (*tian*). What the sage is able to do is to understand this principle of generation and action through careful observation and reflection, and to both act and create new things consistently with these patterns. Not everyone, according to the early Chinese texts, can discern the patterns inherent in things, and it takes a sage to properly understand these patterns. Due to this understanding, the sage is able to regulate his own action in such a way as to act consistently with the patterns inherent in nature, rather than out of step with them. It is part of this overall picture that most of us easily fall out of step with the patterns inherent in the world, acting at cross purposes with them, and that this is the primary source of human failure and lack of thriving. One problem here, of course, is that there is no explanation of how, given that all things are generated and develop based on the patterns inherent in the world, human beings could act or develop in ways inconsistent with these patterns.[96]

Since those of us who are not morally developed sages lack the understanding to grasp the patterns inherent in the world and to use these to direct our action, we must rely on the expression of these patterns by the sages in a form we can understand. The patterns themselves are subtle and inherent in things. What the sages can do, however, is to construct rituals that suitably express these patterns—that is, they can enjoin certain kinds of action that follow the patterns inherent in things. If the rest of us follow these patterns (the rituals), then our actions become aligned with the intrinsic patterns of the world, and we thereby gain personal and communal thriving. Thus, the role of the sage in "completing" what we are provided by nature is to discover and establish as normative certain kinds of actions that properly express human development in accordance with principles. Only certain actions will in fact do this, and the sage's role thus is properly seen as one of discovery (of these actions), rather than creation or innovation.

The *Chunqiu Fanlu* and the *Huainanzi* both hold that the sage, through cultivation of understanding of the inherent patterns in the world, uniquely possesses the ability to formulate rituals that enjoin action mirroring these patterns. In this sense, the sage can be understood as *completing* what is inherent in nature. In this way, the *Chunqiu Fanlu* describes the structured cosmos as a collaborative project between the human sage and nature. In the *Huainanzi*, an account of the patterns of nature is offered that makes ritual a construct of humans based on patterns of the world. In the second chapter of *Huainanzi*, *Chuzhen* (Activating the Genuine), a brief description is given of the patterns of nature and the formation of ritual.

> The Way has both a warp and a weft linked together. [The Perfected] attain the unity of the Way and join with its thousand branches and ten thousand leaves. [...] ...they take the Way as their pole, potency as their line, rites and music as their hook.[97]

The *Chunqiu Fanlu* also contains quite a bit on the connection between the sage, ritual, and the patterns of nature. A passage from the *Chuzhuangwang* (King Zhuang of Chu) chapter reads:

受命應天制禮作樂之異

> Guarding allotment and resonating with nature, institution of ritual works to harmonize differences.[98]

The Maya conception of ritual and the world seems to mirror the view offered in *Xunzi* and *Chunqiu Fanlu*, in which the sage—in this case the ruler—completes the patterns inherent in the world, making them available for human understanding and use. In both the Maya and early Chinese views, the sage or ruler must have some special understanding or access to nature and its inherent patterns that the rest of humanity lacks. The source of this special ability in both cases is not completely clear. In the early Chinese case, it seems to depend on an inborn *skill* the sage possesses that can be refined through practice and continual self-cultivation. In the case of the Maya, the ruler (*ahau*) seems to have a special connection with the patterns of nature not reliant on understanding or cultivation. The *ch'ul* essence of the ruler is simply of a different and more rarified kind than that of ordinary people. Just as we can understand *ch'ul* itself as a more purified form of *itz*, there is some *ch'ul* within this category more purified than the rest, and this is just the *ch'ul* of the ruler. This is the reason that the unseen aspects of the world are not revealed to just *any* person as a result of the bloodletting sacrifice. A commoner who attempted to enact the bloodletting sacrifice would not achieve the same effect as the ruler or noble. The ruler or noble is qualitatively different from the normal person—a *superhuman* in some sense. The difference between the sage and the normal person in the Chinese tradition, for the most part, is not a fundamental difference of nature. The early thinkers are often at pains to say that anyone can become a sage—that is, any person has within them what it takes to become a sage, but the difference between the sage and the rest of us is that the sage *actualizes* this potential. On the Maya view, ordinary people do not have the ability to cultivate themselves so as to achieve the abilities of rulers and nobles. The Maya ruler was also shaman, with unique qualities that made him qualified for both roles.[99]

This also suggests a distinction between the two concerning what it is in nature that provides ritual. For the early Chinese texts discussed here, it is the pattern of nature and the effort of the sage (as fully developed person) that establishes and completes ritual, and thus there is a component of agency that is central to this account. For the ancient Maya, however, ritual is manifest by the patterns of nature, combined with the effort of the right kind of person, which is a matter of independently held (non-cultivated) qualities. Another key difference between the Chinese and Maya accounts of ritual manifestation is that for the Maya, the gods and ancestors, as well as the operation of the cosmos, was revealed more fully to the people during ritual than it was in the case of early China. Ritual, in most early Chinese contexts, was a *social* guide primarily. Drawing on the patterns inherent in the world (*li* 理), it supplied people with practices that would allow them to create cohesive, harmonious societies. For the Maya, there was almost certainly a social function of the ruler's rituals, which likely had to do similarly with group creation and cohesion, but most directly, the rituals had a metaphysical and epistemological purpose. Through bloodletting, the rulers enabled the people to see and understand aspects of the world they would otherwise have no access to. Although there has been little preservation of the effect of Maya ritual on ordinary people in the texts and material record, we might imagine that this would create strong group identity—the people of a city would be joined in their observation of the particular aspects of the world pertaining to that city. This could serve to, among other things, legitimize the rule of those responsible for the rituals—the shaman king, or *ahau*.[100] While rulers seem to have been the sole practitioners of the bloodletting ritual, other members of the elite class, including lower level priests, scribes, and certain warriors, engaged in different rituals.[101]

Other important Maya rituals had similar purposes of revealing hidden aspects of the world and facilitating communication with the gods and ancestors. As I explain in later chapters below, what is ultimately revealed through these rituals is the operation of continual creation of the world. The creation stories, such as those of the *Popol Vuh*, represent phenomena in the world that we do not directly witness, but can be revealed through ritual at any given moment. Because these creative phenomena are always happening in a continuum, they are not fixed to particular dates or times. Creation is not something that happened in time, but is something that continually happens at all times. This creation could be revealed through *performance* according to the Maya, particularly (in the Classic Period) through dance. Maya ritual performers dressed as various deities and mythical heroes, after which they performed dances to enact the creation stories. This "re-enactment" of the creation stories through dance was more than what we would think of as reenactment, or memorialization of some past act. The Maya ritual dance performances, through the power of ritual, became *identical* with the creation stories. The performers through the ritual became more than just performers playing the roles of the deities—rather, they became the deities themselves—the individuals were conduits for these deities. We see here the concept of *embedded identity* that I discuss in chapter 2. Just as with the Catholic doctrine of transubstantiation, in which the bread and wine are not simply *symbols* of the body and blood of Christ, but *become* in substance the body and blood of Christ, in the Maya ritual dances, the performers become the characters, and the dance itself becomes the acts of creation.

The Maya dance ritual cannot literally be the act of creation, unless creation is something that does not happen at some zero point "in the beginning," as it is conceived in the Abrahamic religions. There were no rules, as far as we know, concerning when the Maya dance rituals could take place, and we also know that the ritual itself enacted the creation expressed through the ritual. This by itself suggests that the Maya accepted a view of "continual creation." The dance ritual could become the creation because creation was always happening, at every moment, not fixed to a particular time. The story of the Hero Twins, of the creation of people by the first Gods, etc.—these stories represented events that did not happen at a beginning point, but that were ongoing. The dynamism of the world itself can be understood in terms of continual creation (and destruction). The drama of creation is constantly unfolding. The Maya dance rituals (and other rituals) allowed for the curtain to be pulled back on this process that the ordinary person cannot see.[102]

Both the Chinese and the Maya accounts of ritual assume a natural world, animated or constituted by a vital force (*qi* and *itz*, respectively).[103] As discussed above, in the *Huainanzi* this was seen in terms of the patterns inherent in *dao* (the Way). The various texts that discuss the patterns of nature prior to the conceptualization of humans generally offer an account of the sage's understanding of these patterns as being central to the sage's ability to institute ritual. This understanding, however, must be one that is inexpressible in language, as the sage has to construct the language for expressing this understanding from the patterns of nature in which this language is not already constructed. The difficulty that both the Chinese and Maya views face here is that it is impossible to describe the patterns of nature in a way that is ultimately accurate. It is unclear just what the sage adds to the picture to construct language and ritual from these patterns of nature, but the closest the non-sage or non-shaman can come to understanding the patterns of nature is to engage in the ritual and language instituted by the sage or shaman. Not only does this set up the epistemological difficulty that the non-sage must simply trust that one is a sage and trust in the ritual and language that the sage institutes, but it is also impossible to give an account of just what the knowledge of the sage or shaman consists of, since the ultimate reality and its patterns that the sage understands cannot itself be described by language in an ultimately correct way.[104]

Finally, for both the early Chinese and the Maya, it was the *ruler* who held the role of supreme sage and shaman. In early Chinese texts, the sage-like understanding of the ruler was ultimately what legitimized the ruler's control. Likewise, we see in the bloodletting ritual and other rituals of the Maya kings, as well as the control of the calendar, that the shamanic abilities of the Maya ruler provided legitimacy.

DAYKEEPERS AND SUBSTITUTES—CONTEMPORARY MAYA PRACTICE

Looking to the views and practices of contemporary Maya helps to shed some light on ancient practice as well. We must of course be careful how we use such sources, as Maya thought has changed greatly in the many hundreds of years since the pre-Columbian period. Still, given our understanding of the ancient sources, examination of contemporary sources can reveal shared patterns emerging from Maya thought. Some features of the revival of Maya religion and philosophy in recent decades have been adopted directly from the ancient sources, rather than existing in a continuous chain of transmission.

Much of this has to do with the suppression of numerous practices by the Spanish, which led to their extinction. The *Popol Vuh* itself laments such suppression, predicting that the knowledge of the Maya will soon disappear beneath the onslaught of Christianity.[105] While much of Maya culture did disappear, some practices remained. The most important of these for our purposes is the practice of daykeeping. The Maya continued to use their calendars, particularly the *tzolk'in* ceremonial calendar.[106]

The role of the daykeeper (K'iche': *aj q'ij*, Yucatec: *ah k'in*) consists in keeping track of the 260-day calendar, as well as understanding and interpreting the connection of individuals in the community to the aspects of the calendar, divination, and understanding the *nahuales* connected to individuals.[107] Diego de Landa discusses the role of the *ah kin* in the Yucatan during the early part of the colonial period. The *ah kin* apparently helped to facilitate transformation of various kinds, and the *ah kin*'s understanding of the calendar, as a significant aspect of transformation, made this possible. One ceremony of social transformation de Landa recounts was a kind of "coming of age" ceremony in which youth were transformed into active adults of the community.[108] We can see from this that the daykeeper performs some of the functions associated with the *ahau* (ruler) and the *sahalob* (who gain their authority from the ruler) in the pre-Columbian periods.[109] The link between understanding the calendar and understanding the transformations inherent in the world is the person of the daykeeper, and the unique knowledge they gain through their training.

A number of sources discuss the role of the daykeeper as linked with those of the shaman or priest of the Classic Period. The *Popol Vuh* of the K'iche,' written during the early part of the colonial period, discusses daykeeping as a key responsibility of the human race. The failure to properly keep days, according to the text, was ultimately to blame for the demise of the previous attempts at creation of the gods.[110] The ritual calendar plays a major role in the duties of the daykeeper, as it represents the human role in maintaining the order of the cosmos. According to Barbara Tedlock's 1981 account of daykeepers in Momostenango, Guatemala, the responsibilities of daykeepers consist primarily of rituals connected to the calendar, the new year, and divination practices associated with the connection between individual community members and the calendar.[111] Such priests, in certain parts of the Maya world, are also responsible for rituals that ensure renewal of the world—another way in which human rituals complete what is provided by nature. This renewal combines elements of the past in ways that project new structure onto the present and bounds the possibilities for the future. It is for this reason that we find anachronism among the accounts of important figures in texts like the *Popol Vuh* as well as in contemporary historical memory. Allen Christenson writes, of the people of Santiago Atitlán in highland Guatemala:

Francisco Sojuel, as the greatest of remembered culture heroes in Santiago Ati-tlán, is associated in tradition with otherwise anachronistic historic events. In popular myths, he may appear as a creator god at the beginning of the world, be killed and rise from the dead as a Christ figure to inaugurate aspects of Atiteco Easter observances, contend with the Spaniard king in Antigua soon after the conquest, or live a relatively mundane life as a farmer and community priest-shaman around the turn of the last century.[112]

In the same way, in the *Popol Vuh* we find figures such as the "Plumed Serpent" (Yucatec *kukulcan*) presented both as powerful king in early Maya history, and as a creator god responsible (along with "Heart of Sky") for the origin of humanity itself.[113] The *tzolk'in* calendar plays a unifying role in this, as certain days are associated with features connected to events and indi-viduals recurring through history. There is also a seasonal component of the calendar, as it is used in agriculture in addition to yearly rituals.[114] The impor-tant religious, agricultural, and historical role of the calendar, and through it, calendar makers and keepers (that is to say, humanity itself), shows the place of humanity in cooperating with nature to form the intelligible cosmos. Allen Christenson recounts the dance of a shaman-priest in Santiago Atitlán, who explains that his dance is not a *representation* of the creation of the world, but rather part of the creative process itself. He writes:

> Following the performance of this dance, the *nab'eysil* sought me out to ask if I had seen "the ancient ancestors giving birth to the world." He explained that they had filled his soul with their presence as he danced, guiding him in his steps, and now everything was new again. In the eyes of the *nab'eysil* the dance was not a symbol of the rebirth of the cosmos but a genuine creative act in which time folded inward upon itself to reveal the actions of deity in the primordial world.[115]

With this conception of the role of the priest and daykeeper in mind, we can better understand the power of ritual, why the gods in the first book of the *Popol Vuh* are so insistent on the keeping of days, and how the human con-struction and keeping of time plays a cooperative role in the construction and maintenance of the cosmos itself.

NOTES

1. This is a style of engaging in the history of non-Western philosophy that Roy Perrett refers to (in connection with Indian Philosophy) as the "exoticist" approach.

2. The most influential examples of such work is that of Roger Ames, David Hall, and Henry Rosemont on the early Chinese tradition, Miguel Leon-Portilla on the Mesoamerican traditions, and Sarvepalli Radhakrishnan on the Indian tradition.

3. Radhakrishnan 1957: xxv.

4. Thomas McEvilley argued that both traditions were also further influenced by Persian thought, which brought the two even closer together. McEvilley 2002 (*The Shape of Ancient Thought*).

5. One constructed by people both in Europe and outside of it. Alastair Bonnett argues in *The Idea of the West* that people outside of the West had as large a role in the construction of the "West" as those within it.

6. Houston, Stuart, and Taube, *The Memory of Bones*; Rosemary Joyce and Lynn Meskell, *Embodied Lives: Figuring Ancient Maya and Egyptian Experience*; Stephen Houston, *The Life Within: Classic Maya and the Matter of Permanence*.

7. Prudence Rice, *Maya Political Science*, and *Maya Calendar Origins*; Barbara Tedlock, *Time and the Highland Maya*.

8. Miguel Astor-Aguilera discusses nonphysical elements of Maya metaphysics, including spirit elements such as "*pixan*," which can be understood as "spirit," separable from the human body. Astor-Aguilera, *The Maya World of Communicating Objects*, 103.

9. Joyce and Meskell, *Embodied Lives,* 74–75; xv–vxii. This strikes me as a misreading of Descartes as well. Although Descartes does characterize the self as primarily a "thinking thing" early on in his *Meditations on First Philosophy*, this is done for the purposes of constructing the foundation for knowledge of the self. Later in the *Meditations* he concludes that this view can be revised, and that the person is a "mind-body union," rather than simply a thinking thing. Descartes does not conclude that the self can be identified with the *cogito*, but instead that the self is a "mind-body union," based on the argument of the 3rd–6th Meditations.

10. Astor-Aguilera, *Communicating Objects*, 103.

11. Some philosophical traditions, of course, are more "practically minded" than others. A number of scholars, such as philosophers Roger Ames and Chris Fraser, and numerous historians, claim that the early Chinese tradition as a whole was concerned primarily with social and political questions, and that their philosophy was fully grounded in social practice. Though I agree with this group that certain early Chinese thinkers did have such a pragmatist bent, I disagree with this reading of the early Chinese tradition as a whole.

12. Though there has certainly been *some* work devoted to this, most notably Leon-Portilla, *Tiempo y realidad in el pensamiento Maya*; Pharo, *The Ritual Practice of Time*, Tedlock, *Time and the Highland Maya*, and Friedel, Schele, and Parker, *Maya Cosmos*.

13. Rice, *Maya Calendar Origins*, xv; noted also in *Maya Political Science*, xvii.

14. The "Pan-Mesoamerican" view has been advocated by Linda Schele and Julia Kappelman ("What the Heck's Coatepec?"), and Peter Mathews (*The Code of Kings*).

15. Knowlton, *Maya Creation Myths*, 21.

16. Thompson, *Maya Hierogyphic Writing,* 142; Leon-Portilla *Tiempo y realidad*.

17. Some examples include the deity k'inich ahau and the rulers K'inich Janaab' Pakal of Palenque, K'inich Yax K'uk' Mo' of Copan, and others. Rulers used the "*k'inich*" moniker as an expression of *k'inich ahau*. McKillop, *Ancient Maya*, 218.

18. About 365.25 days to be more precise. This is the reason for the institution of "leap year" days in our Gregorian calendar. The Maya did not recognize such

additional days, and simply allowed the calendars to progress seasons. It is unclear whether they measured years by sidereal or tropical year, but given the emphasis on the equinoxes evident at classic and postclassic sites like Chichen Itza, it is plausible that they thought of it mainly in a tropical sense. Tropical year records helped to determine solstice and equinox dates. Kelley, "Mesoamerican Astronomy and the Maya Calendar Correlation Problem," 66–71. Also see McLeod, *Astronomy in the Ancient World*.

19. According to Scott Hutson (Hutson, *Dwelling, Identity, and the Maya*, 36), being born on one of these days was inauspicious, as one's identity in part relied on having an integrated place in the calendar and thus the world.

20. Literally "Sun-eyed," which is a reference to the Sun God. Stuart, *The Hieroglyphic Name of Altar U*.

21. Colas "K'inich and King," 271. I will return to look more closely at Colas' arguments, as he claims that the use of *k'inich* in the ruler's name is meant to express *identity* with the Sun God.

22. Leon-Portilla, *Tiempo y realidad*, 20–21.

23. Including Rice, *Maya Political Science,* 52–53; Milbrath, *Star Gods of the Maya*.

24. Leon-Portilla 1968: 20.

25. Like many modern terms for Maya sites and objects, *tzolk'in* (*tzol k'in*—day division) is a Yucatec word applied to the calendar by modern scholars of the Maya. Other Maya groups have different names for the calendar. As with most ancient Maya terms, however, modern scholars have had to either guess at pronunciations or substitute modern Mayan pronunciations (usually from Yucatec).

26. Foster, *Handbook to Life in the Ancient Maya World*, 37.

27. Rice, *Maya Political Science*, argues that the *may* system of cycles in which seats of political power were rooted in different cities every 260 years was based on this calendar, in particular the *katun* division. She argues that the name "Maya" itself derives from the term *may*, thus describing the Maya as the "people of the *may* (cycle)."

28. I discuss the astronomical connections of the Maya calendars in McLeod, *Astronomy in the Ancient World*, ch. 1.

29. Leon-Portilla, *Tiempo y realidad*, 20.

30. Personhood is also seen as having necessary temporal aspects: "To be a full person requires having a place in the calendar," Hutson, *Dwelling, Identity, and the Maya*, 36.

31. Pharo, *Ritual Practice of Time*: 21–22.

32. The standard practice of Mayanists is to use letters to name rulers and gods when their names are unknown. The names of cities, on the other hand, follow modern usage, even when the Classic Mayan name is known. The name "Pusilha" is of course not a Classic Mayan name.Other cities for which we do have the Classic Mayan names are still generally referred to using their contemporary names. The city of Tikal, for example, was likely called "Mutul" in Classic Mayan, but is still generally referred to by Mayanists as Tikal, rather than Mutul.

33. Prager, Volta, and Braswell, "The Dynastic History and Archaeology of Pusilha, Belize," 289.

34. Luxton, *The Book of Chumayel,* xi. Vail and Macri, *The New Catalog of Maya Hieroglyphs,* 154.

35. Newsome, *Trees of Paradise and Pillars of the World,* 157.

36. Sharer, *Ancient Maya,* 107. Harris and Stearns, *Understanding Maya Inscriptions,* 13:

> The Maya attached considerable significance to the *completion* of several time periods, including months. As one month ended, the next was to be considered 'seated.' In the inscriptions, a special glyph signifying the 'seating' of a month (the same glyph was used for the seating of a ruler) was used to designate the completion of one month and the beginning of another. Thus, the last day of, say, *Pohp,* is designated the seating of *Wo.*

37. Milbrath, *Star Gods of the Maya*: "Each Katun lord ruled a period of 19.71 years (20x360 days), very close to the interval between successive Jupiter-Saturn conjunctions."

38. Schele and Friedel, *Forest of Kings,* 81.

39. Most importantly for my purposes here, James Maffie reads Aztec metaphysics as representative of a kind of process metaphysics (Maffie, *Aztec Philosophy*). David Hall and Roger Ames interpret much of Chinese thought as accepting (whether implicitly or not) a kind of process view of the world as well (Hall and Ames, *Thinking from the Han.*). While I think there is a much stronger case for the Aztec than for the Chinese in general, certain strains of Daoist thought could plausibly be read as endorsing process metaphysics.

40. Leon-Portilla, *Tiempo y realidad,* 51.

41. McLeod, *Astronomy in the Ancient World,* 17. Diehl, *The Olmecs.*

42. This is the reason scholars have a hard time dating Aztec historical events recounted in texts, given *tonalpohualli* dates.

43. *Timaeus* 38b7–15.

44. Droit-Volet, Fayolle, and Gil, "Emotion and Time Perception: Effects of Film-Induced Mood."

45. Mbiti, *African Religions and Philosophy,* 17. While some disagree with this, including Kwame Gyekye, who argues that this does not hold true for the Akan view of time (although he takes issue only concerning the Akan view, not making a wider claim).

46. The Yogacara school advances such a view.

47. Gerardo Aldana argues for a somewhat similar view, with a different time period focus of over 800 years in Aldana, *The Apotheosis of Janaab' Pakal.*

48. Tedlock, *Popol Vuh,* 65: "There will be no high days and no bright praise for our work, our design, until the rise of the human work, the human design."

49. Vail and Macri, *New Catalog of Maya Hieroglyphs,* 162.

50. Prudence Rice links daykeeping with the ruler in later periods (Rice, *Maya Calendar Origins,* 49–50).

51. Victoria Schlesinger writes (Schlesinger, *Animals and Plants of the Ancient Maya,* 62): "Maya day keepers of the past and present study the cycles of people,

plants, animals, and celestial bodies, looking at the correlation between them. For the ancient Maya keeping track of time gave practical and spiritual order to their lives; they knew when to plant corn and when to give thanks to the gods."

52. Tedlock, *Time and the Highland Maya*, 3.

53. Spencer-Ahrens and Wren, in Foster, ed. *Handbook to Life in the Ancient Maya World*, 262.

54. Pharo, *Ritual Practice of Time*, 2–9.

55. The Gregorian date of August 13 did not exist in the pre-Columbian calendars, of course, but the date can be marked similarly by the fact that one of two zenith passages in the Maya region takes place on this date. The other is February 5, which is also connected with the creation mythology. Friedel, Schele, and Parker, *Maya Cosmos*, 95–97.

56. Friedel, Schele, and Parker, *Maya Cosmos*, 96.

57. *Sahal* refers to a class of nobles rather than scribe/priests, but the scribe/priests uniformly came from this class, as did the ruler (*ajaw*). As with the caste system in India in which only those of the *Brahmin* class had the authority to learn and perform Vedic ritual (although not all *Brahmins* did), being a *sahal* was a necessary, but not sufficient, condition for service as a scribe/priest. Schele and Mathews, *The Code of Kings*, 89.

58. Sharer, *Ancient Maya*, 491.

59. Eberl, "To Put in Order: Classic Maya Concepts of Time and Space."

60. Eberl, "To Put in Order," 80–81, 89.

61. Eberl, "To Put in Order," 91.

62. Eberl, "To Put in Order" 94.

63. Eberl, "To Put in Order," 94, Ruppert and Denison, *Archaeolgical Reconnaissance in Campeche, Quintana Roo, and Petén*, plate 48c.

64. Fasquelle and Beyl, *Copan: reino del sol*, 51.

65. The text is described and translated in Josserand, "The Narrative Structure of Hieroglyphic Texts at Palenque."

66. Josserand, "Narrative Structure," 27.

67. Christenson, *Popol Vuh*, 68.

68. Christenson *Popol Vuh*, 68–69.

69. Blackson, "The Stuff of Conventionalism," 65.

70. To use the terminology coined by Alan Sidelle.

71. Sidelle, "A Sweater Unraveled: Following One Thread of Thought for Avoiding Coincident Entities."

72. Sidelle, "A Sweater Unraveled," 426.

73. Rice (*Maya Calendar Origins*, 49–50) argues that the daykeeper was central to rulership in the Postclassic Period. Barbara Tedlock (*Time and the Highland Maya*) has studied the practices of contemporary daykeepers in Maya society.

74. Rice, *Maya Calendar Origins*, 49.

75. McKillop, *The Ancient Maya*, 178. She points out that the emergence of stelae erection, including Long Count dates in the Maya region, is itself used to define the beginning of the Classic Period.

76. Sabloff and Andrews, *Late Lowland Maya Civilization*, 101. Lopez Austin and Lopez Lujian, *El pasado indígena*,191. Milbrath, *Star Gods of the Maya*, 5. "During the Early Postclassic periods, the Maya still used Long Count dates to note dates

of astronomical significance, but they no longer recorded historical events involving Maya rulers and city-states."

77. Sharer, *The Ancient Maya*, 171. Sharer discusses this in terms of "supernatural power."

78. Evans and Webster, *Archaeology of Ancient Mexico and Central America: An Encyclopedia*, p. 752.

79. Houston, Stuart, and Taube, *The Memory of Bones*, 74.

80. Houston, Stuart, and Taube, *The Memory of Bones*, 61. Also see Stuart, "Kings of Stone: A Consideration of Stelae in Ancient Maya Ritual and Representation," 148–171.

81. Foster, *Handbook*, 293. Harris and Stearns, *Understanding Maya Inscriptions*, 37.

82. Discussions of the Akan conception of time can be found in Gyekye, *An Essay on African Philosophical Thought*; Adjaye, "Time, Identity, and Historical Consciousness in Akan; and Mbiti, *African Religions and Philosophy*.

83. Monaghan, "Of Calendars and Computers: Comparing Mesoamerica and Bali."

84. Adjaye ("Time, Identity, and Historical Consciousness in Akan") points out that the word *osbsosom* translates as "moon." Yet this may be a later name given to an earlier construction, as 40 days is clearly longer than the synodic month (or lunation), which is about 29.5 days.

85. Adjaye, "Time, Identity, and Historical Consciousness in Akan."

86. Adjaye, "Time, Identity, and Historical Consciousness in Akan," 59.

87. Adjaye, "Time, Identity...," 61–62.

88. This is presumably part of the reason that "creation" (*zuo* 作) was frowned upon in early Chinese thought, not just because of the injunction of *Analects* 7.1, 述而不作 ("transmit and do not create"). Michael Puett discusses these aspects of *zuo* in Puett, *The Ambivalence of Creation*.

89. The early Confucians and Mohists, for example, are socially focused, while the Daoists of the Late Warring States and early Han are less so. The syncretists of the Han are a special case, which I discuss below.

90. McLeod "Xunzi and Mimamsa..."

91. McLeod, "Xunzi and Mimamsa...," Goldin, *Rituals of the Way, ...*

92. Goldin , *Rituals of the Way.*

93. *Xunzi* 19.24. I follow the numbering of Chinese texts on the Chinese Text Project website (ctext.org).

94. *Xunzi* 23.8.

95. *Xunzi* 19.1.

96. One answer to this question is to accord humans a special status in the world, possessing a kind of "free will" that allows them to act or develop contrary to the patterns inherent in the world. Freedom from the deterministic pattern of *li* does seem to mark the human in early Chinese texts. Humans, according to Han texts like the *Huainanzi*, possess a particular kind of *qi* (vital essence) we can call *jingshen* 精神 (pure or essential spirit), which distinguishes them from other beings in the world. Free will and sentience are presumably part of this *jingshen*. There has not been much focus on this issue in scholarship on early Chinese philosophy, mainly because of the tendency to read this literature in a modernistic and naturalistic way.

97. *Huainanzi, Chuzhen* 2.4 (Major, Queen et. al trans., 89).

98. *Chunqiu Fanlu, Chuzhuangwang.*

99. Sharer, *The Ancient Maya*, 70.

100. Foster, *Handbook*, 187. Sharer, *Daily Life in Maya Civilization*, 699. Rice (*Maya Calendar Origins*, 95) discusses earlier ritual practice of Isthmian people having similar function.

101. Ancient Maya society is commonly understood as falling into three overarching classes: the elites, including rulers and their families, the *sahalob*, or lesser governing nobility, priests, scribes, and high-status musicians and warriors; the middle class, including low-level officials, merchants and artisans, ordinary soldiers; and the low class or common people, including workers, servants, farmers, and slaves. Foster, *Handbook*, 124.

102. The *Popol Vuh*'s discussion of the text as an instrument of seeing suggests this as well.

103. I remain neutral for purposes of this discussion whether the correct account is one of animation or constitution.

104. We see these claims in many of the Daoist works, especially the *Zhuangzi*, as well as in the *Huainanzi*.

105. Christenson, *Popol Vuh*: "But this is the essence of the Quichés, because there is no longer a way of seeing it. It was with the lords at first, but it is now lost."

106. Use of the Long Count calendar ended in the colonial period.

107. The *nahual* in contemporary Maya thought is akin to the concept of the *way* in ancient Maya thought—a *nahual* is an animal associated with the individual, with certain properties definitive of the individual. Rigoberta Menchú Tum discussed the *nahual* in her famous biography *I, Rigoberta Menchú* (ch. 3). Vila Selma, *La mentalidad maya*, 100.

108. de Landa, *Relación*, 92–95. Also discussed in Solari, *Maya Spatial Biographies in Communal Memory and Cosmic Time*, 193–4.

109. Rice (*Maya Calendar Origins*, 50) associates the activities of the modern daykeeper with the rulers of the Classic Period. Meredith Paxton also discusses the possibility of a distinct practice of lunar daykeeping in the Yucatan. Paxton, *The Cosmos of the Yucatec Maya*, 56–57.

110. Tedlock *Popol Vuh*, 68.

111. Tedlock, *Time and the Highland Maya.*

112. Christenson, *Art and Society in a Highland Maya Community*, 25.

113. Tedlock, *Popol Vuh*, 64–65.

114. Alvarado, *El tzolkin es más que un calendario.*

115. Christenson, *Art and Society*, 24.

Chapter 2

Reductionism versus Correlativism

A RETURN TO TIME

K'in, as discussed in chapter 1, is understood as both "day" and "sun." Association of the day with the sun is standard in human languages, and perhaps the closest parallel that comes to mind is the Chinese term 日 (pronounced *rì* in Mandarin), the character of which is a pictographic representation of the sun. This character occurs of course in a host of other Sino-Tibetan languages, of course, as well as Korean and Japanese, which they adopted from Chinese systems. Though the Maya glyph for *k'in* is translatable as 'sun,' the pictograph represented by the glyph is not the sun itself, but a flower, likely *plumeria rubra*.[1] The sun itself is suggested by two associations of the glyph *k'in* that are sometimes rendered visible in the glyph. While the earliest and most common depiction of *k'in* is the flower depiction, some versions render the glyph as signifying the five directions (north, south, east, west, and center). The right-hand side of the figure below shows a directional rendering of *k'in*. Comparing it to the standard "flower" depiction on the left, we can see how the directional association may have been made. The space between the petals seems to point to the four cardinal directions. The flower represented in the original *k'in* glyph may have been seen as itself a representation of the model of the cosmos, and used to represent *k'in* for this reason. This fundamental unit of time is glyphically represented not as the sun disk itself, but as a model of the cosmos and at the same time a fruit of the sun's activity. The flower is not only *created by* sunlight (in part), but *includes* sunlight, and thus the sun itself, as well as the directions defined by the sun's movement, as part of what it is.[2] This seems to suggest the kind of correlative view I discuss below, in which flowers, the five directions, and the sun do not *reduce* to time (as some scholars argue), but instead are in some sense contained *within* some more fundamental ground of being, such as with the view of *dao* 道 in Han Chinese texts, or that of *prakrti* (primal force) grounding *satkaryavada* (coexistent causation) in Vedic Indian schools. The issue of transformation and causation in Maya texts strongly echoes that of the two views mentioned.

While I agree with Leon-Portilla that time plays an important role in ancient Maya metaphysics, I disagree that the unit of *k'in* plays the role of fundamental constituent of reality to which all other phenomena reduce, akin to the *dharmas* for the Buddhist Abhidharma school in India. It is unclear from the texts alone whether the status of *k'in* as the smallest unit of time discussed in Maya texts and memorialized on monuments shows that it has a privileged status in Maya thought. We must remember that there are at least two distinct issues in play here: that of ontological dependence and priority and that of constitution. One does not entail the other.[3] It can be the case that a *uinal* (eighteen-day time period) is constituted by twenty *k'in* without

a   *b*   *c*   *d*

e   *f*   *g*   *h*

i   *j*   *k*   *l*

Figure 2.1 A number of distinct ways of rendering the *k'in* glyph. From Sylvanus Morley, *An Introduction to the Study of Maya Hieroglyphs*, 1915. Bulletin / Smithsonian Institution, Bureau of American Ethnology no. 57 (1915), Figure 34. G.P.O, 1901. http://library.si.edu/digital-library/book/bulletin571915smit.

it being the case that a *uinal* is ontologically dependent on a *k'in*, that *k'in* is the "more basic or fundamental" concept. Thus, if time is central for the ancient Maya, this does not necessarily mean that *k'in* is the central and basic time concept.

K'in clearly plays an important role in Maya thought, as its imagery is ubiquitous. But there is suggestion in some places that other units, particularly the *uinal*, may have played an even more basic or central role. The *Chilam Balam of Chumayel*, for example, focuses on the *uinal* in giving an account of the creation of the world and human beings. Indeed, the term *uinal* is sometimes said as *uinic*, a word that is also used to mean "human being" (as well as signifying the number 20, although the *uinal* in the Long Count is eighteen rather than twenty days, in order to fit properly into the 365-day solar year).

The "Lords of the Night" glyphs show us additional temporal concepts that challenge the view of the primacy of *k'in* in Maya metaphysics of time. The importance of the time cycle in Maya memorial texts is clear from the focus of the memorials. Nearly all of the memorial stelae of the Classic Period begin with series of calendric glyphs,[4] beginning with the ceremonial glyph known currently as the Initial Series Introductory Glyph (ISIG), which is generally the largest glyph of the text, and sometimes occupies a central position, and receives more ornate detail than other glyphs in the text.[5] The ISIG introduces the "Long Count" date that generally begins each memorial text, generally marking the date of the erection or dedication of the stela. *Tzolk'in* and *haab* dates are also usually included after the Long Count, along with other calendric and religious information such as the "Lords of the Night" placement glyphs,[6] the current day of lunation (at the dedication of the stela), and the number of days of lunation in a given month[7] Important dates in the ruler's timeline are then situated with respect to this initial Long Count date.

The role of the Lords of the Night in the Initial Series tells us about the importance of their representative place *as* elements of time. Raphael Girard, in his classic study of the religious rituals of the contemporary Chortí Maya, argues that the Lords of the Night represent the cycle of time itself. He discusses the Chortí winter ceremony, in which nine elders take part in a ritual in which they act as representatives of the nine Lords of the Night:[8]

> The procession of the nine elders and assistants personifying the Nine Lords of the Night, represents a time cycle of nine nights and its respective numerical order in accordance with the position they occupy in the ceremonial parade. This shows plainly that in the mind of the present-day Maya the gods are both gods and sacred numbers. Like their distant ancestors, the Maya of today deify their time periods. . . . Another feature of the Maya chrono-theogonic system, illustrated in Chortí rites and beliefs, is the elevation of time periods—groups of days, equivalent to groups of gods—to higher power. In light of these ideas, the

procession of the Nine which the Chortís perform every nine days symbolizes
the cycle of Nine days—or gods—and, at the same time, the Nine months of
twenty days of the winter cycle.[9]

The *k'in* glyph, although absent in eight of the Lords of the Night group
glyphs, figures prominently in the most common of the Lords of the Night
glyphs, G9. This glyph is associated with major period endings, and contains the *k'in* glyph as its major component.[10] It is unclear whether *k'in* was
made part of G9 to emphasize the significance of major period endings in
the broader calendric system, or for less ideological reasons, such as its phonetic value. We know that certain logographs first associated with concepts
in the Classic Mayan language of a region were sometimes later adopted as
phonetic markers, based on the word in a particular language expressing the
concept. We see similar developments in other languages that combine logographs and phonetic signs, such as Chinese. One example is the Maya glyph
for the third-person personal pronoun, *u* (he/she/it), initially a logographic
sign, visually representing a human face. Although the word retained this
meaning through time, it also eventually took on phonetic significance of
its own, being used to phonetically render words including the syllable '*u*'
that had nothing to do with reference to persons, such as *uti* ("to happen") or
iyuwal (continuous action marker).[11]

The view that the gods are identified with or are aspects of time, and vice
versa, is an influential one in certain Mayanist corners. Miguel Leon-Portilla
attributes the view to the late Eric Thompson, who was an influential Mayanist
in the twentieth century.[12] While it certainly is the case that *memorials* erected
by rulers had a major concern with time, this alone is not enough to show that
the Maya had a metaphysics in which time was seen as the sole fundamental
constituent of reality, and in which the major deities were all associated with
time. Time is *one* component of the natural world, and insofar as some Maya
constructions were overly concerned with time, they may have focused specifically on time deities in their construction. Time is a fundamental feature of
Maya metaphysics, but it makes more sense of the textual evidence to understand the Maya as offering a view in which time can *become* deities, persons,
and other entities, rather than one in which these things reduce to time. There
is a more fundamental ground of Maya metaphysical thought, akin to the view
of *dao* (Way) we find in Han dynasty Chinese thought.

One interesting feature of some Initial Series glyphs, such as those at
Copan on Stela D, is that the numbers and time periods are represented as
full figures, generally of humanoid deities and other beings. Each word at
least connected to the Initial Series, then, has both a "standard" glyph and a
"full-figure" glyph. We know that this is true for the numbers and for the units
of the Long Count calendar. And these full-figure glyphs were standardized

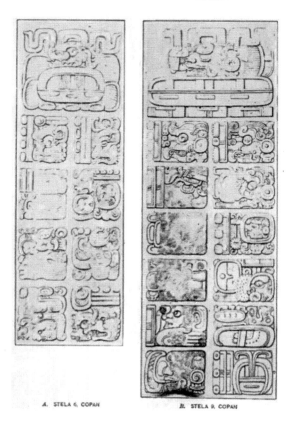

Figure 2.2 Initial series glyphs, from Copan stelae. From Morley, *Introduction to the Study of the Maya Hieroglyphs*, 1915. Bulletin / Smithsonian Institution, Bureau of American Ethnology no. 57 (1915), Plate 8. G.P.O, 1901. http://library.si.edu/digital-library/book/bulletin571915smit.

throughout the Maya world it seems, as we find them at numerous sites, just as with the standard glyphs.

Stephen Houston discusses views on the significance of the full-figure glyphs, advocating a view expressed by Elkins. Houston and Elkins argue that the full-figure glyphs are meant to express a *unity* between the deities, numbers, and time periods—all of the elements expressed in the Initial Series. The full-figure glyphs in the Long Count are generally intertwined with one another, some in embrace or even seemingly growing from one another. Houston adds:

Elkins points exactly to the full-figure glyphs as examples of flux, tension, and possibility. The full-figures invite a blurring of preconceived categories. They interact not just linguistically but as embodied, legged, armed forms. A few seem to go beyond the visual. Open mouths imply speech, song, cries, all in a howling, murmuring, squeaking, orating performance.[13]

This may lend support to the view that correlative cosmology underlies Maya metaphysical thought. Numerous scholars have discussed the seemingly correlative metaphysical nature of ancient Maya thought. While it is still somewhat vague in many sources just what is meant by correlativity here, it can be helpful to look at ancient Maya thought in comparison to other systems that have often been called "correlative" to see what parallels we can draw, and whether these are useful in helping to reconstruct the ancient Maya correlative metaphysics.

Figure 2.3 "Full-figure" Initial Series from Copan Stela D. From Morley, *Introduction to the Study of the Maya Hieroglyphs*, 1915. Bulletin / Smithsonian Institution, Bureau of American Ethnology no. 57 (1915), Plate 14. G.P.O, 1901. http://library.si.edu/digital-library/book/bulletin571915smit.

First, we should understand the sense in which scholars have thought of Maya metaphysics as involving correlative elements. Miguel Leon-Portilla associates *k'in* with the central grounding feature of ancient Maya metaphysics, as discussed in chapter 1. According to Leon-Portilla, Maya thought represents a *"chronovision* of the universe,"[14] in which each deity is associated with and personified by a time period, and the temporal aspect of these beings is their most essential feature, and the one on which they depend for their reality.[15] Leon-Portilla associates the fundamental unit of time with *k'in*, which he claims is the "primary reality, divine and limitless."[16] Leon-Portilla's basic view concerning the centrality of time has been adopted by a number of other scholars, including Timothy Knowlton, who understands time as the basis of what he calls "correlative monism" in Maya thought. Similar to a kind of temporal reductionism, Knowlton claims that time is the central (or constitutive) reality from which everything else derives its existence and can ultimately be understood in terms of.[17] Knowlton offers an explanation of this correlative monism:

> mathematics is employed to interpret all phenomena as interconnected at a single fundamental plane. This single fundamental plane is time. From movement in the heavens, meteorological events, treatment of illness, political fortunes, down to the quotidian activities of weaving, fishing, and carving, all had their effect within this single system. The correlation of celestial and terrestrial events according to divinatory calendars was the method by which persons in ancient Maya society acquired the knowledge necessary to better harmonize human activity with the temporal rhythm of the cosmos to effect greater success. It is reasonable to conclude this orientation from the commensuration of the great many calendars that compose the Initial Series, the calendrical apparatus that dominates the text of a large proportion of ancient Maya monuments. A related metaphysics of the relationship between cosmos and human action also underlies the operations of the tables and divinatory almanacs in the surviving pre-Hispanic Maya books. I refer to this aspect of ancient Maya metaphysics as correlative monism.[18]

While neither Leon-Portilla nor Knowlton offer their views as a kind of temporal reductionism, this is ultimately what their positions amount to, as I argue below. While its identity as reductionism does not disqualify the view, ancient Maya thought has elements that actively resist a reductionist interpretation, and the temporal reductionist position should be amended and rethought. In addition, one thing Knowlton brings up here but does not go on to elaborate on later in the text is the view of "the relationship between cosmos and human action" inherent in many Maya texts and iconography. Insofar as time is a central element of Maya metaphysical thought, it should be thought of as related to other aspects of the universe in *this* connective sense—a connection very similar to the concept of *ganying* 感應 ("reso-nance") in the early Chinese philosophical tradition. I offer an account below of the ancient Maya view of the human-cosmos connection as involving time as the essential link, thus resisting temporal reductionist accounts while still accepting that ancient Maya philosophy does have a substantial "correlative" element, with time as a central feature.

Reductionist views are based on theories in which a particular phenomenon can be wholly explained in terms of another more basic phenomenon without a loss of meaning. Whether a theory is reductionist or not has to do not with constitution or construction, but rather whether the entities in question are taken as fundamental constituents of a basic ontology. Thus, although most philosophers today will agree that all physical things are ultimately *consti-tuted by* atoms, few are atomic reductionists, in the sense that all things can be reduced to atoms and fully understood by understanding the interaction of those atoms. Part of the reason for resisting such atomic reductionism is that we may think different relations apply between constituted objects than between collections of atoms, and also that *reasons* apply differently to both. Macro-level objects cannot simply be understood as collections of atoms if they have properties that collections of atoms cannot. To reduce language about objects to that about atoms would require an ability to say everything that can be said about objects while referring only to atoms.

Although much of the discussion in contemporary philosophy concerning reductionism has to do with reduction of *theories*, this kind of theoretical reductionism is less useful for purposes of understanding the interpretations of the Maya view of time than reduction of *entities* or phenomena. The main idea behind the positions of scholars like Leon-Portilla and Knowlton is that all existent phenomena can ultimately be reduced to time. And such a claim would make much better sense of ancient Maya positions than a theoretical reductionism. They would not have been concerned with the question of whether one theory of the world's workings—say the political, reduced to another. Thus, the kind of reductionism I consider here is one of entities.

Why think that the "correlative monist" view Knowlton offers is a form of reductionism? If we *don't* understand it as a form of reductionism, then it is unclear what import the theory has, and just how it stands out from a fairly pedestrian view that *all* humans have held—that all activities happen in time and can be correlated with one another temporally. We still hold this latter view today. My birth, my writing of this paragraph, the lifespan of Clive of India's tortoise, Richard Nixon's resignation, an instance of calculation of 2+2, and the last appearance of Halley's Comet can all be related via our calendar—they all happen within and are related to time. Yet this does not say anything particularly unique or special about our concept of time and its relationship to a general metaphysical view. If this is all the Maya view amounts to, why should we consider time as playing a special role in their metaphysics different from the one it plays in *every* metaphysical system? I do not know of any metaphysical systems, with the possible exception of a theoretical metaphysics of transcendent realms such as Plato's realm of Forms or the medieval conception of God, that do not hold that all existent things are within time and can be related to one another temporally.

For the theory to be more than trivially true, time must play some foundational or grounding relationship in the Maya metaphysical system. This appears to me to be what Leon-Portilla, Knowlton, and others who stress the importance of time for the Maya are trying to say. The theory is not well worked-out, however. While the centrality of time is stressed, when the theory is explained, it appears to be a version of the trivial position I mention above.

If the "correlative monist" view amounts to a kind of temporal reductionism, then it means that the ancient Maya held that all existent things and all phenomena can be thought of as and ultimately expressed in terms of time. We can explain all activity and entities in temporal terms, having to do with the relationships between different aspects of time. This is an extreme view, but an interesting one, and there is certainly *some* reason to think that the ancient Maya may have held a view like this one. I suspect that scholars who hold positions concerning the centrality of time in Maya metaphysics have something like this view in mind, mainly because of the temporal associations of so many elements of Maya thought, beyond anything we see in other traditions. It is well attested, for example, that Maya deities are closely associated with periods of time, and that the calendar days represent aspects of these deities. This is not simply an association between a day and a *celebration* of a particular deity, as in the Catholic tradition, where various saints have their own "feast days" associated with them on which they are remembered and revered. Rather, the Maya view more closely relates the deity and time period, relating them to one another in terms of either identity or constitution.

The key to correlativity, at least as it is discussed in connection with systems like that of the ancient Maya elites and of the syncretistic schools of Han dynasty China, is the effect of each action in one part of the world on every other, determined by a link between all elements of the system by one active medium. Accounts of correlative thought in the ancient Maya world are generally based on the seeming ubiquity of time elements in all Maya text of which we know. *Time*, according to this view, plays the role of the metaphysical substrate that links all existing beings. Yet time is also linked to specific deities, and different periods of time seem to be characterized by or identified with these distinct deities. One way to try to make sense of this is to attribute to the ancient Maya a henotheistic view akin to contemporary versions of Hinduism influenced by the Advaita school. Are the deities themselves simply aspects of some more general deity (or other undefined) being that represents or is identical to time? According to Leon-Portilla, Knowlton, Rice, and others, *k'in* is such a unifying deity, and also the ground of being.

Numbers and time periods as interchangeable with or identified with human-figured deities may suggest a kind of "unity between nature and humanity." The Han dynasty philosophers in China coined a phrase meant to capture just this idea: 天人合一 (*tian ren he yi*). In early Han texts, we see an explicit construction of a robust correlative cosmology staggering in its scope and detail. A brief look at this conception of correlative cosmology in Han dynasty China can be useful for our purposes here, as similarities between the ancient and modern Maya materials and early Chinese correlative cosmological texts can perhaps help us fill in some holes in the Maya account.

The key concept in early Han correlative cosmology is 感應 (*ganying*, "resonance"), which is meant to explain the causal connection between various seemingly separate aspects of the cosmos. The unity of nature and humanity is explained in Han texts by the attribution of a relationship of *ganying* between the two (the two major components of the cosmos, according to early Han thinkers). This picture was in part meant to offer a more theoretically coherent and detailed explanation for the efficacy of divination in early China, a practice that extended back long before the Han period. The Chinese, like the Maya, had long used the sky, particularly astronomical phenomena, as a roadmap for both prognostication about future events as well as an aid in determining proper action.

GANYING AND CORRELATIVE COSMOLOGY

The ancient Maya (as represented in the available texts) and the correlative thinkers of the Han dynasty China shared a similar view concerning the connection between time, objects, and events. A look at a couple of the correlative systems of the Han can be useful in helping us piece together what the ancient Maya correlative system may have looked like. What we see in the Maya context is certainly much more similar to Han correlative thought than anything in the Western tradition I have come across.

The concept of the *way*, or "co-essence"[19] as well as the association between features of days, deities, persons, and events, shows us a correlative structure underlying Maya metaphysics. There does not appear to be, as there was in early Han thought, an underlying base structure for mapping the correlations based on "elements" or "phases" as we see in ancient Greek or Chinese correlative cosmology. Or at least we do not have any extant texts that give us any indication of such. The closest we have is the concept of time grounding the connection between entities, playing a somewhat similar mediative role to the "phases" (行 *xing*) in Chinese correlative thought. A correlative system does not strictly *require* such a system of minimal components serving as glue, as we see numerous correlative systems that either did not develop such, or developed them only relatively late. The early Chinese correlative metaphysical system was of the latter type. The "five phases" (五行 *wu xing*), although they have a fairly early origin, were not robustly used to ground the correlative metaphysical systems when they first began to appear in a robust way in the early Han. It was only in later texts that the *wu xing* were systematically used to explain the connections between elements of the metaphysics explained in early texts such as *Huainanzi* and *Lushi Chunqiu*.

This section (as many in the book) should be seen then as outlining a number of interpretive *possibilities*. We certainly cannot demonstrate that the Maya held anything close to the specifics of the particular correlative views of the early Han. But it is plausible that the ancient Maya held correlative views of time and other entities (as argued above), and looking to the early Chinese tradition shows us another philosophical system in which correlative thought took center stage, and developed in particular ways. The divergences of Maya thought from early Chinese correlative thought will no doubt be numerous, but through the use of the analogical method, we can find a number of ways in which correlative thought might be developed, to discern whether we can find implications of Han correlative thought matching with positions (explicit or implicit) we find in ancient Maya systems. In this section I argue that we can find exactly these. The correlative metaphysics of early Han texts lines up well with a number of positions we find in the ancient Maya context, and it is thus likely that the ancient Maya held something to some extent similar to Han correlative systems. There are certain positions at which the ancient Maya view comes apart from Han correlative metaphysics, and from these divergences I piece together a possible correlative view using the basic structure of Han correlative thought read through the lenses of Maya texts.

Han correlative thought is developed most fully (for our purposes) in texts such as the *Huainanzi* and *Chunqiu Fanlu* of the western Han period. We can find the roots of correlative thought in other texts in the period and also before, in the Warring States, but it is in the two texts mentioned that we find the expression of correlative metaphysics closest to what we find in the ancient Maya tradition. In the early Han we find the roots of the system that develops later into the full-fledged "five elements" correlative theory and the claims that "heaven and humanity form one unity" that we find in Neo-Confucians such as Zhang Zai many centuries later.

The role of time in unifying various features of the world or explaining their transformation does not strictly *require* a temporal reductionist metaphysics like the one Leon-Portilla and Knowlton describe as "correlative monism." A different kind of correlative system linking all elements of an ontology through a time *without* requiring time to serve as ground of reality is available, and makes sense of the independence of elements of the Maya ontology that we see suggested in the available texts. The notion of *transformation* is at the heart of Maya metaphysics, as it is in numerous other indigenous worldviews of the Americas, North and South. The system of correlative metaphysics with most similarity, I argue, to that of the ancient Maya, is not a correlative monism, but a different kind of system often called "correlative cosmology" but which I will here for purposes of clarity call "non-reductive correlative metaphysics," tied to the system of "embedded identity" that can also be found in Maya thought. This non-reductive correlative metaphysics is most clearly and thoroughly developed in early Han Chinese texts such as the *Huainanzi*.

The *Huainanzi* was written in the mid-second century BCE by a number of scholars in the employ of the Han vassal Liu An, vassal ruler of the state of Huainan. This was the same time as the end of the Preclassic Period in the Maya world, when the highland cities began their decline and the cities of the southern lowland such as Tikal were beginning their rise to dominance that define the Classic Period. During this period in China, the Han dynasty, the first major Imperial dynasty of China (setting aside the short-lived Qin) was still finding its footing, attempting to formulate the ideologies and machinery of government to rule an expansive and ever-growing territory, including not only vast amounts of space but also different regions, cultures, and peoples. Elite thought concerning rulership, virtue, self-cultivation, and even metaphysical issues was undergoing a radical change from what it had been in the period before the unification of the "Warring States" of the region in 221 BCE under by the state of Qin. It was in the period before the Qin unification that most of the Chinese texts most famous in the West were constructed (though some argue most of them were *compiled* in the Han), texts such as the *Analects* of Confucius, the *Mengzi* and *Xunzi*, the *Daodejing* and *Zhuangzi*. Most of these early texts, with the exception of perhaps some sections of the *Zhuangzi* (itself related to the *Huainanzi*), were concerned with ethics and political thought, in particular the cultivation of virtue, attempts to fashion a harmonious society, or attainment of thriving. In texts such as the *Mozi* we see some consideration of language, logic, and metaphysics, but even here there is relatively little, and it is primarily in service of Mohist ethical and political theory.

Part of the reason for the primarily ethical and political concern of Pre-Qin texts may have to do with the social situation during the period. The "Warring States" period, as it is referred to today, was one in which numerous systems of social organization competed for supremacy, through both philosophical dispute and outright warfare. Often, certain philosophical systems are explicitly connected with political entities such as states. The Qin infamously adopted Legalism, formulated and advocated by major advisors of the Qin government, such as Han Fei and Li Si.[20] The philosophy of the *Mozi* was the purview of a paramilitary organization headed by the philosopher-mercenary-political organizer Mo Di. The "Confucian" texts were linked to scholars from the *Ru* (Classicist) school, who were experts on Zhou ritual, generally employed by rulers in the Warring States to teach the intricacies of Zhou ritual (seen as necessary for rulership) to heirs. All of these schools were concerned with broadly political questions that tied into the issues of ethics and moral self-cultivation. It is not until very late in the Warring States period, with texts like the *Lushi Chunqiu*, and in the Han period, that we begin to see robust consideration of metaphysics. Part of the reason for this is almost certainly the radically changed social situation. Scholars in the Han period, in a unified empire in which there were no longer small states fighting one another for supremacy, could not link themselves to a particular cause in the way Warring States figures did. Scholarship was still largely the domain of the elites, as it remains today, and reflected elite interests. But these interests during the Han period were focused on the questions of how to *unify* a disparate and vastly distributed population of different peoples and cultures under a single political entity. There were certainly social and political issues at play here, but one new issue we see move to the forefront is that of metaphysics, as well as that of methodology. In the desire for unity of the empire, elites endorsed or employed scholars concerned with understanding how unity is attained and maintained. A natural direction for such a concern becomes metaphysics. If we can explain the origin and cause of a unity between all things, then we can attempt to organize society along the lines of this unity inherent in nature. This is the source of the non-reductive correlative metaphysics of the *Huainanzi*.

The key here is that a metaphysics of *transformation* in some traditions is taken as grounded in an ineffable source of change that itself is unknowable, and certainly not definable as substance, process, deity, or time. This fundamental ground of being that scholars like Knowlton take to be associated with time for the Maya *cannot* be time, if the ancient Maya understood time itself to transform into beings in the way suggested in the Classic Period and later texts. A better way of making sense of the Maya concern with time is understanding it as playing a key role in a correlative system similar to that of the *Huainanzi*.

TIME AND TRANSFORMATION

Are the various time deities *identical* to time periods, or do they have features beyond this? The temporal *aspect* of these deities, I argue, is one among others—they are not fully identical to the time periods they represent, just as the representative is not fully identical to the representative thing in ceremonies, though the person takes on those aspects of the identity of the represented thing. How can we make sense of this? A separate entity *becomes* identical to another for some period of time, having features additional to those of the object it has become, yet we can say that the two things are identical for this point of overlap. In the same way, the time deities *are* the period of time when it exists, but they also have additional features not contained in that time. To explain this, I coined the phrase "embedded identity." There are a number of different ways to make sense of embedded identity. Some are inclined to look to process metaphysics to make sense of these issues.[21] Do we need a process metaphysics to make sense of this? Is it plausible that the ancient Maya had something like a process view? Or was there something else going on?

A number of scholars have pointed out the seeming contrast between the Maya way of thinking about ontology and that of much of (but not all of) Western thought, epitomized by the concept of *substance*. Stephen Houston voices the discomfort many Mayanists seem to feel with attributing a concept of substance to the ancient Maya:

"Substance," "matter," and "thing" sit uneasily in Mayan languages. English emphasizes the concreteness and weighty reality of these words. In general, present and past Maya thought appears to look toward innate potential, an implied future of workable matter, one thing made into another thing.[22]

Such a conception of a thing, if it is indeed one that was a dominant view among the ancient Maya, is actually not at all incompatible with the notion of substance. In fact, substance in its philosophical sense (rather than the colloquial English sense Houston may have in mind here, and on which I can say little because the concept is vague) is almost exactly in line with what Houston says about the Maya idea. Aristotle's concept of substance, which is the basis of most later Western understandings of the concept (a concept that has in philosophical circles largely been consigned to the history shelves) was closely linked with his concepts of potentiality and actuality, which he used to explain how substances could change. Every substance (aside from the perfect substance, the Unmoved Mover, or God on Aquinas' adaptation of Aristotelian thought) contains potentiality in a number of ways—in particular, it contains the potentiality to become whatever it *can* become but currently is not, including to *do* what it can (in multiple senses) do but currently is not. It is in Aristotle's *De Anima* (On the Soul) that he offers the most robust account of this, as is necessary for understanding any changing and changeable substance.

While this is the case, however, I think the Mayanists are right to suggest that the classical Aristotelian way of thinking about substance, which has shaped general contemporary ways of envisioning them, does not map exactly on to the Maya understanding of "things." One way the substance view has sometimes been challenged is through the language and concepts of *process* metaphysics, which privileges events, rather than objects, as the primary constituents of reality. Process metaphysics reverses the Aristotelian position that holds substances as fundamental and events as comprised of the movement and interaction of substances. Instead, processes are fundamental and basic, and substances can be seen as abstractions of event stages. A.N. Whitehead, Charles Hartshorne, and others developed theories of process metaphysics in the modern period, which were later further developed by philosophers such as Nicholas Rescher.[23] But process metaphysics also may not be the best way to capture Maya ontology, even though it may be closer than the Aristotelian substance approach. Maya metaphysics of things is, I argue, unique, and cuts a path through substance and process metaphysics that makes it distinct from both. *Time* plays a more central role in Maya metaphysics than in either. And objects or things, the fundamental "furniture" of the universe, are envisioned as possibly noncontinuous. That is, it is certain temporal, physical, and other *properties* that instantiate objects.

The Maya view is a transformative metaphysics in which there are both substances and processes, but neither of them has ontological priority over the other. The view closest to this one that I can find in philosophical history is that of the *Huainanzi* in the early Han dynasty China and its associated texts. Although the *Huainanzi* does not advocate an embedded identity metaphysics as we see in the case of ancient Maya thought, the "Huainanist" view does similarly resist categorization either as a substance or process metaphysics, with the fundamental ground of being as *dao*, an uncharacterized (and perhaps not fully knowable) substrate, that is neither process nor substance, but conceptually prior to both. There are also similarities between the Maya view and certain conventionalist views of metaphysics in contemporary philosophy, in which an undifferentiated "world-stuff" is conceptualized by minds as containing distinct objects (or processes)—that is, objects are distinguished or "carved" from the world by convention.[24]

The problem we are presented with in the Maya texts and tradition is that the various time deities, according to a number of scholars, are identified with certain periods in the time cycle. But it is unclear whether the deities are *composed* by these periods, or whether these periods are simply *features* of the deities, who exist separately on the basis of something else. That is, are the deities themselves time, or is time something that belongs to them? The descriptions of the deities such as the Lords of the Night in the monumental texts are always associated with time. The glyphs representing these deities never occur outside of the context of the date series beginning with the Long Count that usually begin these monumental texts. There are *other* deities that are discussed outside of this context, but never the Lords of the Night. This is one reason that the Lords of the Night glyphs have not been fully reconstructed, concerning their pronunciation and other aspects of the glyphs.[25]

EMBEDDED IDENTITY THROUGH THE POPOL VUH

The *Popol Vuh* and the books of the *Chilam Balam* all contain numerous pre-Columbian stories and images, as attested in images found in monuments from the Classic Period and before.[26] Some of these stories and figures from them can also be found in the four extant Maya codices, all from the Postclassic period. The Postconquest texts, *Popol Vuh* and the various *Chilam Balam* books, may seem a strange place to look for information about concepts and philosophy of the ancient (pre-Columbian) Maya, given the clear influence of Spanish ideas through Christianity in these texts. But these texts are important for a number of reasons. First—they do contain much of pre-Columbian thought. Second—while these texts are syncretistic in nature, *all* of recorded Maya thought is syncretistic in similar ways. The Preclassic codices contain Aztec and other Mesoamerican ideas, and even the earliest known images and monumental texts in the Maya area contain influences from elsewhere in the region, especially Teotihuacan.[27] The creation of synthesis with new modes of thought is itself a Maya characteristic (as it is throughout the world, whether admitted or not).

According to the text, the *Popol Vuh* itself is a tool for broadening the human vision of the world—for making seen the unseen elements of the cosmos that were blocked from human understanding.[28] The use of the imagery of *vision* and *sight* here is important—what the *Popol Vuh* allows is a comprehensive access to what numerous scholars refer to as *cosmovisión*—a single, complete, and authoritative access to the whole of the cosmos through special or unusual vision, that exhaustively expresses the entirety of the worldview, or *cosmovisión*, of a tradition.[29] We find such an idea in other global traditions as well. One that comes to mind is the comprehensive cosmic vision outlined in the classical Indian text *Bhagavad Gita*. In Chapter 11 of the *Gita*, Krishna, representative of the universal spirit and ultimately the cosmos itself, reveals his true form to Arjuna, and we are offered a description of this all-encompassing vision. The words used to express the vision are seeking and not fully adequate to the task (as no words could be), but poetically attempt to express the inexpressible, and offer us a sense of the grandeur and completeness of the vision. In the *Gita*, it is Krishna himself who serves as the tool through which we can come to have a comprehensive *cosmovisión*.

Tedlock claims that the *Popol Vuh* as a seeing instrument, or *ilb'al* in the *K'iche'* Maya language, helped people to see "distant or future events," thus having a kind of divinatory quality. I think that a more important sense of the vision allowed by the *Popol Vuh*, however, is that it allows a window onto the processes of continual creation and transformations that humans are generally unable to see (those of us without the special vision of the shaman). It shows us not other worlds or other possibilities, but the elements of our own world to which we have been blinded, and the unfolding of the patterns of creation that continually take place. One of the contentions of this book is that for the ancient Maya, creation is not a single act undertaken by a deity in some distant past. Rather, they offer a view of *continual creation* or re-creation, in which humans play a pivotal role. All of this can be found in the opening parts of the *Popol Vuh*.

The nature of the *Popol Vuh* itself is not obvious from what we find in the text. Although it is a tool for seeing the hidden aspects of the world that show us comprehensively the continual creation of the cosmos, the authors claim that the *Popol Vuh* can no longer be seen. They write:

> There is no longer a place to see it, a Council Book, a place to see "The Light That Came from Beside the Sea" ... a place to see "The Dawn of Life"[30]

According to Tedlock, the text is referring to the original glyphic version of the *Popol Vuh*, which has either been lost or hidden away to avoid confiscation by Spanish authorities. The text is also discussed as a *performance* in Part One, however, suggesting that the true nature of the text is in its ritual performance. I contend here that the *Popol Vuh* as tool for vision is the *performance* of the Popol Vuh, which involves substitution/impersonation (*k'ex*), in which the performers literally *become* the characters from the *Popol Vuh*, representative of aspects of the cosmos. The reason the *Popol Vuh* is able to pull back the curtain and show us the continual creation of the world is that it, in its performance, *represents* this process. It is akin to opening up the hood of a running car to observe the engine in operation. The story of the *Popol Vuh* would have been best known to the general public through performance,[31] as the majority of the people in the Maya area were illiterate during the Classic Period.[32] The story of the *Popol Vuh* would not have been something limited to the elite classes, however, even if only elite scribes and other literate people could access the written text. The primary form of the stories may have been in performance, with the textual versions only given later, or having lesser importance. There are numerous sites from the Classic Period throughout the Maya area that suggest the importance of performance of various stories found in the *Popol Vuh*—a number of images on monuments at Izapa suggest that stories from the *Popol Vuh* were performed in processions through various areas of the site.[33]

We must be careful when looking to a Postconquest text to distinguish between what is of ancient origin and what is borrowed from Christian ideas brought by the Spanish. As a significant philosophical and religious text in itself, of course, this is of no import. Every text and cultural phenomenon borrows aspects from outside groups and cultures. But since our concern here is with ancient Maya thought specifically, the question becomes an important one. Which ideas in the *Popol Vuh* did earlier Maya people in the Preclassic and Classic Periods hold, and which did they not? As Allen Christenson points out, there is little *direct* influence of Christianity in the *Popol Vuh*, though there is certainly influence.[34] Parts Two and Three of the text, which focus on the two pairs of Hero Twins, have the greatest antiquity in Maya thought. Indeed, we find much iconography throughout the Maya area corresponding to aspects of the stories contained in Parts Two and Three, consistent with their telling in the *Popol Vuh*.

Part One discusses the "original" creation in a way that sounds clearly influenced by Christian thought. Indeed, one of the reasons for this I suggest is that it is distant from the earlier Maya view of continual creation, which we see suggested deeper into the text. A passage from Part One reads:

> Then came his word. Heart of Sky arrived here with Sovereign and Quetzal Serpent in the darkness, in the night. He spoke with Sovereign and Quetzal Serpent. They talked together then. They thought and pondered. They reached an accord ... Beneath the light, they gave birth to humanity.[35]

There are numerous passages in the first part of the *Popol Vuh* reminiscent of Christian texts and creation myth. Despite this, some of the material we might be inclined to see as borrowed from Christianity does indeed have a deeper history in Maya thought. The story of the dissatisfaction of the gods with the created world ending in its being destroyed in a flood to make way for a new people—imagery (and text?) recounting this story can be found on Classic Period Maya monuments and other texts.[36] What is less clear is that the stories told at the very beginning of Part One represent something of an older Maya tradition. Christianity is mentioned explicitly early in the text, as the *K'iche'* author(s) write that the introduction of Christianity is the reason that the *Popol Vuh* "can no longer be seen."

Allen Christenson argues that the limited use of Christian terms in the text (the terms *Christianoil* and *Dios* appear only in this passage and again in Part Five in the *Popol Vuh*'s account of history near the end when the Spanish arrive) shows that the *Popol Vuh* should be taken as an authentic and unadulterated by Spanish ideas—an accurate account of pre-Columbian Maya thought.[37] It does not follow, however, from the fact that Spanish-derived words are not used throughout the majority of the *Popol Vuh*, that there was no influence of Spanish ideas on the text. Indeed, the account of creation beginning with the "word" of the god Heart of Sky, creation of the light, and other aspects of the first creation story all suggest possible Christian influence here. This is especially so given that we have multiple distinct creation accounts later in the *Popol Vuh*, and numerous accounts of the origins of a number of important institutions, such as that of rulership.

For my purposes, Part Three of the *Popol Vuh* offers us the most interesting and useful material. The account of the Hero Twins and the story of their struggles in Xibalba contains a wealth of ideas and expresses a number of concepts I have focused on in this book. We might take the story of Part Three of the *Popol Vuh* to offer a kind of summary of Maya philosophical views. The story certainly traces back well into pre-Columbian Maya history, as the Twins and their exploits are memorialized throughout the Maya area. From the beginning of the story, we see symbols of important ideas in Maya metaphysics, ethics, and political thought.

First, the idea of the *dual principle* represented by twins, and the multiple sets of twins in the *Popol Vuh* is clearly central to the text. In Part One, there are in *two* creators in the beginning (rather than one), Heart of Sky and Plumed Serpent,[38] who fashion the world from a preexisting sky-and-sea (another dual-aspect, the "pre-created" cosmos). There are numerous twin characters in the text, perhaps most importantly the Hero Twins, Hunahpu and Xbalanque, and their father/fathers One Hunahpu and Seven Hunahpu (as well as their Xibalban counterparts One and Seven Death). Representing dual principles in the world through the characters of twins or pairs (such as the half-brothers of the Hero Twins, One Monkey and One Artisan) seems to be a common feature of Mesoamerican literature and mythology, and is accounted in Aztec thought as well.[39] Given this association of twins with gods and heroic characters with them, the general Mesoamerican attitude toward twins may come as a surprise. Twins were seen as monstrous or abominations, and often at birth one of a pair would be killed.[40] The Aztec pair of Xolotl and Quetzalcoatl are thought by some to mirror such a pair of twins, with Queztalcoatl as the survivor and Xolotl as the killed twin, inhabiting the underworld.[41] This pair, as with those found in the *Popol Vuh*, represents the fundamental duality of nature, and the reciprocal codependence of each of these various dualities. Life and death, day and night, above and below, male and female—dualistic pairs are seen as together forming an essential unity, while being not completely distinct. On a fundamental level, there is never a *One* in Maya thought, because even the most basic oneness has a fundamentally dual nature. Thus even in the beginning before the creation of the world, there is both a dual-natured cosmos (sky-and-water), and dual gods (together understood as one divine principle).

This dual principle can also be understood in terms of the two "worlds" that are the primary settings of the drama of Part Three of the *Popol Vuh*, the human world (for lack of a better term), and *Xibalba*. We can see in the

Popol Vuh that while Xibalba and its inhabitants are antagonists, they can also be on the side of humanity. The relationship between the Hero Twins (and by extension all of us) and Xibalba is a complicated one. Xibalba is not something we can simply reject and dismiss. For a portion of our lives, we have the responsibility to struggle against the Xibalbans (death). But, like the Hero Twins toward the end of their story, we ultimately must sacrifice ourselves in Xibalba, in order to ensure the continual creation of things, and the continued existence of the entities that we stand in substitutional relationships with (more on this below).

The idea of unity in duality as fundamental is common to Mesoamerican thought,[42] and can be found throughout the *Popol Vuh*. The significance of the foundational characters in Part Three being twins is important, especially given particular aspects of the story. As numerous scholars have pointed out, the names of people and characters hold significance beyond what we find in names in other parts of the world. Many of the characters in the Popol Vuh, as well as rulers and other figures whose names we have access to, have names that include *numbers*. Numerology played an important role in ancient Maya culture.[43] Numbers were associated with particular gods, periods of time, and characteristics. This can be seen (as mentioned above) through the glyphic representation of numbers in full form (as deities), in head form, or dot and bar form. Many of the glyphs and their variations reveal this element of transformability and the interconnectivity of all things in Maya thought. No being in the world can be understood as autonomous and distinct—rather it includes both in a manifest way and in potential a host of other things within it. Beings are part of a transformational process that is in the midst of change. We can at best attempt to take a snapshot of this change, but what we grasp in this snapshot cannot be said to comprise the whole being itself, or give us the qualities of such a being.

We find duality throughout Mesoamerican culture as a central aspect of creative power and foundational things. In Maya texts, we find pairs in almost every significant role. This is apparent in the *Popol Vuh*, in which we have the pair of gods Heart of Sky and Plumed Serpent at the beginning, engaged in the project of crafting humanity—the Hero Twins, One Monkey and One Artisan, and others. The creative nature of pairs is a central theme of Maya thought. The complimentary dual (also thought of as unified) is the principle of creation. This understanding must have come from observations of the world. The individual human is created by the combination of male and female, rather than by one alone. The existence (which entails continual creation, as I argue below) of everything in the world is in terms of the creative pair.[44] This principle of duality carried even into daily life, including the institution of provincial government among the Itza of Yucatan during the Postclassic and Postconquest Periods, in which the Ahau Batab was assisted by a junior partner, the Batab.[45] There may have been similar governmental structures in earlier periods. Numerous Maya rituals involved pairs and the principle of duality as well. In a ritual with connection to the Classic Period, chickens are sacrificed in pairs, in a ceremony intended to facilitate communication and other connection to the gods and to the dead—a common concern of much of Maya ritual and thought.[46]

Numbers also have significance in Maya thought. In the extant texts, they are often seen as elements of names (as they are in Aztec texts).[47] They are also elements of the ritual *tzolk'in* calendar (structurally identical to the *tonalpohualli* calendar of the Aztecs), and represent aspects of the world, of the gods, and of transformation.

The names of the Hero Twins from the *Popol Vuh* themselves have numerological significance. The name "Hunahpu" (Hun Ahau in Yucatec, which is generally used to render Classic Maya) signifies one of the days in the *tzolk'in* calendar. *Hun* is the number one, so the day being referred to is One Ahau. "Ahau," of course, is the word for *ruler*, in addition to being a day sign. Thus, "One Hunahpu" roughly translates to English as "One One-Ruler." The suggestion here is that the number one has to do with *origination*. We will see that Hunahpu, one of the Hero Twin sons of One and Seven Hunahpu, can be understood as the original ruler, and the model for rulership. Thus his name, "One Ruler." *One* Hunahpu, then, might simply be taken as the originator of the originator of rulership. The two *together,* One and Seven Hunahpu, may have a different significance—the combination of One and Seven can indicate the entire thirteen days associated with a particular day name in the *tzolk'in* calendar, because the first occurrence will fall on a 1 day, and the final (thirteenth) occurrence will fall on a 7 day.[48] There may be astronomical significance to the numbering as well. But certainly there are other meanings to the names—just as we see in the origin case with One Hunahpu. One and Seven Death likely have similar significance. Rulership and death. But what of Seven Hunahpu? This character, like Xbalanque in the later story, is a trickier case. It is One Hunahpu who has his head cut off by the Xibalbans, whose head is placed in a tree in which it multiplies and mirrors the calabash fruit. But there is an essential connection between One and Seven Hunahpu such that the head of One Hunahpu is *also* the head of Seven Hunahpu (despite the text explicitly claiming that only One Hunahpu's head was cut off, and Seven Hunahpu was merely buried).[49] This is intentional—as with the squash incident with Hunahpu in Xibalba later in Part Three, the authors intend to show us that *substitution* can take place while retaining original identity—what I refer to above as "embedded identity"—which is one of the most unique features of ancient Maya metaphysics. After referring to the head in the calabash tree as that of One Hunahpu, the text reads:

"Now go up there on the face of the earth; you will not die. Keep the word. So be it," said the head of One and Seven Hunahpu—they were of one mind when they did it.[50]

Embedded identity is part of what makes both substitution and transformation possible. We see both of these as important symbols throughout Part Three of the *Popol Vuh*. In the case of One and Seven Hunahpu, intentional states made them the same individual. To think the same is in an important sense to *be* the same. James Maffie discusses what he calls "inamic dualism" in Aztec thought, and explains how the concept of *olin* is meant to unify the dual principle, just as we see such unity in duality in Maya thought. Maffie writes:

Olin motion-change bounces, curves, swirls, oscillates, and pulsates inamic partners into a single, unified process.[51]

This unified process from duality is very much found in Maya thought as well, and can be seen in the duality of the creative gods, One and Seven Hunahpu, and other pairs, but interestingly absent seems to be a conception of a transformational principle such as *olin* that unifies dual principles. Transformation is certainly dynamic as well as largely unpredictable, but there does not appear to be a particular named concept expressing this for the Maya, unlike what the Aztecs called *olin*.

In the case of Hunahpu and Xbalanque we also see association in a similar way. They represent another dual principle that in the end is visualized as the sun and moon. They also represent the dual principle of the living and the dead—the visible world and Xibalba. It is not an insignificant feature of the story that the mother of the Hero Twins is the daughter of one of the lords of Xibalba. The Hero Twins, then, while they have in them the principle of life and rulership, also contain the principle of death, of Xibalba. In this way they are representative of humanity and the human experience. Death is not, according to the Maya, a failure of the human animal, something that happens to us when our bodies give out and are no longer able to hold up against destruction. Rather, death is *part* of our nature, implicit within our bodies, and a natural process of the generation and transformation of the human. Ultimately, Xibalba is not the enemy, it is a necessary part of human life and the continual creation of the cosmos. While we resist Xibalba throughout our lives (just as the Hero Twins, who emerge victorious from the hosts of tests associated with means of death), in the end we must submit to or be sacrificed to Xibalba. The Xibalbans appear as enemies of the heroes of the *Popol Vuh* in some places, such as in the stories of the Hero Twins (for the most part), but they also appear as advocates and friends.[52]

One way this can be understood is in terms of substitution and transformation.

EMBEDDED IDENTITY, SUBSTITUTION,
AND TRANSFORMATION

ͺ Transformation is a feature shared with the Daoist tradition in early Chinese thought, while the Maya conception of substitution is unique to the Maya tradition (and perhaps other Mesoamerican traditions). Understanding the connection between transformation and substitution, however, will give us a better grasp of the Maya conception of embedded identity, and how this conception added to an approach to transformation very much like that of the Daoists leaves us with a concept of substitution at the heart of Maya metaphysics.

Hunahpu and Xbalanque, as we see toward the end of Part Three, have the ability to sacrifice themselves and one another, and return to life. The twins first jump into an oven (or pit of fire) prepared by the Xibalbans. They reappear in a very different, fish-like form, and then as humans again, in different forms, unrecognized by the Xibalbans.[53] The theme of transformation through sacrifice continues on throughout this text and Maya thought in general. The gods themselves are sacrificed (a theme we also see in Aztec philosophy), and human sacrifice is instituted first as an exchange—in Part Four of the *Popol Vuh*, it is the secret of fire for which humans exchange sacrifice, in an agreement with Tohil.[54] This attainment of fire is important both for cooking and agriculture. The maize god is sacrificed and reborn underground, in a key symbol of the life cycle for the Maya.[55] Corn is harvested for the sustenance of humans and the plant is cut down, to be buried again and reborn from the ground anew.[56] This key cycle of death and rebirth may lie at the very center of Maya thought concerning transformation and substitution.[57]

The new maize plant, when it arises from the old, cannot be considered a *distinct* entity. Rather, the new plant represents a part of the same entity as the old. If we consider the way in which the plant (like the human) develops, this appears plausible. A seed from the prior plant becomes the ground from which the new plant develops. This seed is surely *part of* the prior plant, and is also part of (in the sense of being the basis of) the new plant. Thus the prior plant and the new plant are not completely independent, but are representative of the same thing—the *maize plant* itself. They may be understood as different stages of the maize plant. This is how we should understand sacrifice and rebirth, for the human as well as for the maize plant.

Indeed, some Maya rituals suggest recognition of a key connection between the maize plant and the human. There is the well-known story of the *Popol Vuh* of humans being crafted by the gods from maize.[58] There is also the practice in the highlands of Guatemala described by the seventeenth-century Dominican priest Francisco Ximénez of Maya burial of their dead in maize fields.[59] In addition, there is the story of the Hero Twins themselves, representative of both maize and the origins of rulership (Hunahpu= 1 Ahau,= 1 Ruler).[60]

In the *Popol Vuh*, One Hunahpu (through his head in the calabash tree, that is identical with that of Seven Hunahpu) fathers the Hero Twins Hunahpu and Xbalanque. The head of Hunahpu says to the maiden of Xibalba who has just been impregnated through the head's saliva:

> This, my head, had nothing on it—just bone, nothing of meat. It's just the same with the head of a great lord: it's just the flesh that makes his face look good. And when he dies, people get frightened by his bones. After that, his son is like his saliva, his spittle, in his being, whether it be the son of a lord or the son of a craftsman, an orator. The father does not disappear, but goes on being fulfilled. Neither dimmed nor destroyed is the face of a lord, a warrior, craftsman, orator.[61]

Here, we see a view of rebirth and substitution that makes the primary entity—the lord, warrior, maize, etc. in a way immortal through its continual creation and rebirth. The language of *rebirth* in connection to Maya texts might remind us of the concept of rebirth in the Indian tradition, but something very different is going on in the case of the ancient Maya. A standard view of the Brahmanist schools in Indian thought is that the soul or self (*atman*) is reborn into new persons upon the death of an individual.[62] What continues on is the *atman*, rather than the larger structure of the person that the atman is connected to.[63] This is a similar conception to that of Plato in the Greek tradition, and which certain schools of Christian thought adopted, of the separability of the soul from the body (and mind, to different degrees).

The notion of rebirth in the Maya tradition is not of a single separable soul that reemerges in a new body or person, but rather the continual perishing and reemergence of the same entity or person in a new guise. In a sense, we see here the *inverse* of the Indian view mentioned above. What survives (or rather, is continually reborn) is the entity comprised of the individual. The *ruler* is continually reborn, the father, the scribe, the entity seemingly attached to a particular role—not the individual who at any given time constitutes this entity.

We can understand this idea better perhaps through importing the idea of *constitution* from Western philosophical thought. Constitution, in the Maya view, is indeed identity, but the constitution of objects can change while retaining their identity. The Ship of Theseus[64] is identical to the material constituting it at the beginning of its journey, but as pieces are replaced, it simply becomes identical to new material, such that the Ship at the end of its journey, with completely new parts, is still the Ship of Theseus. Allowing for *transformation* is what enables the Maya view to avoid this problem. And this transformational view can be understood in the context of embedded identity. The entity in question, in this case the Ship of Theseus, is neither identical with the material parts making it up *nor* the function and historical activity. Rather, the Ship of Theseus would be understood on the Maya view as an entity that is composed of transformable or substitutable parts that are each *identical* with the Ship of Theseus. Thus, at the beginning of the journey, the wood of the ship is identical with the Ship of Theseus, and later when the replaced parts comprise the ship, these are identical with the Ship of Theseus. This seems to privilege the "function/historical activity" conception of identity, but in the Maya case something different is going on. The Ship is identical to what comprises it in terms of material at any given time, but what comprises it as material is a matter of *creative* connection. The identity and endurance of things then must be understood in terms of the Maya conception of continual creation. The Ship of Theseus example is here not the best one to explain what is going on, because replacement parts of a ship can be understood only in a very vague way as creatively connected.

The primary example we see throughout Maya texts is that of the *ruler* (*ahau*), and this example works very well to explain the features of substitution and embedded identity. A particular *ahau* is identical to the person who composes it—who through *substitution* inhabits the identity. According to the Maya view, substitution, often attained through enacting a role or engaging in a performance in which features of a particular entity are represented, makes an individual attain the essence of that identity, and the individual *becomes* the entity in question. Thus, an entity such as a ruler, scribe, or other things we might associate with roles, is largely an *extra-human* role.

There are a number of physical and other associations with the concept of rebirth in Classic Maya thought. The color red (presumably due to its connection with blood), the east (because of its association with the rising sun), and cinnabar and hematite (which bodies would be covered with at death) were all connected to the concept of rebirth.[65] A perhaps more mundane conception of rebirth or transference of essence can be seen in Traci Ardren's interpretation of northern lowlands burial practices (shared in many parts of the Maya region). Bones of children in particular, she argues, were kept, cared for, buried, and reburied in particular households as a way of personalizing or "ensouling" the house. This suggests a kind of transfer of identity or essence from the original person represented by the bones to the house.[66] The child is in some sense *reborn* as the home, similar to the way that a ruler is reborn as the next in the lineage, or in the stelae, monuments, glyphs, and other artifacts manifesting his essence.

Figure 2.4   **Interior of plats showing the rebirth of the maize god from a crack in a turtle's back.** Drawing by Linda Schele © David Schele. Photo courtesy Ancient Americas at LACMA.

TRANSFORMATION IN EARLY CHINA

Above I discussed the Maya view of the unity of dual principles as found in the *Popol Vuh* and suggested that the concept of transformation had to do with embedded identity, which also explains substitution. In the early Chinese tradition, we can find an explicitly spelled-out conception of transformation and unification of multiplicity that, while it is not exactly like the Maya case, can help us to explain how the *transformational* aspect of the Maya view may have worked. Looking to early Han metaphysics concerning the origination of things in *dao* and the principle of transformation of things can help to understand what is going on in Maya thought, as can (we have seen) a number of other features of early Chinese thought. I propose here that there is (in many texts, at least), a conception of a correlative cosmology ultimately reducible to *qi* 氣 (vital essence) in explanation of effective action in the world—generation, destruction, and change. There is resistance in those same texts, however, sometimes in the same passages, that seems to suggest such a reductionism, to the idea of *qi* as fundamental. We can understand, I propose, what seems like a *qi*-based reductionism as actually a *qi*-bound correlative cosmology. This is structurally similar to the picture I offer of Maya correlative cosmology, where it is not time (*pace* Knowlton[67]) that plays the binding role, but something much more akin to the *dao* of the *Zhuangzi* and *Huainanzi*. Time in Maya philosophy plays a similar role to *qi* in the Han correlative texts I discuss here.

The earliest text discussing the issue of transformation in anything like the way we see it in Maya texts is the *Zhuangzi*. According to Zhuangzi, the myriad things (*wan wu* 萬物) are constantly in flux, seemingly in an unpredictable way. This is based on the spontaneity of the action of *dao* in concert with the natural propensities (*tian li* 天理) of things. In the *Huainanzi*, transformation and change was a major concern, as it directly connected to the overarching focus of the text, on creating unity between seemingly disparate schools, positions, peoples, customs, and other elements of the world.[68] In the early chapters of the text, the *Huainanzi* offers a cosmogony explaining how multiplicity was achieved from a primordial single *dao*, or ground of being.[69] The authors associate this primordial *dao* with perfection, complete understanding, and the original unity of all things. They read the creation or beginning of multiplicity as a decline from this original unity. This is meant as both a cosmogony and an explanation of how there come to be disparate views, teachings, peoples, etc. In the third chapter of the *Huainanzi*, they write that from heaven and earth (and presumably *dao*) *yin* and *yang* developed, which are the principles of change, creation, and destruction, and from these the *wan wu* (myriad things) ultimately developed.[70]

In order to explain diversity, the *Huainanzi* first gestures to *yin* and *yang*. The problem is that when there is but a single entity or principle, it becomes impossible to explain how anything additional could come to be or how this entity or principle could change, with nothing additional to change it. Thus, at least a dual principle is necessary to explain change. Indeed, this could be part of the reason for the importance of the dual principle in Maya (and other Mesoamerican) thought. We notice that the creator deities, as well as other important deities who serve as agents of change, are presented in double, as dual creative, destructive, or transformative powers.[71] The Parmenidean problem of change persists in the Chinese and Maya contexts as well: How can something that does not exist come to be, and how can something that exists ever come to not exist? The issue of change is intimately connected to that of generation and destruction—how can things change without this? Indeed, this is what led Parmenides to deny the true existence of change. In the *Huainanzi*, we see *yin* and *yang* offered as the dual principle explaining change through their alternation or movement. Neither *yin* nor *yang* go into or out of existence, but they process such that one principle is dominant over the other at one time, and vice versa—they are two processes constantly in flux, along with and against one another. But this raises a new question. How do *yin* and *yang* themselves change, and what is the nature of *yin* and *yang*? Are they general entities that constitute everything else—a kind of psycho-physical substrate out of which everything else is constructed?

The *Huainanzi*, along with later texts, seems to answer this question by referring to the concept of *qi* (vital essence), which is seen as playing a central causal role in transformation of one thing to another, in connection with both the principles of *yin-yang* as well as the *wu xing* (five phases).[72] In the *Huainanzi*, *qi* plays a number of different roles, but the most important for our purposes is the understanding of *qi* as what John Major calls "conveyor of resonant influence." There has been much discussion of the idea of "sympathetic resonance" (感應 *ganying*) in the *Huainanzi*,[73] and while the term itself is not used in the text, the idea behind it seems to be developed there. The general idea is that each thing in the world, including humans and other aspects of nature, has an influence on other aspects of the world, such that when they act a certain way, it affects these other things.[74] This effect, some argue, should not be understood as *causation*, but rather something like *correlation* or *resonance*. Just what the difference between these amounts to is not altogether clear. James Behuniak offers an explanation of the difference:

> The type of causal common sense that sequences such occurrences into prior cause (meteor falling) and subsequent effect (sea swelling) is not that of the *Huainanzi*. Things and events do not *cause* one another; they *correlate* with one another. In this manner, things and events are conceived as embedded in dynamic, relational matrices of mutual shaping and mutual coordination taking place on multiple levels simultaneously.[75]

It is unclear to me that what Behuniak describes *is* distinct from causation. Causation must be understood as more than simply prior cause and subsequent effect. Depending on what kind of coordination we are talking about, cause and effect are perfectly coordinated. Coordination as such must take place within some reference point—that is, multiple things cannot be coordinated unless there is some frame of reference in which they can be coordinated and move or act in reference to one another. In order to be fixed in a frame of reference, there must be mutual coordination. This is as much the case for cause and effect as it is for anything else. In order for some effect to have some cause, the features of the effect must be explainable by the complete description of the cause, and in this way the effect *does* shape the cause. It constrains the cause. In addition, if we look at the standard account of cause and effect in classical mechanics concerning force, we can see that any force involves causation in multiple, not only one, direction. One thing does not simply *act on* another—two things act on one another. And this is the most classical conception of causation possible. Thus, it seems that the description of correlation that Behuniak offers cannot be considered as distinct from causation. Nor need it be. Early Chinese correlative cosmology can be understood perfectly well in terms of causation.

Behuniak follows Joseph Needham's description of Chinese correlative metaphysics as "organic" rather than mechanistic,[76] but again it is unclear to me why we should conceive of causation as mechanistic if this means that it consists of, as Behuniak says, "external relations between discrete entities," as opposed to metaphysically inseperable objects. This is simply an implausible conception of causation, and one not held in the West at least since the age of Newton. Perhaps certain medieval thinkers like Jean Buridan, who accepted the theory of impetus, held such a view, but it is unclear even they would have had such a metaphysically implausible conception of causation. Needham's insistence notwithstanding, the "organic vs. mechanistic" dichotomy used by some scholars of Chinese thought (and others) is as ill-fitting as the "cyclical vs. linear time" dichotomy discussed by Mayanists. It turns out there simply is no robust difference between the two.

Qi (vital essence) is referred to in the *Huainanzi* as the *medium* of this causation or resonance between things. The problem of causation in the West is well known—philosophers worried throughout Western history how to make sense of the *power* or *force* through which a cause produces an effect. In a sense, the Chinese answer to this question is to point to the role of *qi*. While this may not offer us the kind of explanation most philosophers would have desired, it does give a name to the active component behind causation and resonance, and also associates this active component with a concept that was already well-known and discussed by earlier thinkers—the *qi* of human vital essence, as described above. This earlier sense of *qi* seems very close to the Maya concept of *ch'ul* in the blood, released or sacrificed by rulers in ceremonial bloodlettings.[77]

John Major claims that this understanding of *qi* was first developed in the third century BCE with the work of Zou Yan,[78] but it clearly did not reach the pinnacle of its development until the second century BCE during the Western Han dynasty. A.C. Graham discusses *qi* in a way that makes it sound very much like the *causal power* that medieval and modern Western philosophers were so concerned about (and could never find, which led David

Hume to give up on the whole thing).[79] *Qi* is seen in the *Huainanzi* as both the basic operative *stuff* constituting the universe (a meaning it retains in later Han texts) and as a kind of energetic vital *force*.[80] Thus, *qi* has elements of physical atomist views of the cosmos, but the fundamental stuff composing the universe is itself active, playing the central role in the causation/correlation between things that is the basis of the correlative cosmology most fully developed in the Han.

Yin and *yang*, according to the *Huainanzi*, operate primarily through the expression of *qi* and certain features of *qi*. We may read the connection as a *reductive* one—many passages from the *Huainanzi* and other texts of its time explain the operation of the *yin* and *yang* principles in terms of *yin* and *yang qi*:

> For this reason, the sages inhaled and exhaled the *qi* of yin and yang, and none of the myriad living things failed to flourish.[81]

> The hot *qi* of accumulated yang produced fire; the essence of fiery *qi* became the sun. The cold *qi* of accumulated *yin* produced water; the essence of watery *qi* became the moon.[82]

It is ultimately *qi*, according to *Huainanzi* and other Han texts, that has effective power in causation/correlation between things in the world. There are regularities between every component of the universe—the *ganying* (resonance) between things extends to humanity and the rest of nature. When an action happens somewhere in the cosmos, this creates resonant effects elsewhere, effecting the patterns of nature, whether in the human or non-human realm.[83] *Qi* seems to be the basic force (and material) which can have *yin* or *yang* characteristics and thus effect change. The suggestion in the *Huainanzi* is that there are different *kinds* of *qi*, and the distinctions between these kinds account for the differences in properties of various entities in the world. At its most basic, there is *yin qi* and *yang qi*, but then there are the various *qi* of particular entities, which distinguish them from others. The *Huainanzi* refers to human *qi* as *jingshen* (pure or quintessential spirit), which is a kind of "refined" *qi*, connected with, one imagines, sentience. According to the *Jingshen* chapter (ch. 7), there are grades of refinement of *qi*, and the refined and pure *qi* became that of humans.[84] This distinction between refined and turbid *qi* is likely meant in part to explain why human beings are sentient, for example, while other things with *qi*, such as plants, rocks, and other non-sentient things, do not. It is not quite as simple as this, however. The *Huainanzi* suggests that we can *lose* our *jingshen*, that it can be dispersed or depleted. Thus it cannot be sentience itself, for that is only lost when one dies or has massive brain injury. The *Jingshen* chapter itself is a treatise instructing us how to secure and retain our *jingshen*, and explaining the advantages of retaining it. A passage from *Jingshen* reads:

When the blood and vital energy are agitated and not at rest, then the *jingshen* courses out [through the eyes and ears] and is not preserved. When the *jingshen* is not preserved, then when either good fortune or misfortune arrives, although it be the size of hills and mountains, one has no way to recognize it.[85]

Jingshen, then, as a particular kind of *qi*, is compatible with a more basic kind of human *qi*—the minimal *qi* one needs to have to be alive, for example. The effective power of the sage is based on the sage's possession of a purer and better *qi*, that is, the *qi* of *jingshen*, than the rest of us possess. Of course, according to the *Huainanzi*, this is due to the fact that the sage has been able to retain *jingshen*, rather than attain it. All of us are supplied with *jingshen* by nature, but most of us lose it because we don't understand how to retain it. Still, *qi* here is clearly the force through which effectiveness is explained. *Qi* is responsible for causation/resonance between elements of the world as well as the human realm. While there are passages that seem to contradict such a reading throughout the *Huainanzi*, it appears as if the authors hold a kind of *qi* reductionism. All of the variety of actions and things in the cosmos that are explained in terms of *yin* and *yang* and other properties can ultimately be understood as possessing certain types and quantities of *qi*. Despite passages like 7.1 ("[heaven and earth] differentiated into the yin and yang and separated into the eight cardinal directions"),[86] *qi* does appear to be the most basic force and entity in much of the text. In 2.1 there is a discussion of the generation of things from the original nothingness:

The *qi* of Heaven beginning to descend, the *qi* of Earth beginning to ascend, yin and yang mixing and meeting, mutually roaming freely and racing to fill the interstices of time and space.[87]

This makes *qi* the operative force even in the first organization of the cosmos, which suggest that it is the most direct expression of the primordial (and ultimately ineffable) *dao*. How can we understand this as anything other than a kind of *qi* reductionism which makes *qi* the basic force in the cosmos of which everything else is ultimately constituted, and which connects and correlates the myriad elements of the cosmos? It turns out to be the case that different texts in the Han and before understand *qi* and its role in different ways. In the *Huainanzi*, there appears to be a heavy strain of *qi* reductionism, although due to the nature of the text, which is constructed of many elements that were independent and perhaps even offered sometimes contradictory views, we can find passages which seem to suggest otherwise. In other Han texts, however, we find alternative conceptions of the operation of *qi*.

A number of scholars accept a general *qi*-reductionist view as accepted by early Chinese thinkers in general.[88] Franklin Perkins writes:

[*qi*] eventually became the dominant label for the basic stuff of the world, used
to explain all kinds of dynamic processes, from the formation of heaven and
earth to the patterns of weather to the processes of the human heart. It was
closely connected with life and the generative power of nature. [89]

Another Han text relevant to the discussion of the origination of correlative
cosmology in China, much of it dated to the period immediately surrounding the production of the *Huainanzi*, is the *Chunqiu Fanlu* (Luxuriant Gems
of the Spring and Autumn), traditionally attributed to the Han "Confucian"
scholar Dong Zhongshu. Texts like *Chunqiu Fanlu* show us that the latter part
of above statement from Perkins can be true (*qi* as explanation of dynamic
process, i.e., causation, and the generation of nature) without the first part (*qi*
as the "basic stuff of the world") being true. That is, *Chunqiu Fanlu* and a
number of other texts seem to show us alternative ways to construe *qi* such
that it has the effective power claimed for it in the majority of Han correlative
texts, without being a basic stuff to which everything is reducible. Ultimately
I will, using this as a comparative backdrop, argue for a similar position with
respect to ancient Maya thought.

The relevance of this *Chunqiu Fanlu* for understanding correlative cosmology in China and also its parallels to the ancient Maya case is enormous. It
offers us a different conception of *qi* than what we find in *Huainanzi* (though
there are some echoes of that text), and it also introduces a new category of
"forces" beyond what we see in *Huainanzi*, the *wu xing* (five phases).[90] It is
generally the *Chunqiu Fanlu*, rather than the *Huainanzi*, that is given credit
for inaugurating Han correlative cosmology,[91] but as I show above, both had
a central role in the expression of correlative thought in the Han.

The discussion of the metaphysics of *qi* in the *Chunqiu Fanlu* is contained
mainly in chapters concerning *yin-yang* and *wu xing* (five phases) thought
toward the end of the text. We see a picture of *qi* emerge in this text along
the lines of how it is developed in the *Huainanzi*, but the *Chunqiu Fanlu* goes
further in offering a more robust explanation of the connection between *qi*
and the categories of *yin-yang* and five phases. It is less clear in this text that
we see the kind of "*qi* reductionism" we can find in the *Huainanzi*. *Qi* in the
Chunqiu Fanlu, I argue, should be seen as an *aspect* of the myriad things,
rather than as something that the myriad things are ultimately reducible to.
The *qi* aspect of these things helps to explain their interconnection, the ways
in which they can cause effects in one another and can be correlated in the
way suggested by the correlative cosmological texts. But what we see here
is not a kind of *correlative monism*, to use Timothy Knowlton's phrase, but
rather a correlative pluralism. One thing has resonance with another in the
world because each *has qi*, not because each *is qi*. In order for this to work,
however, we have to read *qi* differently from the way Major et al. read it in

the case of the *Huainanzi*. *Qi* cannot be both matter and energy, but rather must be understood as a particular energetic and causal property that a thing possesses, that explains its causal potency. Notice that on this definition of *qi*, it will still be the case that if a thing "runs out" of *qi* it will cease to exist. But this is not because it is made of *qi*, but because *qi* is necessary for causal efficacy—and for a thing to lose causal efficacy is for it to cease to exist. *Qi* then can be seen as a *thing-making* feature. The other elements of a being that are *non-qi* can only have effective interaction with the rest of the world insofar as they are supported by *qi*. This does not make them *qi*, however.

RELEVANCE FOR MAYA THOUGHT

We have seen from the Chinese material that there are (at least) two possible ways of reading a correlative metaphysics that makes a particular concept central to the causal and resonance connections between different elements of the world. The dominant ancient Maya view that we find in much of the extant literature (ancient and modern) suggests something much closer to the view in the *Chunqiu Fanlu* than the *qi*-reductionism of texts like *Huainanzi* (if that is indeed the correct way to read the *Huainanzi*). Time is indeed fundamental in Maya philosophy, but if it plays a role akin to *qi* in Han correlative thought, it should be seen as playing the causal role of *qi* in *Chunqiu Fanlu*. That is, ancient Maya thought was not reductionist about time. This position sets my view at odds with Knowlton, Leon-Portilla, and a number of other scholars of Maya thought. But the available textual evidence, as well as other anthropological and sociological evidence based on contemporary practice, is more consistent with a picture of correlative cosmology along the lines of the *Chunqiu Fanlu*. We might call the two structures *reductionist* and *correlationist*, with the Chinese views described above giving us a clear picture of the structure of such views. Using the analogical argument, we can put the Maya position into relief, and try to determine whether either of these structures fits the ancient Maya position. Did the Maya offer a reductionist (or, correlative monist) or a correlationist metaphysics?

One may wonder at this point whether another relevant metaphysical dispute among scholars of the history of philosophy, especially in Chinese philosophy, does not rise to the surface. In numerous studies of the early Chinese philosophical tradition, it has been proposed that a kind of process metaphysics was the dominant position in the tradition, rather than the substance-based metaphysics that tended to dominate in the West.[92] I contend here that the issue of whether one accepts a substance or process metaphysics (I think we can find *both* in the early Chinese tradition, just like we can find both in the Western tradition) can be sidestepped when considering the question of whether a reductionist or correlationist metaphysics is being offered, because both reductionism and correlationism are compatible with both process and substance conceptions of the world. I think there is good reason for the distinction between process and substance metaphysics to be collapsed in the first place, and Maya thought may help us find a way to do this. Here, however, I want to leave this aside, and so offer some argument to demonstrate the independence of these metaphysical categories. Ultimately, even if one rejects the position that the Maya tradition should be seen as collapsing the distinction between process and substance (as indeed I think we see in some Chinese texts as well), one can still accept that the Maya tradition offered a correlationist rather than reductionist metaphysics.

How can a process metaphysics be reductionist? As we have seen above, most of the philosophers who accept a *qi*-reductionist position in early Chinese texts also accept that they offered a process metaphysics. *Qi*, on this position, can be understood in terms of both matter and energy. The larger processes that make up the world, such as the five phases, can ultimately be understood in terms of more fundamental processes involving *qi*. *Qi*, as a fundamental constituent of reality, itself has to be conceived as a process. There is not, on the face of it, any reason why we could not understand processes as related to one another in terms of reduction, any more than we could understand substances as so related. Reductionism of this kind only commits us to the view that there are certain aspects of the world that are more explanatorily fundamental, and that all other aspects of the world that are not understood in terms of those entities are explanatorily reducible to them. Of course, there are different kinds of reductionism. For our purposes, we can overlook the specifics of these kinds of reductionism, because the reductionism I propose here is general. Whether we see it in terms of derivation of the claims of any theory from one foundational theory (say *qi* theory for early Chinese thinkers),[93] or whether we want to make stronger claims about translatability, or weaker claims about explanation, these are all a version of a more broadly construed reductionist position in which the base theory is the foundation and more basic than other theories of the world which can ultimately be understood in terms of it.

The basic elements of the fundamental theory of the world are thought to be the "basic stuff" or basic constituents of reality. One might object that the reductionism involved in early Chinese or Maya thought cannot be seen as the same as the "theory-based" reductionism of contemporary philosophical and scientific thought. But in the Chinese tradition, at least, the textual evidence we have from Han texts seems to show that they did think of the reduction in something like this way. Texts like *Chunqiu Fanlu* offer *yin-yang* as well as five phases explanations for different phenomena in the world, and develop robust accounts of how both of these theories work. Yet they also discuss things in certain places in what seems like more fundamental terms of *qi*. If there is reductionism at work here, it does seem to have to do with something we can call "theory." Theoretical reductionism is not, that is, a feature only of contemporary Western thought.

We can also make sense of reductionism on substance accounts of metaphysics. The only requirement of theoretical reduction is that the target theories be understood in a way amounting to reduction to the base theory. We could even combine process and substance, as we see on many metaphysical views. One may take process, for example, to be reducible to substance—that is, every theory that refers to processes as components can ultimately be reduced to a theory referencing substances and their interaction. Likewise, one could construct a position in which substance is reduced to process. Whether a reductionist metaphysics ultimately counts as process or substance metaphysics has to do with the ontology of the base theory.

It is a bit more difficult to show that a correlationist system is compatible with either a process or substance metaphysics. First, I have to give a more detailed explanation of just what the correlationist system amounts to, as unlike reductionism, it is not well known in Western philosophy. The idea of correlationist metaphysics itself comes from a particular reading of early Chinese texts (particularly Han dynasty texts). If we think of correlationist metaphyics in terms of *theory* (as with reductionism), the general view is that the numerous elements referenced in the ultimately correct theory of the world (in contemporary terms perhaps our current best explanation) are causally connected to one another via their possession of some other metaphysical entity—in the early Chinese texts, *qi*. *Qi* is itself a member of that ontology that has both material and energetic elements, but it should be understood as operating on the *same* theoretical level as the other elements of a most basic theory of the world. There is no *reduction* from five phases or *yin-yang* theory to *qi* theory. Rather, *qi* operates alongside of these elements, and explains the causal efficacy of these elements insofar as they represent the causal power of these elements. Note that this position seems to have a strange implication. If possession of *qi* is required for causal efficacy, then a thing that loses its *qi* is no longer in any sense causally efficacious—it cannot interact with anything in the world. How can we then say that such a thing still exists? On the correlationist view, such a thing indeed does cease to exist. But it does not cease to exist because the thing is ultimately *composed* of *qi*. Rather, there is a thing (substance, process, undecided) that has *qi* as a necessary property for effective action. Effective action, in the Chinese tradition, is closely tied to the issue of existence. I argue elsewhere[94] that in Han texts (and suggested earlier) we can find a view not altogether different from the view of substances and their properties found in Aristotle. It has always been more of an assumption than anything else that substance metaphysics as found in

Aristotle is contrary to the metaphysical positions found in ancient Chinese texts. Aristotle's view of causal efficacy is close to the correlationist view, in which particular properties of a thing are causally efficacious, and there is an underlying substrate that possesses those properties. Aristotle seems committed, because of this, to the position that there is an ultimately feature-less matter that perhaps cannot exist on its own with no properties, but is not identifiable with any of the properties—the *prime matter* discussed in greater detail by Aquinas. The *qi* correlationist view in early China would make an *qi*-less, causally impotent entity something like this prime matter—perhaps something that could not exist on its own, but conceptually distinct from the properties (in this case *qi*) that make for its causal efficacy.

The views offered by Knowlton, Leon-Portilla, and others read ancient Maya thought as primarily offering a kind of *time reductionism*. Generally, reductionist interpretations of Maya thought make time the basic entity, due to the clear focus on the importance of the concept throughout the extant literature. However (as I argue above), we should be careful to assume the ontological centrality of a concept on the basis of how much it is discussed in the texts. The concerns of the authors of these texts and their patrons may not have been with the most fundamental features of the world—just as when we write philosophy, we do not always (or even most often) discuss the question of fundamental ontology. While time was clearly important to the ancient Maya, as I argue above we tend to overestimate its ontological centrality because of its inclusion in almost every extant Maya text. Time had a fundamental role in Maya thought, but the fact that most of the texts we have today were commissioned by and served the purposes of the *ahauob* (rulers) who themselves wished to fix the significant dates of their own lives and reigns with the events of mythical time and continuous creation,[95] can largely explain the extent to which time is discussed in the extant texts. What specific reason do we have to think that the elements of the world *reduce* to time for the ancient Maya, rather than gods, or number, or other seemingly fundamental elements of the world?

That most of the entities in the Maya texts are *associated* with time is beyond question.[96] The various gods, numbers, individuals, and other elements of the world can be connected to particular time periods, time units, distance numbers, or other temporal elements. But as I have shown above, the pervasive association of particular entities with some element does not entail a *reduction* of those entities to this element, as this can equally well be explained by a correspondentist view. And there are additional features of the Maya texts that suggest correspondentism rather than reductionism.

The correlative metaphysics we see in Maya texts uses time along with the concept of *itz* (discussed in chapter 3) to tie together all objects into a single order. We see a correlative system here because it is not simply that time and *itz* form the medium in which things affect one another. Instead, the temporal aspects and the *itz* aspects of objects have effect on one another, and there is a regular and accessible order to the effects that changes in *itz* and these other elements create in one another. If we understand *itz* as playing a role similar to *qi* in early Chinese correlative metaphysics, we can make sense of Maya correlative thought. Elements of the unseen world, such as Xibalba, respond to the rituals using the *ch'ul* (essence) of rulers, because this *ch'ul* shares features with these elements of the unseen world—it is of the same essence. In this way, the *ch'ul* contained in the blood of the ruler is the *ch'ul* of the unseen aspects of the world that the ruler can reveal through his or her ritual activity. The various kinds of *itz* respond to one another in like, and it is thus that the ruler, whose particular *itz* (as *ch'ul*) is of a kind with powerful forces of the unseen world, is able to communicate with and manifest these aspects of the world through ritual.

NOTES

1. Milbrath, *Star Gods of the Maya*, 58.

2. I look particularly to the *Avatamsaka Sutra* and its commentaries for the Huayan view, and the *Samkhyakarika* for the Samkhya view.

3. Thus it possible for some realists about objects to claim that the fundamental "furniture" of the universe in a complete ontology includes objects like trees, chairs, and other macro-level objects, rather than just atoms and collections of atoms. See Elder, *Real Natures and Familiar Objects*.

4. The use of memorial stelae was common well before and after the Classic Period, even extending to non-Maya cultures such as the Aztec, up until the Conquest Period. The Classic Period stelae, however, are noted for the use of Long and Short Count dates and other calendric information. It is in part this calendric focus on monumental texts that Mayanists used to define the Classic Period, as distinct from the Preclassic and Postclassic.

5. Scott Johnson discusses the ISIG in his *Translating Maya Hieroglyphs*, 81–83.

6. The "Lords of the Night" glyphs have not been given phonetic spoken readings as have many other glyphs. Their meaning has been deciphered but the possible pronunciations of the glyphs is still a mystery. The glyphs are given the classification "G," so the glyph representing the second Lord of the Night is referred to as G2.

7. Each month is one of 29 or 30 days of lunation, generally alternating. This variation is due to the fact that a synodic lunar month (the time for the moon to go from one phase to return to the same phase) is 29.53 days.

8. I discuss the concept of "substitution" or "representation" in chapter 4.

9. Girard, *Los Mayas*, 175.

10. Johnson, *Translating Maya Hieroglyphs*, 94.

11. Montgomery 2002: 225 (*Dictionary of Maya Hieroglyphs*).

12. Portilla : xvii, Thompson 1954: 162.

13. Houston, *The Life* Within, 107.

14. Leon-Portilla, *Tiempo y realidad*, 95.

15. Leon-Portilla, *Tiempo y realidad*, 86. "Time … is the life and origin of all things. That is why its study and measuring is the supreme concern of the wise men the *ah Kinob* ('those of the solar and temporal cults') as they were designated by the Maya of Yucatán."

16. Leon-Portilla, *Tiempo y realidad*, 54.

17. Knowlton, *Maya Creation* Myths, 19. Leon-Portilla's position seems to have been influential in interpretation of Maya thought, but his book on the subject is not often mentioned in statements of the claim.

18. Knowlton, *Maya Creation Myths*, 19.

19. Discussed in chapter 4. The concept bears similarity to that of the *nahual* in contemporary Maya thought. The *nahual* is an animal spirit associate of an individual that expresses some important aspect of the individual's essence. The term *nahual* comes from Nahuatl, but the concept mirrors that of the *way*. Arata, "The Testimonial of Rigoberta Menchú in a Native Tradition," 82; Miller and Taube, *The Gods and Symbols of Ancient Mexico and the Maya*, 122.

20. The text attributed to the former, the *Hanfeizi*, is today taken as the central presentation of the ideas of the Legalist "school" (法家*fa jia*).

21. Examples include the work of Roger Ames and David Hall on the Chinese tradition, and James Maffie on the Aztec tradition.

22. Houston, *The Life Within*, 5.

23. See Rescher, *Process Metaphysics*.

24. For example, Alan Sidelle and Amy Thomassen argue for versions of such a conventionalist position. Crawford Elder, an opponent of conventionalism about kinds, characterizes the view thus: "Conventionalism is the view that the borders of nature's kinds, and the courses of existence traced out by individual members of those kinds, are functions of our conventions of individuation." (Elder, *Real Natures and Familiar Objects*, 2.)

25. The Lords of the Night glyphs are given the designation "G," and the nine Lords of the Night glyphs are then categorized as "G1"–"G9" or alternatively "Lords of the Night glyph 1," etc.

26. Coe, *Lords of the Underworld: Masterpieces of Classic Maya Ceramics*, 58–60. Taube, "A Representation of the Principal Bird Deity in the Paris Codex."

27. Culbert, "Maya Political History and Elite Interaction: A Summary View," 315.

28. Tedlock, *Popol Vuh*, 63–4.

29. Matul and Cabrera, *La cosmovisión maya*. Lima Soto, *Aproximación a la cosmovisión maya*. I will use *cosmovisión* here rather than "worldview," as there are connotations of the former term not included in the latter.

30. Tedlock, *Popol Vuh*, 63.

31. Solari, *Maya Spatial Biographies in Communal Memory and Cosmic Time: The Franciscan Evangelical Campaign of Itzmal, Yukatan* (Ph.D. dissertation, University of California, Santa Barbara): 84–85.

32. O'Neill, *Engaging Ancient Maya Sculpture at Piedras Negras*, cites Houston and Stuart.

33. Rice, *Maya Calendar Origins*, 68.

34. Christenson, *Popol Vuh*, 26.

35. Christenson, *Popol Vuh*, 59–60.

36. Vail and Hernandez, *Re-creating Primordial Time*, 5.

37. Christenson, *Popol Vuh*, 55.

38. Kukulkan for the Yucatec, Quetzalcoatl for the Nahua/Aztecs, this figure seems to be common god in the shared heritage of Mesoamerica, appearing in many cultural contexts in the wider region.

39. Maffie, *Aztec Philosophy*, ch. 3.

40. Maffie, *Aztec Philosophy*, 205.

41. Seler, *Commentarios al Códice Borgia* I, 144. Maffie, *Aztec Philosophy*, 205.

42. Maffie, *Aztec Philosophy*, ch.3.

43. Rice, *Maya Calendar Origins*, 112.

44. Pellicer, *Maya Achi Marimba Music in Guatemala*, 54. Tedlock writes that the dual is "the very nature of the primordial world and of anything that might be created in that world." Tedlock, *Popol Vuh,...* (1986).

45. Jones, *The Conquest of the Last Maya Kingdom*, 95.

46. Scherer, *Mortuary Landscapes of the Classic Maya: Rituals of Body and Soul,* ... Vogt, *Zinacantán: A Maya Community in the Highlands of Chiapas,* 70.

47. Maffie, *Aztec Philosophy*, 216.

48. Attributed to Andres Xilój, in Tedlock, *Popol Vuh*, 207.

49. Tedlock, *Popol Vuh*, 97.

50. Tedlock, *Popol Vuh*, 99.

51. Maffie, *Aztec Philosophy*, 241.

52. The emissary from Xibalba to Tohil on the behalf of humans is an example. Tedlock, *Popol Vuh*, 154–156.

53. This may remind us of the story of Jesus' reappearance after his resurrection in the Gospels of Luke and John, where he is unrecognized by his disciples as having a different form. It is unclear the extent to which (if any at all) these Christian stories influenced the story of the Hero Twins in the *Popol Vuh*.

54. Tedlock, *Popol Vuh*, 154–156.

55. Scherer, *Mortuary Landscapes of the Classic Maya*, 53. Looper, *To Be Like Gods*, 115. Friedel, Reese-Taylor, and Mora-Marin, "The Origins of Maya Civilization: The Old Shell Game, Commodity, Treasure, and Kingship," 77. The image included below has the Maize God reborn from the back of a turtle (Kappelman, "Carved in Stone"; Taube, "The Olmec Maize God," 62). Sometimes the image of rebirth of the Maize God is from water rather than soil (Guernsey 2010, *Ritual and Power in Stone*. 137).

56. Vail and Hernandez 2013: 13.

57. Scherer, *Mortuary Landscapes of the Classic Maya*, 53. ("The Maya liken the concept of soul rebirth to the life cycle of plants, particularly maize.").

58. Tedlock, *Popol Vuh*, 145–146.

59. Peterson, *The Highland Maya in Fact and Legend*, 27.

60. Looper, *To Be Like Gods*, 115.

61. Tedlock, *Popol Vuh,* 99.

62. For the Advaita Vedanta tradition this "self" is disembodied and dis-minded.

63. Phillips, *Yoga, Karma, and Rebirth: A Brief History and Philosophy*, ch. 4.

64. To use an example discussed by the ancient Greek scholar Plutarch that contemporary analytic philosophers commonly draw upon.

65. Fitzsimmons, *Death and the Classic Maya Kings*, 82–83.

66. Ardren, *Social Identities in the Classic Maya Northern Lowlands*, 122.

67. Knowlton, *Maya Creation Myths*.

68. See McLeod, "The Convergence Model of Philosophical Method in the Early Han."

69. *Yuan Dao* and *Chuzhen* (chs. 1 and 2) lay out this cosmogony. Ch. 3 (*Tianwen*) and Ch. 7 (*Jingshen*) cite *Daodejing* 42.

70. *Huainanzi* 3.1 (*Tianwen*). I follow here the text numbering of the Chinese Text Project (www.ctext.org).

71. In *Popol Vuh*, we find the creator gods as dual, the Hero Twins, as well as One and Seven Death, lords of Xibalba, representing death principle. Aztec thought also emphasizes the dual principle. Indeed, this seems to be a theme in a number of philosophical and religious traditions.

72. Major, *Heaven and Earth in Early Han Thought*, 30.

73. See Major, Queen, Meyer, and Roth, *Huainanzi*, 207.

74. John Henderson argues that *ganying* was a rationalization of the effects of resonance or indirect causation noticed between things in the world by Han scholars. Henderson, *The Development and Decline of Chinese Cosmology*, 40.

75. Behuniak, *Mencius on Becoming Human*, 31.

76. Behuniak, *Mencius on Becoming Human*, 30. Behuniak attributes this view to John Major as well.

77. Foster, *Handbook*, 190–192.

78. Major, *Heaven and Earth in Early Han Thought*, 30.

79. Graham, *Yin-Yang and the Nature of Correlative Thinking*. Michael Loewe also discusses *qi* in a way that, for its organic imagery, also seems to suggest causation. He writes (Loewe, *Faith, Myth, and Reason in Han China*, 69): "[*Qi*] conveys the idea of creative energy or life-giving force."

80. Major et. al., *Huainanzi*, 883: "*qi* is both matter and energy, the basic substance out of which the entire universe is composed."

81. Major et al., *Huainanzi*, 99.

82. Major et al., *Huainanzi*, 115.

83. As Major et al. point out, the term *ganying* itself does not appear in the *Huainanzi*, but the concept seems to develop here. They mention a number of passages in which *gan* and *ying* are used together to express the idea, though it is only in later texts that the formulation of the term "*ganying*" is used to express this idea.

84. *Huainanzi* 7.1. Major et al. add on p. 234 of their translation, "*Shen* can be thought of as composed of the most highly rarefied and purified kind of *qi*, and *jingshen* as the quintessence of *shen*."

85. Major et al., *Huananzi*, 244. (7.4).

86. Major et al., *Huainanzi*, 240.

87. Major et al., *Huainanzi*, 85. (2.1).

88. Including Perkins, "Metaphysics in Chinese Philosophy"; Liu, "In Defense of Qi Naturalism," 33.

89. Perkins, "Metaphysics in Chinese Philosophy."

90. The idea of the five phases begins with the work of Zou Yan in the mid-third century BCE according to the Han dynasty historian Sima Qian, but it is in the early Han that the concept comes to be most fully developed.

91. Although correlative cosmology itself has much deeper historical roots than the *Chunqiu Fanlu*, the project of combining Confucian moral theory with a particular metaphysics of correlative thought specified using the categories of *yin-yang* as well as *wu xing* is widely seen as a quintessentially Han dynasty project, with *Chunqiu Fanlu* as the major representative.

92. Some notable process interpretations of Chinese thought include Hall and Ames, *Thinking From the Han*; Franklin Perkins, "What is a thing (*wu*)?"

93. Nagel, *The Structure of Science*, for the classic statement. Also see Schaffner, "Approaches to Reduction."

94. McLeod and Brown, *Transcendence and Substance in Early Chinese Thought* (forthcoming).

95. Rice, *Maya Calendar Origins*, 172.

96. Houston, Fernando, Mazariegos, and Stuart, *The Decipherment of Ancient Maya Writing*, 207.

Chapter 3

Worlds and the Question of Essence and Truth

The ontology of the ancient Maya, as I argued in previous chapters, involved time as a central component (though not the basic component to which all other things are reduced). There are however, other aspects of their view of the basic components of the world that can help us to understand the scope and outline of their philosophical thought. In this chapter, I offer accounts of the Maya views of *worlds* and *essence/truth*, and the connection between these two. I argue for the view that the Maya conception of the cosmos is monistic, rejecting the view advanced by a number of scholars that there are numerous transcendent realms represented by deities and other aspects of the Maya cosmos. Instead, there is an essential connection between the elements of the world most humans have access to and the "unseen" elements of the world, accessible to us only through the rituals performed by the ruling class. A central concept linking all things in the cosmos, seen and unseen, is *itz*, which I interpret as both "essence" and "truth." As in previous chapters, I use a striking parallel between Maya and Chinese views to offer a more developed possible account of the ancient Maya position on these concepts.

THE ONTOLOGY OF WORLDS—ONE, TWO, OR MANY?

While there is little doubt that the ancient Maya accepted the existence of at least two distinct "realms," that of human beings and perhaps the deities, and that of *Xibalba*, or the underworld,[1] a better case can be made that the Maya thought of these worlds as different parts of one fundamentally unified world (in the sense of physical, temporal, and causal continuity), rather than as ontologically distinct realms along the lines of Plato's physical realm and the realm of the Forms. A claim on distinction between worlds might be either an ontological or a focus or value claim, at least. For example, Plato's distinction between the world of Forms and the physical world is an ontological distinction, while the distinction between the "human world" and the "natural world" in our language (a distinction the early Chinese also held) is not an ontological distinction, but one of focus.

The distinction between the worlds discussed in ancient Maya sources, and which we can draw from Postconquest sources, is not that of ontologically distinct worlds, but rather that of the relationship between two (or more) parallel centers of significance within a single world, defined by its sharing of principles of activity, explanation, laws, and its constitution and the causal connection of each of the parts of the world with the other. Transcendent worlds, such as the realm of the Forms for Plato or that of God for the medieval Europeans, do not operate according to the laws of other worlds (such as the physical world), are not constituted by the same things, and have different grounds, even if there can be a causal connection between the two (though this connection, given the ontological distinctness of every other feature of the worlds, can be as much a mystery as that between the substances of mind and body for Cartesians).

Does the same hold in the ancient Maya case? Clearly, the rulers were seen as having access to features of the world (or other worlds) out of the reach of others.[2] But was this access *supernatural*, akin to Platonic and theistic views, or was it akin to that of the sage in early Chinese thought?

Perhaps the best case for many-world views in ancient Maya thought comes through consideration of the relationship between the living world and that of Xibalba (the place of fear), the Maya "underworld." The theme of Xibalba is an important one in the Maya creation story, recounted in the *k'iche' Popol Vuh*, but also present in parts on a number of monuments and texts in earlier periods.[3] Xibalba is also prominent in consideration of the shamanic power of rulers, and as an abode for both certain sets of gods and deceased rulers.[4] One of the most famous images of the ancient Maya world is from the sarcophagus lid of the Palenque ruler Janaab Pakal, and shows Pakal descending into Xibalba, which is linked with the "world tree," which will be another important part of the discussion below, and which links the living world, Xibalba, and all other realms. I argue below that the World Tree plays a somewhat similar role to *dao* in Han dynasty Chinese thought, and that it can be seen as the adhesive for a single unified world, accessible by those with special or developed insight. The World Tree is the basis of existence *everywhere*, both in the world we see and Xibalba, but the majority of us are not developed enough to *see* these other aspects of reality. Stories from the *Popol Vuh* and the ancient texts show us, I argue, that Xibalba and other "realms," rather than being distinct worlds, exist side-by-side with, or *within*, our own world, accessible in principle but invisible to most, due to lack of vision. The Maya view of the cosmos shares much in common with that developed in early China, and while they diverge in certain areas, the early Chinese position can inform our investigation into the Maya view. It will become apparent the variety of ways in which the Maya view diverges from that of the Han, for all of their startling similarity.

The story of the *Popol Vuh* has much to say about the realm of Xibalba, seemingly consistent with much of the iconography from ancient sites. Xibalba is spoken of as some distance from the place of persons, and there is a road to Xibalba that is open to the Hero Twins and presumably others who care to take it. The conflict between the Hero Twins and the lords of Xibalba is precipitated by a ballgame played by the Twins along the road to Xibalba, which disturbs the lords of Xibalba. In return, the lords of Xibalba call the Twins to the underworld to defeat them. The lords of Xibalba are described in terms of their work, causing the numerous necrotic difficulties of humanity, including death of the human itself. These natural activities that happen in the world, the decay and ultimate death of biological individuals, are attributed to the workings of the lords of Xibalba. Thus, regardless of the status of the realms under consideration, the Xibalbans have a great deal of causal influence on the human world. This alone, however, cannot show that the two realms are part of a single ontologically unified world. Theistic views, as shown above, hold that there is a completely dependent one-way causal relationship between the worlds, but this is not the basis for the collapse of the two into one ontologically unified world. Presumably part of the reason for this is the asymmetry of the causal relationship. While the human world is caused by and completely dependent on the divine, the divine is neither caused by nor at all dependent on (and arguably even not *affected* by) the human world.

There is an impressive range of different lords of Xibalba responsible for particular necrotic processes, some of which the *Popol Vuh* describes:

> There are the lords named Scab Stripper and Blood Gatherer. And this is their commission: to draw blood from people. Next are the lords of Demon of Pus and Demon of Jaundice. And this is their domain: to make people swell up, to make pus come out of their legs, to make their faces yellow, to cause jaundice, as it is called ... . Next are the lords Bone Scepter and Skull Scepter, the staff bearers of Xibalba ... and this is their staff-bearing: to reduce people to bones, right down to the bones and skulls, until they die from emaciation and edema.[5]

The account continues like this discussing other effects of the workings of the lords of Xibalba. The Hero Twins are granted access to Xibalba as a result of invitation from the lords, who conspire to defeat them. The Twins are killed in Xibalba, but are also resurrected, and the story of the Twins in Xibalba as

Figure 3.1   Janaab Pakal descending into Xibalba, connected to the World Tree/cross, from the sarcophagus lid of Janaab Pakal at Palenque. Sarcophagus cover inside the temple of the inscriptions. Shown is the double-headed serpent that undulates through the branches of the tree, with enlargements of the *k'awiil* ("god k") and jester god figures who emerge from the open jaws of the serpent. Below is the image of *k'inich* Janaab Pakal and the quadripartite monster. Drawing by Linda Schele © David Schele. Photo courtesy of Ancient Americas at LACMA.

a whole is meant to represent the cycle of death and rebirth to life. Indeed, the famous Maya ballgame as well as the well-attested practice of human sacrifice had links to this mythology. The sacrifice made by the twins led to the rebirth of society and the defeat of the lords of Xibalba in part through the ballgame.[6] Likewise, the sacrifice of humans was meant (at least on an ideological level) to represent the sacrifice that would allow for the continual rebirth and continuation of the human world.

The image from Janaab Pakal's sarcophagus lid itself suggests such a sacrificial connotation. Pakal himself descends into Xibalba, the realm of the dead, but from this realm itself grows the World Tree representative of the cosmos. The world of the living and the world of the dead are clearly linked, with Pakal, even in death, forming the nexus between the two. In sinking into Xibalba in the image, the memorial is not making the claim that Pakal is descending into oblivion—indeed, this would be an extremely bizarre statement for a ruling dynasty to make on its own monument to a beloved leader. Rather, Pakal's descent here represents his continuing identity as the conduit between the "worlds." Pakal's death is not an annihilation or flight to the underworld, but rather a *transformation* while retaining the same features he had in life, of the connection between the myriad seen and unseen aspects of reality. This aspect of rulership, I will show below, is important, because rulers in the lineage are seen as fundamentally *sharing in* the identity of rulers past. Thus, not only is Pakal simply transformed rather than eliminated at his death, but the entity of which Pakal was part, the ruler of Palenque, which is itself/himself the connection between aspects of reality, continues on in the form of Pakal's successor. The ancient Maya conception of rulership requires a discussion of metaphysics, as it is not simply a *role* that can be filled by a given individual, in the same sense as our contemporary understanding of roles. While it is a role, it is one linked with an individual identity and in that sense an individual *person* or *agent*. Again, as in the case of worlds, we will see that there are strong parallels between the Maya views here and those of early Chinese philosophers. Although in the case of agency and identity, the Maya have a position that may seem to us even more extreme than those found in early China.

Megan O'Neill discusses an interesting practice in Classic Period Tikal of burying stelae and sculptures as expressing the transition and presence of potent things in the world without being seen. This suggests further the "monistic" view of worlds I argue for in this chapter. Xibalba and elements of other "realms" are not in ontologically distinct worlds, but are rather features of our own single world, active within this world that simply cannot be seen (by most, at least). O'Neill's claim concerning Xibalba here is instructive:

> Earth and Xibalba are parallel worlds that cannot be seen from either location,
> though sound and visible signs provide connections between them.[7]

The idea of *parallel* worlds here requires some consideration. O'Neill recognizes that it is not correct to think of Xibalba and the human realm as *separate* or *distinct* realms. They have a connection that is not completely explained in the Maya texts, but one that is far too robust to suggest ontological distinctness. O'Neill goes on to explain a way in which we might understand access to the "unseen" aspects of reality, that is in line with my own position on worlds in ancient Maya thought:

> This passage [the Hero Twins' acts in Xibalba corresponding to the growth and sprouting of maize in the human realm] is one of many examples of sensitivity to and exploration of the line between the visible and invisible in Maya culture, past and present. Vision, although of great import, is only one mode of perception, among others; and beings—even if unseen—can be considered present and perceived through modes other than sight, whether through hearing, through signs that marked and reflected their existence and behavior, through dreams, or through memory.[8]

It is often unclear what will count as evidence for a dual-or-many-world ontology, outside of the explicit claim that there are numerous worlds, which we see in texts like Plato's *Republic* and other works, the work of Christian and Islamic philosophers. Here I look to some features of clearly multi-world ontologies, to ultimately determine the extent to which we see something like this, or fail to see something like this, in ancient Maya texts and thought. My position concerning the Maya is that we see something there much closer to the early Chinese single-world position described by the phrase *tian ren he yi* (天人合一), and characterized by correlative monism. The correlative monist picture has room for features and forces of the world which most humans do not have conscious access to, but it does not require ontologically distinct worlds to make sense of this.

Even in contemporary physicalist conceptions of the world, we can make perfectly good sense of the idea of parts of the world or certain abilities only accessible by the talented elite. Top-level athletes, for example, can perform physical feats impossible for most of the population, even with constant training. Those with eyesight greater than 20/20 are able to discern things in their environment most others cannot see. It is not that such people have access to any ontologically distinct realm, but rather that they have abilities to access things in the single world that most people cannot.

This holds also in the case of early China. *Tian ren he yi* 天人合一 ("heaven and humanity form one unity") is at its core a claim that every element of the nonhuman world has an effect on the human world and vice versa—the kind of causal effect through *ganying* 感應 (resonance) that entails that each thing that exists, human and nonhuman, not only has the potential to causally interact with any other thing, but that the same patterns (*li* 理) govern the generation, development, and activity of everything in the cosmos. Philosophers who adopt a separation between worlds or substances have difficulty explaining interaction across these disparate worlds or substances. We see such difficulty also in the case of Descartes' substance dualism concerning the person. The early Chinese never faced such a difficulty of explaining causal interaction between worlds because the dominant strain within the tradition accepted a one-world ontology, with no ontologically distinct worlds or substances. *Ganying* can take place between human and nonhuman elements of the world simply because *ganying* can take place between any two (or more) things sharing the same causal space.

The *Huainanzi* offers an explanation of *ganying* along just these lines, likening it to physical causation. A passage from Chapter Six (*Lanming*) reads:

> Now when a person who tunes a *se* plays [the note] *gong*, [another] *gong* string responds; when he plucks a *jue* [string], [another] *jue* responds. This is the harmony of notes that are the same.[9]

Striking one string of a *qin* vibrates the surrounding strings, as well as the air around it. This is a clear example of resonance between two ontologically similar objects. This example could not serve as an adequate explanation of *ganying* if the relation were between things in distinct worlds, such as Plato's Forms and material objects.

Notice that the image that Plato uses to explain the relationship between Forms and physical objects, namely *resemblance*, leads to immediate and obvious problems. What does it mean for something in the physical realm to resemble an entity that is ontologically completely unlike it? Answering this question leads to a number of problems Plato himself considers in the *Parmenides*, all of which can be taken as hurdles to multi-world views in general. How can one explain in ways that do not lead to the problems of *Parmenides* how ontologically distinct worlds or substances can interact with one another in any way? Descartes notoriously takes on this difficulty when he makes the distinction between mental and physical substance in his *Meditations on First Philosophy*.

The fact that this issue never arises in the early Chinese correlative tradition suggests that something different is going on here. *Ganying* is not problematic, and is illustrated in terms of the kind of causation we understand within a single-world frame. It is thus likely that *ganying* and the connection between humanity and *tian* was understood as expressing (among other things) a kind of one-world naturalism. As I argue further below, to call this position naturalism is *not* to claim that the early Chinese accepted a kind of physicalist naturalism such as that seen in contemporary Western thought. Rather, the position here is that in early Chinese correlative monism, features that in some other systems are attributed to a transcendent divine world outside of nature are "naturalized" in the sense of being accepted as elements of the single natural world.[10] To "naturalize" a thing is not necessarily to explain it in terms of what is empirically accessible. Presumably even the staunchest physicalist must hold that there may be certain physical elements of the world that we cannot detect with our senses or even our best instrumentation. Dark matter, for example, is not seen as transcendent or in a different world, even though we cannot sense it. Neutrinos presumably existed even before we could (very faintly) detect them with modern techniques. So the inaccessibility of a particular feature of the world (even in principle—there may be features of the world so different as to be impossible for humans to ever detect) in itself does not render that feature supernatural.

"Naturalism" itself is difficult to define. It seems to have come to serve as a banner for the nonacceptance of entities inconsistent with a conception of the world determined by the entities required to make sense of physics, or reducible to physics. Hardly anything that goes by the name of "naturalism" in philosophy meets this stipulation, however. Thus, perhaps a more adequate description of naturalism is a general philosophical attitude to stay as close to or attempt to render positions as compatible with a physicalist understanding of the world as possible. Areas such as mathematics or ethics, that might be plausibly understood as cutting against naturalism, are understood in various ways by naturalists as ultimately reducing to physicalistically respectable elements, or elements that can be countenanced in the physical sciences. Of course, it is possible to be naturalist about certain entities and nonnaturalist about others, but naturalism tends to be more of a general outlook and tendency among philosophers. Naturalism is most properly seen as a guiding philosophical intuition concerning the commitment to *rejection* of certain kinds of entities seen as violating a broadly physicalistic worldview.

To refer to metaphysical views in traditions like those of the ancient Maya or Chinese as "naturalistic," then, is somewhat misleading. Naturalism as it has developed in the contemporary philosophical context is dependent on modern science as the ground for understanding reality. Neither Maya nor Chinese thought can be considered naturalistic in this sense; thus if we call either of them naturalistic, we must have some different conception in mind. Janghee Lee offers an account of the early Chinese philosopher Xunzi as accepting a kind of naturalism distinct from contemporary forms. He explains:

By "naturalism," I mean an ancient Chinese philosophical orientation that seeks the source of normativity in the natural realm. In ancient China, the notion of "transcendence"—the notion of absolute deity or the conception of the Platonic "Forms"—never occupied a central position in philosophical discourse. As a result, it seemed perfectly natural for philosophers to turn to the "naturalness," or "spontaneity" of nature to find the source or value of guidance for a way of life.[11]

This definition of naturalism is still somewhat vague, as it uses the concept of nature and the idea of naturalness to explain what naturalism is. What we should want in a definition of naturalism is some account of just what one means by "nature" or "naturalness" in the first place. I think we can modify Lee's account, however, by referring to *worlds* as the key to the idea of naturalness. He notes the "natural realm" as a commitment of the Chinese naturalist, and I think it is the "realm" part of this that we should focus on. While neither the ancient Maya nor the ancient Chinese could be considered naturalist on a contemporary conception, they do both accept the view that there is a single unified world, a cosmos in which everything can *potentially* interact with everything else. This view must be qualified, of course. While "naturalists" in this sense in early China accepted what they called "the unity of nature and humanity," the early Chinese tradition as a whole cannot be called naturalist in this sense. That is, I disagree with Lee's view that the notion of transcendence played a minor role in early Chinese philosophy. The kind of "one world naturalism" found in certain texts was opposed to a conception of transcendence found in other, sometimes opposing, texts. Much like we today see a dispute between scientific naturalism and religious nonnaturalism, somewhat similar oppositions played out in early China—though of course the issues and the sides were not exactly the same as they are in our contemporary debates.

Since it is the issue of the unity or duality of worlds that is primarily at issue in both the Maya and the Chinese case, I suggest that we dispense with "naturalism" as a way of framing the issue, and instead focus on the issue of worlds—the number, interaction, and nature of worlds. I argue below that for the Maya, as for a certain tradition in Chinese thought, there is a single world containing potentially interactive and ultimately unified objects. The Maya and Chinese views about the first of these claims—potential interaction—is almost the same. It is in their explanation of the second—the unified nature of objects, that the Maya and Chinese views show interesting differences.

We can put the issue here in terms of monism versus pluralism (including dualism) about worlds. The monist view, roughly, is that there is a single world including potentially interacting objects, governed by the same laws (although these may act differently in different locations in this single world), and that there are no existent entities that are not subject to these laws, that is, transcendent or potentially non-interacting. The pluralist view is that there is more than one world, independently governed by different laws that do not apply to one another, and that entities in these worlds are potentially noninteracting with entities in other worlds. The issue of monism versus pluralism (generally dualism) comes up in other related areas as well—most importantly for our purposes, monism versus dualism about the substances of mind and body. According to a monist view, mind and body are not distinct substances, and should be understood as ultimately constituted by the same thing. (Cartesian) dualism, on the other hand, is that the two are wholly distinct (but potentially interacting) substances, neither of which contains any aspect of the other. This substance conception of mind and body is not generally accepted in contemporary philosophy of mind, and is far more at home in seventeenth- and eighteenth-century Western philosophy. But for purposes of understanding Maya thought, understanding mind and body as substance(s) is far more illuminating, as the Maya conception of the person relies on the person as something like a substance, with "essences"

In most Western philosophy after the medieval period, consideration of ontological monism versus dualism tended to surround issues in the philosophy of mind and the relationship between mind and body. In the realm of *worlds*, there is relatively little consideration of the possibility of ontologically distinct worlds, outside of the considerations of ontology of modality and possible worlds, which is based on very different considerations than those we are concerned with here.[12] Despite the issue of ontologically distinct worlds being a major feature of the thought of major Western philosophers such as Plato, the medieval Christian philosophers, and perhaps Immanuel Kant, in contemporary philosophy there is little focus on the issue, likely due mainly to the widespread contemporary acceptance of scientific naturalism. There is a single world, and its principles are physicalistic and causally unified. This monistic position is somewhat close to that of numerous early Chinese schools and the Maya view, but there are also key differences between these views. The most important distinction is that while the early Chinese and Maya views are *monistic*, they are not *physicalist*. One of the features definitive of physicalist monism is that all causal interactions are ultimately physical. There is only physical causation, as the single kind active within our world. In other systems, causal connection is understood in terms of more fundamental processes that involve physical but also nonphysical elements of the world.[13]

The nature of basic ontologies and thought about them tends to cluster into consideration of the *number* of different kinds of entity in any account of reality, and the relationships between these entities. At perhaps the most basic level, the ontology concerning the *world* or cosmos is center stage. While this issue is not prominent in most contemporary philosophy, it was a major issue throughout the history of philosophy both in the West and elsewhere in the world. There are numerous historical philosophers who held the view that there are numerous (two or more) ontologically distinct worlds, and others who hold that there is only one, but who deal with the possibility of numerous worlds and argue against it. Perhaps the earliest Western conception of a many-worlds view is that of Plato.[14]

Other kinds of dualism have received less philosophical attention, and are subtly different than Platonic dualism. Scholars of religion have paid more attention to these distinctions, as the issue of multiplicity of worlds (most often dualism) is still seen as a *live* issue in religion, unlike in philosophy. Many, perhaps even *most* religions (certainly all theistic religions) accept many-world ontology.

Religious scholar Ugo Bianchi has a useful definition of dualism (of the *worlds* kind with which I am concerned here). Bianchi's position is that what determines ontological distinctness is causation. Causal principles are key, in that a world can be determined on the basis of a causally closed system.

> dualism may be defined as a doctrine that posits the existence of two funda-
> mental causal principles underlying the existence ... of the world. In addition,
> dualistic doctrines, worldviews, or myths represent the basic components of the
> world or of man as participating in the ontological opposition and disparity of
> value that characterize their dual principles.[15]

That is, everything existing in some particular world is causally connected to some world-initiating principle, and all things not so connected are not inhabitants of that world. This is a difficult definition of a world to maintain for those who accept numerous ontologically distinct worlds, however, because there is generally a *connection*, including causal connection, between these distinct worlds. Indeed, any view holding there to be numerous worlds with no causal connection between these worlds would collapse into a form of what we might call "agnostic monism"—nothing could be known or said about any possible other worlds, as this would entail causal connection between the worlds that would undermine their status as distinct worlds.

It may be difficult to offer a general account of dualism or many-worlds ontology that avoids this pitfall. Many-worlds accounts all offer *some* connection between worlds, or access points between worlds. We have to look at particular accounts to understand how worlds can be seen as ontologically distinct and yet having some effect on one another. The causal account cannot supply a good explanation. Indeed, a causal account like that of Bianchi runs into the very same problem that ultimately derailed Descartes' substance dualism concerning mind and body. If two things, substances, worlds, etc. are completely causally distinct, insofar as they contain nothing of one another, how can they have any effect on the other whatsoever? That is, there can be no causal connection between two ontologically completely distinct things, and so to make the claim of ontological distinction is to sever the causal link. In which case, mental causation of the physical becomes impossible. The problem with Bianchi's definition of dualism is that in accepting a radical Cartesian view of dualism as applied to worlds, it is rendered impossible for there to be any kind of connection between worlds, including even knowledge of other worlds.

THEISTIC VIEWS OF WORLDS

There is a somewhat different conception of distinct worlds in theistic views. The human realm and the divine realm are the two fundamental aspects of reality, and the two can be understood in terms of ontologically distinct worlds, as the human world is subject to laws, contingent, non-eternal, and separated from the divine world, which is God itself. In the Christian and Islamic traditions, the Platonic distinction between the physical world and the world of Forms was applied to this human-divine distinction. Thus, it is no surprise that we see echoes of the Platonic view when looking at early Christian and Islamic philosophy. One of the key distinctions between the human and divine realm, according to many theistic thinkers, is the absence of critical features such as time in the divine realm. The Andalusian Sufi thinker Ibn Al-Arabi (1165–1240) wrote:

> even if we describe ourselves as He [God] describes himself, in all possible aspects, there would still remain an inevitable factor of distinction [between Him and us]. This [factor] is our dependence on Him for existence, which, in our case, derives entirely from Him because we are originated while He is free of all dependence whatsoever. Thus is He rightly called the One without beginning, the Ancient of Days, contradicting all priority in the sense of existence starting from nonexistence. For, although He is the First, no temporal priority may be attributed of Him. Thus He is called also the Last.[16]

Here, it is the cause, origin, and features of the worlds (humanity and the divine) that make them ontologically distinct. This kind of dualism fits well with Ugo Bianchi's definition, and indeed this kind of theistic many-world ontology was just what Bianchi was motivated to capture with his definition of dualism. Even the fact that he refers to it as "dualism" suggests this. There is no particular reason that a many-world ontology should limit itself to two, rather than five or twenty-two worlds, but in theistic many-world views we tend to see only two, a natural human world of physical objects, change, and (normal) time, and a divine world, uncaused, eternal, and necessary. This dualism in much of Western (particularly Christian and Islamic) theology and philosophy owes much to Plato's world dualism. The divine "realm" is the realm of the Forms, and plays much the same role in these systems of thought as the Forms do in Plato's thought.

Ibn Al-Arabi's theism, however, is an interesting case, because while he does not seem to deny the fundamental Islamic view of the distinction between God and the world, the human and divine realms, he also holds that they are fundamentally united through one reality. This is the core of Al-Arabi's mysticism, and Sufi mysticism in general. Does this give us a different kind of picture than that we see in early Chinese thought? The view that there is overall one single unified reality is one we find in a number of different traditions and philosophical contexts, even where it would otherwise seem that there are ontological distinctions made concerning worlds. Not all monistic views concerning worlds are the same. One key issue at stake here is the question of just what unifies these worlds, or if there are any fundamental distinctions between worlds to be unified in the first place.

As I argued above, there can be no system of thought that coherently posits causally distinct, completely separate, and ontologically distinct worlds. We would have no way of accessing these distinct worlds even to gain knowledge of their existence. The most we could do would be to *guess* concerning their existence, and it is even doubtful that the results of these guesses would be *about* the other worlds in question. *"Some* other world exists" would be the result of our guesswork, and this may turn out to be true. But it could neither qualify as *knowledge* nor could it be *about* whatever other world exists.

The answer Ibn Arabi offers to this problem, similar to Plato's answer, is to make the human the meeting point between two worlds, in some sense inhabiting both. The connection between these worlds is primarily through the human, and thus we do not need to access other worlds because we are already fundamentally part of them. R.W.J. Austin writes, in his introduction to his translation of *Fusus al-Hikam*:

> within the context of the divine-cosmic polarity, man, and especially the Perfect Man, constitutes the all-important link or medium between the two poles of Reality; the Isthmus [*barzakh*] as Ibn al-Arabi calls him. Having called man the link, however, it is necessary to point out that any link is important only so long as it serves to effect communication and relationship between things that are real in themselves, the link itself having no meaning per se, except by reference to the things it links. Thus man, considered in himself and by himself, is an absurdity, while assuming enormous significance when considered within the context of the polarity God-Cosmos.[17]

While there are hosts of gods in ancient Maya thought, it is unclear that they represent different or transcendent worlds in the way seen in theistic systems. It is even unclear that the numerous gods inhabit a distinct divine world separate from the human world, so that we have a kind of dualism somewhat akin to theistic dualism.

Alfredo López-Austin argues that there is nothing like a mind-body substance dualism to be found anywhere in Mesoamerican thought in general, and that "the embodiment of psychic entities is quite apparent."[18] If this is the case, then it also damages our reasons to believe that there is a multi-world ontology in ancient Maya thought as well. There are scholars on both sides of this divide, with Knowlton, Lopez-Austin, Maffie, among others, on the side of some kind of monism, and those we have seen above, such as Kappelman, Schele, Friedel, and Thompson on the side of dualism or many-worlds. If López-Austin is right that the evidence we have is not enough to show that there is an ontological mind-body distinction, then insofar as the evidence for a multi-world ontology is of the same kind, it also cannot show that the Maya held such a view.

But this, notice, is insufficient in itself to show that the Maya had either a single-world ontology or no distinction between mind and body as substances. To establish that, we need positive evidence of such views, not just a criticism of the evidence brought to establish it. While perhaps we cannot offer such positive evidence directly from the written and other materials of the ancient Maya, the analogical argument drawing from the similarities between early Chinese views on worlds and what we see in Maya thought can be helpful for offering a possible reconstruction.

Ultimately there is a better way to explain the Maya view than deferring to numerous worlds. The ancient Maya view is much closer to a position found in early Chinese thought concerning worlds (especially in the early Han dynasty) than it is to the views of the theistic philosophers of the West.

WORLDS IN EARLY CHINESE PHILOSOPHY

In much of early Chinese thought, there is a focus on seemingly distinct worlds as unified in one single *dao* 道(Way). The philosophy of the early Han period in particular is focused on such metaphysical issues, concerning the generation and nature of the cosmos. The question that motivates Plato seems to be in the background here as well—that is, how can we make sense of stability within change? The early Han thinkers offer a very different solution to this problem than does either Plato or Aristotle, however—but one that shares some elements with both.

Early Han thinkers in general tend to prefer a response that tends toward the Parmenidean response or that of the Vedantic schools of India that gives ontological priority to the single and unchanging over the multiple and changing. The truly real (in terms of having the greatest *degree* of reality—an idea discussed in medieval European thought but not much since the early modern period in the West) is *dao*—the Way itself. All things both *arise from* this Way and are unified in it. While the early Han thinkers do not deny the reality of multiplicity and change, they view these as manifestations of the single and unchanging *dao*. As such, the single world is understood as grounded in *dao*, and knowledge as well as thriving comes through understanding of this single *dao* inherent in all things.

The opening lines of the *Huainanzi* discuss the relationship between the "myriad things" and *dao*:

> As for the Way: it covers heaven and upholds earth. It extends the four directions and divides the eight end points. ... It embraces and enfolds heaven and earth, it endows and bestows the formless. ... Therefore, pile it up vertically: it fills all within heaven and earth.[19]

This all-pervading quality of *dao* is also understood as having a causal connection to the essential features of all things (akin to the claim in the *Bhagavad Gita* of Krishna's potency). It is *dao* that makes all things what they are, that gives them their characteristic features. The first part of *Huainanzi* continues:

> Mountains are high because of it. Abysses are deep because of it. Beasts can run because of it. Birds can fly because of it. The sun and moon are bright because of it. The stars and timekeepers move because of it.[20]

Dao seems to be a creative principle, a ground of being, and also an animating force. At the same time, *dao* is something humans can intuitively comprehend, and this comprehension leads to skillful action and ultimately thriving life. It is a complex and puzzling concept, which the *Huainanzi* and other texts that discuss it seem perfectly content in letting us struggle with understanding. In Daoist and early Han syncretist texts, from *Daodejing* and *Zhuangzi* through *Huainanzi, Shizi*, and others, we see two main categories of views concerning *dao*: *dao* as creative principle or source, and *dao* as source of (often intuitive) knowledge or skill. The first chapter of *Huainanzi, Yuandao* 原道 ("Origins and the Way"), discusses *dao* as origin, and the origin of *dao*. The title as given is somewhat ambiguous. To render it as literally as possible, it could be called "Source/origin Dao." This could mean a number of different things, however; all consistent with the Chinese rendering. Most importantly, the two main possibilities are that it is discussing the origin of *dao* or alternatively that it is discussing origins of the world in *dao*. There is no consensus on this among translators. Major et al., render it "Originating in the Way" while Roger Ames translates it "Tracing *Dao* to its Source." These both involve choices concerning the subject matter of the chapter, which is difficult enough to discern. The chapter does open with a discussion of *dao*, what it is, where it is, and its other important features. But it is unclear whether the purpose of this is to explain the origins of *dao*, or to explain the features of *dao* relevant in the generation of the cosmos. After the opening passages of the chapter, it becomes clear that the focus shifts to the second meaning or property of *dao* as something that humans can access and understand that leads to skillful action and thriving life. The decision then must be largely based on whether one thinks that the title refers to the information in this second section concerning understanding and use of *dao*, or the beginning passages speaking of origins and creation. Whichever is chosen, the other can be understood as in the service of it. So the text, as so often happens in ancient thought, does not ultimately help us determine the proper understanding. It is possible, of course, that this is purposeful. The authors of the *Yuandao* chapter could have left this purposefully ambiguous so as to suggest that *both* of these readings are correct, and thus point us toward an important feature of *dao* first discussed in depth by *Zhuangzi*—that is, *dao* is not found in oppositions and selection of "this" over "not-this." Indeed, this is one of the major themes of the *Huainanzi* itself, which (among other things) attempts to create a synthesis between seemingly disparate schools, traditions, texts, and thinkers, in an attempt to explain how they are all rooted in a single *dao*.[21]

In an early passage of *Yuandao*, the authors discuss the creative activity of the mythical Fuxi and Nuwa, who were responsible for the creation of the cosmos. It explains their efficacy in terms of the use of *dao*, which was prior and all-pervading even then.

> The two August Lords of high antiquity grasped the handles of the Way and so were established in the center. Their spirits mysteriously roamed together with all transformations and thereby pacified the four directions. ... they ended and began together with all things.[22]

Humans often fail to fully understand *dao*, but this is not due to any ontological distinction between worlds. The cosmos is unified completely through *dao*, and there is no other world than this. While the human ignorance of the Forms and thus lack of knowledge is attributed to failure to access the realm of the Forms according to Plato, in *Yuandao*, human ignorance of *dao* is attributed to the silent, unapparent, and *xuan* 玄 (mysterious) quality of *dao*. One important passage concerning this reads:

> The most exalted Way generates the myriad things but does not possess them, completes the transforming images (*ba gua*) but does not dominate them. Creatures that walk on hooves and breathe through beaks, that fly through the air and wriggle on the ground, depend on it for life, yet none understands its Potency.[23]

Perhaps the most potent statement of one-world naturalism in early Chinese thought comes in the *Chunqiu Fanlu*, which speaks about the "unity" between nature or heaven and humanity. The formulations seen in the *Chunqiu Fanlu* itself are numerous:

> 天人之際，合而為一
>
> The boundaries between nature and humanity unify and become one.[24]
>
> 以類合之，天人一也
>
> Unifying the types, nature and humanity are one.[25]

The *Chunqiu Fanlu* speaks in terms of *unifying* nature and humanity—a unity that would not be possible if the two inhabited or were the bases of two ontologically distinct worlds. Nature and humanity, while possibly alienated from one another through human actions or ignorance, are essentially connected to the same *dao*, and thus understanding of this *dao* allows the sage understanding of how the two are unified, and enables him or her to express, make clear, and more importantly practically use this unity.

This can be further seen in a statement made by Han dynasty philosopher Yang Xiong in his *Fayan*, concerning the efficacy of the sage's action:

> 聖人存神索至，成天下之大順，致天下之大利，和同天人之際，使之無間也
>
> The sage preserves the spirit and seeks finality, completes the great following along of the world, achieves the great benefit of the world, harmonizes and brings together the boundaries between nature and humanity, causing there to be no space between them.[26]

According to the text *Hanshi Wai Zhuan*, proper governance can eliminate or unify the boundaries between nature and humanity. This comes very close to something we see in Maya thought, concerning the role of the ruler in accessing and using information that only he can understand and a skill that only he possesses to bring into alignment two *aspects* of the cosmos. A passage reads:

善為政者、循情性之宜，順陰陽之序，通本末之理，合天人之際

Those who well establish proper governance follow the correct (dictates) of
affective states and human nature, go along with the ordering of *yin* and *yang*,
express the principle connecting root and branches, unify the boundaries of
nature and humanity.[27]

Clearly in much of the early Chinese tradition through the Han dynasty
nature and humanity are *unifiable* and not ontologically distinct worlds. The
knowledge and ability of the sage is not a kind of supernatural or shamanic
ability that allows the sage to access transcendent worlds or accords on him
an ability to move between otherwise inaccessible realms. Rather, becoming
a sage is a matter of attaining an understanding of *dao*, in which nature and
humanity and all things are unified, in order to bring back into alignment with
dao people and things that have moved away from understanding, through
conceptualization and other obstacles that have got in the way of human
understanding. Thus, the sage's (re)discovery of *dao* is more akin to the person with developed vision being able to see things that those with corrupted
vision cannot (but that are within the same world that those others inhabit)
than it is to a person's shamanic access to distinct worlds that normal people
simply cannot access.

Indeed, in the Chinese case, the widespread and clear belief in a single
ontologically unified world was so strong that outside traditions attempting
to justify themselves in Chinese terms strove to make their many-world views
more palatable by putting them into unified naturalist or monist terms. We see
such in the writings of the sixteenth-century Chinese Islamic thinker Wang
Daiyu. In Wang's "Real Commentary on the True Teaching" (*Zhengjiao
Zhenquan*), a basic overview of Islamic teachings including responses to
(real and imagined) questions of non-Islamic interlocutors, he describes the
creation of humanity and a verse from the *Quran* suggesting that there are
different time scales for humanity and God—"one day with the Lord is one
thousand years to your counting." (*Surat al-Hajj*, 22:47)[28]

In the Chinese case, it is clear that the realms of nature and humanity
are not distinct but rather part of the same world, and the *unification* that
the early texts speak about is in terms of discovery, expression, and transmission of this fact. In the same way that the sage brings order to society
through expression and transmission of the *natural* rituals that order human
behavior and society,[29] the sage "unifies" nature and humanity through the
expression and transmission of his knowledge of the contours of nature and
how to follow them. This following is suggested in the *Fayan*'s use of the
expression 天下之大順 ("the great following along of the world") from
the above-cited passage. We can see then that the ability of a specialized

individual (or group) to access certain key features of reality and bring them into alignment with the normally accessible world does not in itself entail a many-world ontology. This picture is complicated, of course, by the existence of an alternative strain of thought running through Chinese philosophy that appears to accept a kind of dualism about worlds, and which is fortified by the adoption and thriving of Buddhism in China during the early centuries CE.

ITZ, UNIFICATION OF WORLDS, AND TRUTH

Kappelman follows a number of other authors in making the claim that the shamanic system of the ancient Maya was based on a multiple world position, in which the shaman has access to other worlds.[30] These worlds are connected by a central axis—the tree of creation, or some other central construction.

The explanation of the god Itzamna and the property of *itz* is read through this multi-world ontology. I think the multi-world ontology makes a bit of a mess of the mythology of Itzamna and the property of *itz*. As Kappelman discusses,[31] *itz* is associated with a number of natural substances in Yucatec, such as "milk, nectar, dew, juice, and bodily fluids such as sweat, semen, and tears."[32] Barrera-Vasquez's dictionary also points out that it is "a morpheme, whose significance is related to ideas of knowledge, magic, and occult power."[33] I argue in this section that *itz* should be seen as a concept expressing the unification of different aspects of the world, seen and unseen, and that we might profitably understand this unification along the lines of the early Chinese view outlined above. An additional feature of *itz*, I argue below, is its expression of a concept of truth in Maya thought, one that shares features with the concept of truth outlined in the *Zhuangzi* and *Huainanzi* in the Chinese tradition, which focuses on truth primarily as a feature of persons and things (物 *wu*), rather than statements (言 *yan*). Thinking about the parallels between the Maya and Chinese views here can help us reveal an element of the concept of *itz* as "core" or "essence." This can also show how *itz* may be related to *truth* more generally, in its non-semantic as well as semantic forms.

Itz is a difficult concept in Maya texts, and is not well understood. It may be understood as "cosmic essence," "sap," "spirit," or "vital fluid." There seems to be a connotation to liquid essence in colonial dictionaries of Yucatec Mayan, with meanings of *itz* including "milk, tears, sweat, sap, resin," and the above-mentioned elements.[34] *Itz* as vital energy is closely related to the concept of *ch'ul*, as Friedel, Schele, and Parker note.[35] *Ch'ul* is the vital essence or spirit seen as contained within human blood. One way we might understand *ch'ul* is as the particular human aspect of *itz*. *Itz*, as pervading the cosmos, is manifest in humans as *ch'ul*. We can see in a number of rituals the connection between these two concepts—particularly in the well-known ritual of royal bloodletting. The practice is well attested in Maya imagery and texts. Rulers and other important nobles drew their own blood by piercing their genitals, lips, or tongues. This was offered as sacrifice in rituals that were intended to give access to the invisible spiritual elements of the world. The rulers, through this sacrifice, played the role of intermediary between the people and the spiritual elements of the world. It was through the *ch'ul* of the blood, which manifested a particular human *itz*, that this was possible.

A set of carved lintels from the city of Yaxchilan demonstrates the significance of the bloodletting sacrifice. In the first of these, the queen Lady Xoc draws blood through piercing her tongue, kneeling before her husband, the ruler Itzamnaaj Balam II. This depiction of the bloodletting ritual is followed in the second lintel by the appearance of an anthropomorphic serpent before Lady Xoc, representing the access to the unseen and extramundane aspects of the world that the ritual creates.[36] The serpent rises from the ritual vessel containing Lady Xoc's blood, suggesting that the blood itself has the power to conjure this vision. It is the *ch'ul* in this blood that allows for the manifestation.

A number of scholars have concluded that *itz* is a more general potency of fluids, and that it is linked to esoteric knowledge.[37] Barrera-Vasquez wrote that *itz* is "a morpheme whose significance is related to ideas of knowledge, magic, occult power."[38] *Itz*, like *ch'ul* as a particular type of *itz*, has the potential to reveal unseen or hidden aspects of the world to humans, because it serves as a link between these various elements of the world, human and nonhuman, visible and esoteric. It is in this way that the *itzam* (one who manipulates *itz*) accesses the unseen world and makes it manifest to humans. The *itzam* is a sage or shaman who understands and can direct *itz*.[39] This direction or control of *itz* is not a matter of manipulating it based on the will of the *itzam*, but rather of revealing the full operation of *itz*, including its hidden features, to humans. The *itzam* is able to pull away the veil to show the operation of *itz*.

How might we understand the connection between *itz* and *ch'ul*? The most likely explanation is that *ch'ul* is a particular type of *itz* possessed by humans. We see a very similar view in the early Chinese text *Huainanzi* concerning the relationship between *qi* 氣 (vital energy) and *jingshen* 精神 (pure spirit). *Jingshen*, according to the text, is a particular human manifestation of *qi*. It is a type of *qi* that only humans possess, and what distinguishes humans from nonhumans. All things in the cosmos have (or are constituted by) *qi*, but there are different kinds of *qi*, and the *qi* of humans is a more purified *qi* than that of other things in the world. This is what allows humans to understand *qi* and the inherent patterns in the world in a way that other things cannot. We might

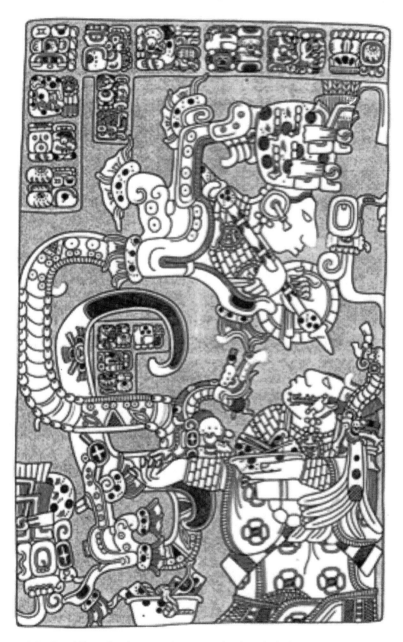

Figure 3.2 Yaxchilan Lintel 25. Lady Xoc (right) kneels before an anthropomorphic vision serpent rising from the blood she has drawn in the bloodletting sacrifice. Lintel 25, waxaklahun-uban-kan (the war snake) appears with tok'-pakal and lady k'abal xok. Drawing by Linda Schele © David Schele. Photo courtesy Ancient Americas at LACMA.

understand the connection between *itz* and *ch'ul* along these same lines. While *ch'ul* is a particular human quality, it is nothing more than *itz*. This of course raises the question (for the Maya and Chinese views both) of how *itz* (or *qi*) can be obscure, turbid, or less than fully manifest, if it is understood as simply the vital essence of things. Some Chinese thinkers[40] refer to the *amount* of *qi* a thing possesses as making the difference in its abilities as opposed to the abilities of others. But on the account of the *Huainanzi*, and on the Maya account of *itz* and *ch'ul*, this quantity answer seems problematic. Nowhere in Maya accounts do we see any evidence that things possess varying quantities of *itz*, or that *itz* is even the kind of thing that permits of quantity. To call it, as Friedel, Schele, and Parker do, the "cosmic sap" captures the pervasiveness of *itz*, but incorrectly suggests a quantity account. One thing might be more "sappy" than another, for example. *Itz*, however, is within everything. There is nowhere it is not. It is evenly distributed through the world, as it is the vital essence that allows the world to act as it does. Even this language does not capture it, however. *Itz* is not distributed at all, because it does not admit of quantity. In this way, *itz* is a concept closer to that of "the good" or "the noble." Goodness or nobility exists where it does, not in greater or lesser quantity, but as itself whole or not at all. Even closer to *itz* is a concept like "life." A plant lives and a human lives—although they live in very different ways, one is not *more* alive than another. Life is a concept that does not admit of quantity. In some philosophical traditions, the concept of life is very relevant, as it suggests motion, purposiveness, and perhaps agency. In Native American traditions more generally (including that of the Maya and Aztecs), life is seen as a pervasive quality animating the cosmos.[41] *Itz* is close to this conception, as is *qi*. *Qi*, however, diverges from this enough to be understood in terms of type, quality, and quantity of *qi*. It is for this reason I think that *itz* is best translated as "vital essence," as many translate the Chinese *qi*. It plays a similar determinative role, in fixing the capacities of individuals and things. It is also the medium through which we can understand and communicate with everything else in the cosmos, including that which is unseen. This is only possible if it is the same and single *itz* that links and ultimately unifies all things.

This understanding of *itz*, as unifying essence of things, suggests another meaning of *itz* that may have been accepted by the ancient Maya—*itz* as *truth*. While there are no direct statements in Maya texts suggesting that *itz* is used to predicate truth to statements, persons, or anything else, we can find indirect evidence in the use of *itz* in connection with certain deities as well as its etymology to suggest that *itz* was understood as expressing a concept of truth.

There is a connection between the concept of *itz* and the centrally important god Itzamna of the Yucatan Maya tradition. The term as a number of senses that are linked to a single concept. *Itz*, in addition to the "vital essence" described above, refers to a causally efficacious property of things that links entities of the world in a correspondentist metaphysics as well as a broader concept of truth (both semantic and non-semantic). Truth here

Figure 3.3   The itz glyph. Drawing by the author.

should be understood in terms of having an essence that matches an ideal, in the way we might call someone a "true friend" or a "true person." We can see this by attending to features of the god Itzamna as well as various uses of the term *itz*.

The god Itzamna (in Yucatec Mayan), also referred to as "God D," while accounted for in numerous regions of the Maya area, was the central god in the Yucatan, prized in importance over all the others.[42] There is some controversy behind the meaning of name of the deity, as a number of views have been advanced. An early view by scholars in the 1960s and 1970s held that Itzamna should be translated as "lizard house," with *itzam* meaning "lizard" or "iguana."[43] It is more likely, however, that *itzam* is meant in another sense, "sage" or "shaman." This sense of the word draws on the concept of *itz*, with the *itzam* being one who understands and can direct *itz*.[44]

Itzamna was associated with scribes and with knowledge, among other things, and can be understood as the first or quintessential scribe. Like the other gods of the Maya, Itzamna included a variety of different aspects, and could be manifest in many ways, including as the serpent (associated with Kukulcan)[45] and the Milky Way itself,[46] which also represented the World Tree linking all aspects of the world to one another. Itzamna, as chief god (in the Yucatan) was associated with the ruler as well. And most interestingly for our purposes, Itzamna was associated with the ruler/shaman's ability to see the unseen aspects of the world and to see into the future. This association is made through the identifying glyph sometimes associated with Itzamna, *akbal*, which means "darkness, blackness." Lynn Foster writes:

> [this] may represent the polished black surface of an obsidian mirror. The polished black surfaces of such mirrors were important devices that allowed shamans to see past and future events. As an attribute of Itzamna, the obsidian mirror suggests an important function of the god.[47]

These features of Itzamna all suggest a connection between the god and the essence represented by *itz*, manifest in rulership, literature, and shamanic vision. All of these capture a sense of *truth* in terms of fulfillment of an ideal. One way to understand the concept of truth, although one that has gone neglected for the most part in much contemporary philosophical literature on the topic, is truth as concept of *substantiality* or *fullness*.[48] When we use truth in the sense of "true person" or "true friend," this is the operative concept. One can make a case that there is a general concept of truth including this sense of truth and the semantic sense of truth meant when we call something a "true statement." Truth as substantiality or fullness can capture both of these. The true friend and the true statement share in common that they both fully meet an ideal of the entity in question. The fullest expression of the statement is the one that mirrors reality, and the fullest expression of the friend is one who acts in the ways a friend is expected to—their actions match the ideal of friendship.

We see just such a conception of truth developed in the Han dynasty in early China, I argue. The concept of *shi* 實 is just such a concept of truth, and the etymology of this term tracks the development of the kind of concept I discuss above. The concept of *shi* has a rich and complex history in early Chinese thought. According to the *Shuowen Jiezi*, it has the sense of the core of a plant, a fruit.[49] This led to its early use in a sense close to our "substance"—the substantial or valuable part of a given thing. This could be a property of anything—persons, governments, or teachings. It is not limited to an appraisal of language. In the Western tradition, truth tends to be seen as a linguistic property, and a certain kind of linguistic property, belonging to a narrow subset of linguistic entities. This is certainly how it is seen in most contemporary Western philosophy, but this conception of truth is nothing new to Western thought. It reaches back all the way to the beginnings. The early modern French philosopher Rene Descartes, for example, thought of truth as a property of certain (linguistically accessible) ideas. It is only *judgments*, of all of the classes of ideas we can have, that can take a truth value.[50] Perceptions, as such, cannot take a truth value, nor can volitions—these being the two other classes of ideas. The reason that these two other kinds of ideas cannot have truth value is that something is only true or false insofar as it makes a statement about matters of fact. A perception is a representation, perhaps of anything. The perception itself does not include an assertion, however, that this perception is based on matter of fact, rather than simply being a figment of one's imagination, a hallucination, etc. Descartes sees truth as narrowly applicable to statements asserting claims about the way the world is independently of our perception of the world. Thus truth, according to Descartes, is epistemological and linguistic in basis—it has to do with the accuracy of our assessments of our perceptions, insofar as they mirror the mind (and idea)-independent world.

Such a conception of truth is probably the most influential on contemporary conception of truth, but even this has its origins earlier in Western thought, in the Ancient Greeks. In the work of Plato, the concept of truth is broader than the linguistic/epistemological concept of Descartes, but this is one *aspect* of the more robust concept of truth as a whole. We might see the history of Western philosophy as focusing ever closer in on this single aspect of the original Platonic conception of truth, until in contemporary thought philosophers only really ever deal with the issue of truth insofar as it concerns a property of assertoric linguistic entities.

Figure 3.4   Maya World Tree, with Itzam Yeh (the bird deity) perched on the top, emanating from the crocodile. Detail of world tree, sarcophagus cover, temple of inscriptions. Drawing by Linda Schele © David Schele. Photo courtesy of Ancient Americas at LACMA.

Itz expresses a concept of truth very close to that of *shi* discussed here. It also turns out that the etymology of the term may be similar to that of *shi*.

The glyph for *itz* is comprised of two major parts: the infixed glyph *ak'ab* in the center, surrounded by petals and stamen of a flower.[51] One of the meanings of the word *ak'ab* is "tongue," and the flower petals and stamen here suggest *potency* or effectiveness. This is very close to the "core" and "fruit" understanding of *shi* that became the basis for a concept of truth. But with the glyph of *itz*, it is possible that the linguistic aspect of truth is built into the word originally. *Ak'ab* (tongue) could very well signify *speech*, such that *itz* originally signifies the potency, effectiveness, or fullness of speech or statements. We see in the development of the Chinese concept of *shi* that it is first applied to nonlinguistic objects and only later comes to be understood as connected to statements. It may be the case for *itz*, if my reading is correct, that it first signified *linguistic* truth and later came to be applied to nonlinguistic entities. The beginnings of the concept of *itz* in linguistic truth would certainly help make sense of the connection of the god Itzamna with scribes, as mentioned above. Scribes aim to produce work that manifests *itz* in the sense of fullness or potency of statements.

There is a clear connection of this sense of *itz* to that of the "vital essence" of all things in the cosmos, linking them all, and through which the *itzam* (sage, shaman, one who directs *itz*) can reveal unseen aspects of the world. Beginning as the fullness or potency of words and language, the concept of *itz* likely expanded over time to mean the fullness or potency of things in general. Both a generalized concept of truth, and a concept of the feature of things that makes them effective or potent, the vital essence that animates them and makes them what they are. The shaman is one who is able to access the *itz* inherent in all things because of the uniquely potent manifestation of his or her own *itz* (in the form of *ch'ul*).

What the *itz* accesses and reveals through this "manipulation" is that *itz* must be considered elements of a single unified world. A multi-world approach here is unsatisfying, because the reason that the *itzam* can access the unseen is through accessing *itz,* which as we have seen is a common feature of all things that links them and through which they can be understood, while the multi-world claim seems to entail that *itz* is accessible by shamans because only they can access the other worlds. If these other worlds are based on *itz* as a fundamental feature, then how can they be considered as distinct from our own in any robust way? Friedel, Schele, and Parker understand the shaman as one with access to the other world or worlds, and can thus control or manipulate *itz*.[52] If *itz* is the substance of the otherworld, then how can it be and why is it associated with features of our own world, such as natural substances associated with humans and natural objects, such as *ch'ul*? If those elements of the world reveal something of the otherworld, then it seems that the two worlds are too closely linked to indeed be two *different* or ontologically distinct worlds. *Itz* is a pervasive feature of our own world, and the ruler/shaman has unique access to it. But is this power closer to the power of the intercessor between humanity and God as we see in Christian and Islamic notions of rulership, or is it akin to the power of sage knowledge that we see in the Chinese tradition?

THE WORLD TREE

The primary image in Maya thought from ancient times to the present of the structure unifying all aspects of the cosmos is the "World Tree" or cross.[53] The tree represents the cord connecting the underworld (Xibalba), the middle world, and the upper world, and rulers are often represented as somehow being masters of or aware of how to travel along the world tree. Some imagery even *identifies* the ruler with the World Tree, as does Stela C at Copan, which presents Waxaklajuun U'baah Kawil in the form of a crocodile with the World Tree emerging from his body.[54] In the tree is the bird deity (Itzam Yeh), associated with creation and often found depicted in World Tree imagery.

The imagery of the memorials of the city of Izapa, in Group A in particular, seems to demonstrate that the ruler also identified himself with the bird deity, and also that there was bird imagery connected to the story of the Hero Twins (best known from the *Popol Vuh*), but there seems to be little evidence that the bird imagery from the Hero Twin imagery corresponds to the ruler-as-bird image, or that the World Tree plays the role of the connection between worlds that the ruler is able to access. Surely, the ruler as shaman has some kind of elemental power that the people in general are unable to access and on which they rely. The *ch'ul* of the ruler is such that, as sharing essence with the World Tree itself, the ruler has broader access to the world than does the average person. This allows the ruler to communicate with and otherwise access entities in parts of the world the rest of us are barred from.

The symbol of a tree representing the cosmos and its branches pointing toward the four directions is a ubiquitous feature of Maya thought. The most famous depiction of the world tree in Classic Period imagery is from the sarcophagus lid of the Palenque ruler Janaab Pakal (discussed in chapter 2). Here, Pakal is represented as entering into Xibalba through the World Tree, which itself serves as link between these parts of the world. In addition to representing the four corners of the world (based on the cardinal directions), the tree also represents the levels of the world, from the underworld to the upperworld. This tree, itself accessible to the ruler, must represent and exist within a single world, to link the various aspects of the cosmos. The World Tree still plays a role in contemporary Maya thought, connected with the symbol of the cross, which came to be associated with Christianity after the Spanish conquest. The decorated cross was an element of Maya culture before the arrival of the Spanish, connected to the World Tree, and representing the four directions. In the religious syncretism that has developed in the Maya region since the Spanish conquests, the Christian cross came to be fused with the Maya cross.[55]

NOTES

1. Xibalba is discussed frequently in the *Popol Vuh*, and is represented in Classic Period images as well, such as possibly the famous sarcophagus lid image of Janaab Pakal. Sharer, *Ancient Maya*, 280. Fitzsimmons (*Death and the Classic Maya Kings*, 16) considers alternative realms for the dead alongside the "horrific" Xibalba.

2. Foster, *Handbook*, 36.

3. Rice, *Maya Political Science*, ... Baudez, *Maya Sculpture of Copan*, 252. Sharer, *Ancient Maya*, 205.

4. Sharer, *Daily Life in Maya Civilization*, 210.

5. Tedlock, *Popol Vuh*, 92.

6. The story of the twins recounted in the *Popol Vuh* is also contained in imagery from the Classic Period. McKillop, *The Ancient Maya*, 211.

7. O'Neill, "Ancient Maya Sculptures of Tikal, Seen and Unseen," 119.

8. O'Neill, "Ancient Maya Sculptures," 119.

9. *Huainanzi, Lanming* 6.4 (Major, Queen et al. trans, 220).

10. Jeeloo Liu argues that a number of early Chinese thinkers held a kind of "liberal naturalist" outlook, which is similar to the view I outline here. Liu, "Chinese Qi Naturalism and Liberal Naturalism." Liberal naturalism, accepted by a number of contemporary philosophers, presents itself as a kind of compromise position between scientific naturalism and supernaturalism. Generally, its proponents want to avoid physicalistic reductionism (generally motivated by concern with morality), while also eschewing "supernatural" entities. See DeCaro and Macarthur's collections *Naturalism in Question* and *Naturalism and Normativity*.

11. Lee, *Xunzi and Early Chinese Naturalism*, 2–3.

12. And indeed most accounts of possible worlds take such worlds to be abstractions and not worlds in a concrete ontological sense. One notable exception to this is the view of David Lewis's famous *On the Plurality of Worlds*.

13. I do not get too deeply into this issue in this book, as it takes us a bit far afield from the focus of this book, but I suggest some ways in which we might use the monistic world conceptions of the Maya and early Chinese to make sense of property dualism about mind and body in a more adequate way than mind-body dualists such as the classical substance dualists like Descartes or more modern property dualists.

14. The clearest exposition of Plato's dualism concerning worlds is given in the *Phaedo*, with another in the middle books of the *Republic*. His particular version of world dualism is motivated by the problem of stability within change, initiated in the ancient Greek tradition by the Presocratics such as Heraclitus and Parmenides.

15. Bianchi, "Dualism." Bianchi's distinction between three fundamental dualistic oppositions is less useful for our purposes here.

16. Austin (trans.), *Fusus al-Hikam [The Bezels of Wisdom]*, 55.

17. Austin, *The Bezels of Wisdom*, 34.

18. Lopez-Austin, trans. in Tate, "The Poetics and Power of Knowledge at La Venta," 158.

19. Major et al., *Huainanzi*, 48.

20. Major et al., *Huainanzi*, 49.

21. See McLeod, *Theories of Truth in Chinese Philosophy,* ch. 5.

22. Major et al., *Huainanzi*, 49–50.

23. Major, Queen et al., 2010: 51.

24. *Chunqiu Fanlu, Shenjiminghu* 1.

25. *Chunqiu Fanlu, Yinyangyi* 1.

26. *Fayan, Wenshen* 4.

27. *Hanshi Wai Zhuan* 7.19.

28. Murata, *Chinese Gleams of Sufi Light*, …

29. McLeod, "Xunzi and Mimamsa."

30. Guernsey Kappelman, "Carved in Stone"; *Ritual and Power in Stone.*

31. Also Friedel, Schele, and Parker, *Maya Cosmos.*

32. Guernsey, *Ritual and Power in Stone,* 108.

33. Barrera Vasquez, *Diccionario maya cordemex*, 272.

34. Barrera-Vasquez and Rendon 1948: 29, Jones 1998: 428 (*The Conquest of the Last Maya Kingdom*), Friedel, Schele, and Parker 1993:210.

35. Friedel, Schele, and Parker 1993: 210.

36. This image on the first lintel, Yaxchilan Lintel 24, is one of the most famous of the Maya world. The lintels are currently in the British Museum in London. They are discussed in numerous works, including Tate, *Yaxchilan: The Design of a Maya Ceremonial City.*

37. Friedel, Schele, and Parker, *Maya Cosmos*, 411, Barrera-Vasquez, *Diccionario,* 272.

38. Barrera-Vasquez, *Diccionario,* 272.

39. Friedel, Schele, and Parker, *Maya Cosmos,* 211.

40. Such as Wang Chong, in the *Mingyi* chapter of his *Lunheng* ("Balanced Discourses").

41. Astor-Aguilera, *Communicating Objects*, 114. He claims that the view is that all things have the *potential* for agency. Tedlock and Tedlock (*Teachings from the American Earth*, 150) argue that this view is linked to myth in certain Native American traditions.

42. Milbrath, *Star Gods of the Maya*, 285. Thompson, *Maya History and Religion*, 209–233.

43. Thompson, *Maya History and Religion*, 209. Roys, *Rituals of the Bacabs*, 152–153.

44. Friedel, Schele, and Parker, *Maya Cosmos*, 412. Guernsey Kappelman, "Sacred Geography at Izapa," 92: "the term *itzam* also designates shamans or individuals who

had access to the supernatural world and who could manipulate *itz*, or cosmic substance of the Otherworld."

45. Sharer, *Ancient Maya*, 531.

46. Sharer, *The Ancient Maya*, 530. Milbrath, *Star Gods of the Maya*, 284–285.

47. Foster, *Handbook*, 166.

48. See McLeod, *Theories of Truth in Chinese Philosophy*, ch. 6.

49. *Shuowen jiezi* 4564.

50. Grene, *Descartes*, 9–13.

51. Montgomery … The entry for *itz* explains: "Related to the concept of the soul and 'sacred essence.'" Represents a flower with stamen dropping from its blossom. 3.

52. Schele, Friedel, and Parker, *Maya Cosmos*, 412.

53. Paxton, *The Cosmos of the Yucatec Maya*, 25.

54. Foster, *Handbook*, 182.

55. Molesky-Poz, *Contemporary Maya Spirituality*, 80.

Chapter 4

Personhood, Identity, and Substitution

IDENTITY AND MAYA CORRELATIVE THOUGHT

What reason do we have to think that terms such as *k'inich ahau*, time names, and other important names are something like proper names rather than role names? After all, it does not take a particularly exotic kind of metaphysics (or any metaphysical view at all) to see "ruler" or "Lord of Tikal" as a role description akin to "the Pope," that can be held by different individuals at different times. The Maya view seems to go beyond this, however. One reason that it appears that something more is going on is that *attributes* of earlier rulers are associated with the *ahau*, as if there is a more robust connection between these individuals than simply performing the role. But might we say the same thing about the performative expectations connected with roles? Take the case of the president of the United States. While there is no essential connection between the individuals Abraham Lincoln and Andrew Jackson, we might (and should) take it that particular features of Andrew Jackson's personality and traits (as well as others) had an effect on the broader social conception of what is expected of a president. What the Confucians referred to as *li* 禮 (ritual) was a socially constructed set of norms attached to roles. The expectation of the practice and attitudes of a father, a teacher, or a ruler were in part determined by the practices of exemplary or influential individual who performed those roles. Thus, it was not only abstract and independent rules concerning norms constructed by scholars that went into determining how a ruler should act, but patterns woven into the conception of the role by actual rulers living the role. We see the same thing in the case of the pope. Before Andrew Jackson, certain expectations concerning how one was elected as the president were followed, and after his time, a certain kind of charisma was expected of a president (whether ultimately for good or ill). We may ask the question "how and why do these features of particularly memorable holders of a role become normative, attaching to the role itself?" A number of different answers are possible to this question. Perhaps the most relevant is that memorable or particularly excellent role-holders shape our conceptions of the best way to perform particular roles. We do not come into the world fully formed, with understandings of how best to perform certain tasks. We learn how to better perform any task, whether playing guitar, teaching a language, or ruling a state, through the performance of it. It is in part this that was meant by the Confucians when they said (in *Analects* 15.28): 人能弘道 , 非道弘人 "persons broaden the Way, the Way does not broaden persons." We cannot construct norms for action independently of engaging in that action. Exemplars, who come to be associated with the excellent performance of particular roles, themselves discover ways of performing. Thus almost every feature associated with a particular role can be found in some early exemplary practitioner. Independently of whatever the right view is concerning right action or virtue, the norms attached to our roles *are* developed in an exemplarist manner.[1]

Thus, certain features of Abraham Lincoln *qua* president were also features of Andrew Jackson. It is not that, independently of the presidency, Lincoln demonstrated these features, which made him uniquely fit to be president (although we may certainly also argue that certain independent features of character conforming to role expectations make one more fit to perform the role, and thus more likely to succeed at attaining it), but rather that in performing the role of president, internalizing the role expectations and performing them will entail performing (and internalizing) features that were those of Andrew Jackson. And not only are they coincidentally or accidentally features of Andrew Jackson. It doesn't *just happen* to be the case that Abraham Lincoln was also charismatic. The charismatic features of Abraham Lincoln insofar as they were part of the role of the president were *causally* and historically related to the features of Andrew Jackson. They were *Andrew Jackson's* charisma in this sense, rather than just charisma. In this sense, Andrew Jackson himself became part of the role of the president—part of him, his features, have become associated with the normative description of the role.[2]

In this sense, then, we may associate office holders (say holders of the office of the president) with other office holders whose particular traits contributed to the construction of the norms of action, attitude, etc. connected with the role.[3] Is this what is going on in the case of Maya identification of *ahauob* with previous holders of the position? Certainly this is *part* of what is going on. But unlike the explanation I gave above, which is consistent with (and drawn from) a particular interpretation of early Confucian thought concerning roles, the Maya view seems to contain a metaphysical element that goes beyond just the association of roles with features of the practice of particular persons. It amounts to something *close* to the early Confucian view, but with additional metaphysical apparatus involved.

Note that how we understand or define the *self* is relevant to how we will understand what is going on in cases of internalization and performance of roles based partly on the individual characteristics of exemplary past role practitioners. The early Confucians did not advance any particular metaphysics of the self (indeed in the *Analects*, Confucius appears to explicitly reject metaphysical theorizing.[4]) They were much more concerned with the concept of the *person* construed as a social entity.[5] The term *ren* 人 in early Confucian literature refers to this. The person is, according to them, defined by his or her roles and positions in the community. Given the social nature of personhood, to be a person is to have a location in the community, in terms of both relationships and responsibilities. A person is defined by their family relationships and also by the responsibilities attached to the roles they inhabit, which overlap with these family relationships and also go beyond them to broader communal relationships. Unlike in much of the Western tradition, it is not rationality or autonomy that defines the person (indeed, the latter is *impossible* according to the Confucians),[6] but rather social *locatedness*. This is at the root of the Confucian criticism of Daoists and Yangists, who reject society and who the Confucians view then as uncommitted to development of persons and as less than fully persons.[7] We can see here that personhood is not a metaphysical issue.

Given that personhood is based on social locatedness, relationship, and role, it turns out that many of the features individuating persons are not features *of individuals*, but communal features shared between groups past and present. One way of getting at this in our context is to focus on physical and behavioral characteristics of individuals. Our physical features are not merely our own, but they are also features of our parents, grandparents, great-grandparents, etc.[8] It is not only that we *resemble* these people in our physical features, but also that we have similar features because these features are *causally connected* to those of our ancestors. There are sometimes resemblances between unrelated people, and these resemblances are coincidental. But our resemblance to our parents, for example, is not mere resemblance. We look as we do *because* they look as they do. It is their genetics that makes us this way, and insofar as we share their features, it is because we share their genes. Just as future cell states of our parents' bodies are causally related to their previous cellular states, our bodies are likewise future cell states of the bodies of our parents, carrying their genetics. Thus, even more than the Confucians, we in the contemporary world should recognize the sense in which what we are contains what our ancestors are and were. We are not autonomous in that sense—we are continuations of a biological process stretching back to our distant ancestors. The fact that we can interact with our parents and children does not undermine the truth that we are part of them in a broader sense any more than the fact that we can observe and reflect on our own mental states undermines the truth that both the observation and what is reflected on are "our" mental states.

The way we tend to define the *person* in contemporary Western (now global) thought is unintuitive and awkward. In early Confucian material, as in a number of other traditions, the person was seen as both communal and event based. As Roger Ames and David Hall argued, the community and its features are seen as the *locus* of the person.[9] The various features of the person were not seen as things that belong to the individual, and the individual was not seen a discrete, separate, or separable entity independent of the community. In addition to the biological features shared with our ancestors, other properties each individual has comes from the community—one's language, preferences, attitudes, etc.—these are not simply self-created autonomous choices. Rather, it is the community around us that has the primary role in creating these properties. If the individual is committed ultimately to performing certain roles consistently with communal norms, it is because the individual ultimately is a collection of communal properties. This is the reasoning behind the Confucian commitment to social norms as necessary for construction of virtue and maintenance of the thriving society.

All of this, however, is meant to be independent of metaphysical views concerning the self, identity of this self through time, and related issues we see more prominently in the Indian and Western traditions. Certain thinkers within both of these traditions defer to the idea of the soul, Form, or *atman* in order to make sense of the idea of a persistent self that retains identity through time and is distinct from other members of the community, including ancestors and other close community members. Such a view would seem odd to both the Confucians and the Maya, and it ought to likewise seem odd to us, given the facts we understand about genetics, behavior, and the human mind. It is in part due to this understanding of the self as ultimately discrete and autonomous that, led to the contemporary propensity for engaging in what psychologists call the "Fundamental Attribution Error" concerning character traits.[10] Certain studies have suggested that people in East Asian cultures are less likely to make the Fundamental Attribution Error. If this is right, then part of this may be due to these different ways of understanding the nature of the person.

This difference between the Chinese and the Indian/Western understanding of the person may also be one of the main reasons for the influence of the Mahayana Buddhist tradition in East Asia, first in China, then throughout the rest of the East Asian world. Early pre-Mahayana Buddhism never made a major impact on East Asia, with its focus on individual enlightenment and the undermining of existential suffering—which we can see are not major topics of concern in early Chinese thought. The turn toward a metaphysics of "emptiness" and an understanding of *anatman* (non-self) in terms of compassion and the "Bodhisattva ideal" may have presented a conception of the person and its role much closer to the views of early China than the earlier non-Mahayana schools, and in this way became both easier to understand and more palatable to Chinese thinkers.

All of this may be contained in the Maya view, but correlative metaphysics is the missing piece of the puzzle, and it is a position we see develops in Chinese thought as well, during the Han dynasty. Correlative metaphysics concerning personhood (and other elements) is a natural move given the kind of general picture of the person sketched above, which is shared in early China and the Classic Period Maya region. While the exact historical development of a correlative metaphysics is unclear in the case of the ancient Maya, in the Chinese case, it developed from a consideration of the interdependence and non-independence of the person and other things in general, and developed later than more general views about the nature of the person. There seems to be no reason such a historical progression must be the case, though. In the Indian tradition, metaphysical views concerning the self and the person arose alongside of the folk or ethical view concerning the person.

On the Huayan (Avatamsaka) Buddhist view, each thing in some sense contains within it everything that has a causal effect on it.[11] "Containing" here may be understood in a number of different ways: one way of understanding it could be simply that one could come to know every causally connected event by fully knowing a particular entity. There need be no robust metaphysical claim involved here. A metaphysically stronger claim however is that "containing" should be understood as holding that the entity in question can be seen as *itself* in some way materially identical with all other things causally connected to it. It is the latter claim that is made by the Huayan Buddhists. Another similar view is Leibniz' conception of the *monad*, which contains all things and events in much the way the Huayan Buddhist understands this claim.

The Maya conception of an entity containing those causally connected to it is somewhat different. Unlike the Huayan and Leibnizian accounts, the Maya view is not that an entity is *always* identical to (in the sense of being always possibly taken as or seen as identical to) entities causally connected to it. Rather, an entity has the possibility to *become* identical to other entities, independent of causal connection. For an entity to contain all other entities on the Maya view, then, is for that entity to have the potential to become identical with any other entity. What creates this identity is the act of *substitution* (*k'ex*), which I discuss further below. A particular entity can become identical with another, but before the act of substitution (and after it), the two entities are not identical, but merely *potentially* identical. On the Huayan view, on the other hand, each entity is always and necessarily identical with the other entities causally connected to it. Taking entities as distinct is possible on the level of conventional truth, but on the level of ultimate truth, there is no distinction between things. Buddhist schools posit a distinction between two levels of reality, conventional and ultimate, in order to square the correctness of everyday claims such as "I went to the store" with their metaphysics, which does not accept the existence of selves. They explain that there can be truths based on conventions (understood in different ways by the different Buddhist schools).[12] There are difficult questions for the Huayan Buddhists to answer concerning how we can make sense of causal connectivity between ultimately identical entities. But in the case of ancient Maya thought, entities were separable but potentially identical. The conventional/ultimate truth distinction, like the distinction between worlds discussed in chapter 3, would be collapsed on the Maya account. The role of substitution was to create what I call "embedded identity," in which one entity becomes identical with another through ritual (as discussed in chapter 2). Below, I further clarify embedded identity, as well as some metaphysical views in other traditions similar to it, most particularly the Catholic Christian view of *transubstantiation*.[13]

The ancient Maya want to have a way to make sense of the metaphysical separability of objects beyond simply seeing them as aspects of an undifferentiated whole. Things such as time periods, human beings, buildings, etc. are all separable substances with their own essences (indeed, it is the possession of these unique essences that make a substance approach more plausible than a process approach), and it is through special intervention that these things become associated with one another in the relation of identity. This is part of the reason that the rituals of substitution are crucial in ancient Maya society—without them, the entities that rely on these rituals for their continuation will be destroyed.

There is a suggestion in the *Popol Vuh* of just this. The gods early in the story, in their attempt to create humanity, continually destroy the first inadequate creatures they make, due mainly to the failure of those creatures to "keep the days"—to engage in the calendric rituals required to give order to the cosmos and complete the activity of the gods.[14] Humans in particular are required to perform the rituals that associate things that must be associated for the cosmos to operate properly. The entities that can be associated or made identical are themselves separate substances, otherwise there would be no inherent transformation in the ritual act, but simply a shifting of focus or attention to the truth of the entity's identity with some other important entity.[15] A very similar claim can be made for a structurally very similar metaphysical view—the Catholic view of transubstantiation. According to this view, the bread and wine used to celebrate the Eucharist (the ritual expressing the sacrifice of the death and resurrection of Christ) in the Mass undergoes transubstantiation, literally becoming the body and blood of Christ. The bread and wine keep their material form, but the *substantia*, the underlying nonmaterial substrate that makes them what they are, has been changed. This is not, notice, a matter of the bread and wine being identical with the body and blood of Christ in the Huayan sense in which all things are ultimately identical with one another. Rather, the bread and wine have their own substance and are transformed such that they attain such identity with the body and blood of Christ. Since this transformation requires certain conditions, it requires ritual specialists (in this case, ordained Catholic clergy) to facilitate the transformation.[16] Much the same is true in the Maya case. The ritual specialists, such as rulers and nobles, were needed to play the role of creating transformations, including seating of periods of time, keeping of days, and reenactment of the rituals of continual creation.[17] The rituals establishing rulership, time periods, and enacting continual creation included the erection of monuments and stelae, many of which can still be seen standing throughout the Maya region and in museums around the world.

Stephen Houston writes, of this ritual transformation:

> Through representation, one thing is made to change into another. Our pottery bowl, for example, might echo a woven or carved original, although, in the process, something unusual happens too. A little bit of eternity creeps in. The stone image of a Maya king endures far longer than its human inspiration. Similarly, in archaeological sites, buried sherds come close to immortality. With the bowl, however, the potter and painter zeroed in on materials other than human flesh.[18]

There is a good deal of evidence that the Maya constructions in the Classic Period and its adjoining periods, including stelae and monuments, were seen as containing the essence or some important part of the person they memorialized, generally the *ahau*, the ruler of a particular city-state. Archaeologists have presented evidence of widespread destruction of monuments concerning the *ahau* of a city when there is conquest, this being seen as elimination of the *ahau* in various forms. While this in itself cannot show us that there is a different kind of metaphysical understanding of personhood here than in any other society (surely any conqueror wants to eliminate all signs of the power and authority of conquered enemies), there are numerous other signs of evidence that the ancient Maya took these representations of rulers to hold some of the personhood or essence of the rulers, rather than just serving as reminders or likenesses.

In the contemporary Maya context, Miguel Astor-Aguilera has discussed so-called "communicating objects" in Maya ritual. These objects are seen as representing certain aspects of nature or gods.[19] Along with these practices, which are recounted in ancient texts, there seems to have been a sense in which *human beings* could also play the role of communicating objects. Just as a piece of stone can take on part of the personhood of the *ahau* through its carving, a future heir can take on part of the personhood of a previous ruler. This is a theme we see in many of the monumental texts. The recounting of events and lives of *ahauob* in early texts shows us this. The correlative association between rulers, deities, and other elements of the nonhuman world obtains here. Astor-Aguilera writes:

> These acts [recounted in monumental texts] appear to portray practical relational events that demonstrate reciprocal behavior between those living in the flesh and those living in other than human forms. The Mayan hieroglyphic inscriptions leave no doubt that Maya kings ideologically sought to link themselves to mythic history, communing with ancestors, and agricultural bounty self-aggrandizement for the sake of politico-religious legitimacy.[20]

While this is certainly true, Astor-Aguilera's appraisal of the situation is a bit too politically deterministic. There are generally philosophical, religious, and other ideological reasons behind such actions as well, in addition to whatever political and economic expediency there may have been. Political reasons for particular views or ideologies do not rule out philosophical reasons. Political or economic determinism is as impoverished as other kinds of determinism, which fail to realize the complexity of explanation of philosophical positions (or anything else).

When we give an economic explanation for the actions of an emperor or a scholar who had no idea of the concepts of modern economic theory or even thought himself of his actions in anything like these terms, we often defend this methodology by claiming (or arguing) that these theories *really* explain the actions or thoughts of the figure in question, whether he realized it or not. Yet many remain unwilling to do this for the case of philosophy.[21] We have no qualms about applying the conceptual tools of economic materialism to ancient Maya thought, but we resist the application of philosophy. I suspect some of the reason for this is the implicit mistrust of the concepts and categories of philosophy as legitimate aspects of human experience, and the assumption that economic materialism is legitimately explanatory and "real" in a way philosophy is not. If the concepts and methods of economic materialism get at something that is actually there in human thought or the world, regardless of whether ancient Maya thinkers conceptualized it as such, it is a legitimate enterprise to use these concepts and methods to interpret Maya thinkers. If the concepts and methods of philosophy are parochial, culturally dependent, and subjective, then they cannot be used outside of their narrow context. I think such views are wrong about both philosophy and economic materialism.

Philosophers as a v hole are much less likely to see philosophy as culturally dependent in a way that, say, economics and politics are not, than are historians, sinologists, and other non-philosophers. This is why one often sees in work by historians on early Chinese philosophy, for example, a "hermeneutic of suspicion" stance taken on philosophy or ideology, while taking economic or political claims at face value. Taking philosophy seriously as a legitimate explanatory and causal force in the life of humans, and one with universal and not just parochial or culturally determined characteristics will give us a very different sense of its possibility and role in understanding ancient thinkers, whether Maya, Chinese, Indian, Western, or other.

The "hermeneutic of suspicion" is dominant in fields such as history, as is economic or political determinism. There is a lot of evidence, however, that such determinisms are flawed and overly simplistic. Economic or political reductionism simply cannot explain numerous phenomena we observe, without ignoring a great deal. Numerous examples of such determinism can be found in scholarship on Chinese philosophy. It has become standard for historians to read early Chinese texts in terms of political or economic motivations. The *Huainanzi*, in which a model for creating a synthesis between all schools and strains of thought is developed, is most often read as primarily (or only) a vehicle for the political ambitions of Liu An.[22] To do this, however, is to neglect the ways in which philosophical reasons were in play in the construction of these views, unwarrantedly seeing them as reducible to political reasons. The scholars Liu An employed to compile the *Huainanzi* certainly had their own agendas, and those agendas cannot be understood as the kind of imperial political agendas Liu An had. These were scholars, not politicians. If the *Huainanzi* indeed had a political goal (and no doubt it did), that political aim was symbiotic on very real philosophical content, with its own goals. We should not ignore this, as if the political aspect of the project is all there was to it. To do so would simply be to wave off philosophy as an important consideration for no reason at all other than preference for political and economic history.

We can draw an analogy to a situation much closer to home, to make the case even more strongly. Academic institutions as a whole today generally have as their aim economic and political goals. They aim to maximize their influence in academia and the wider world, and also to maximize prestige, endowment, money, etc. This is why university presidents and administration often have very different aims and motivations than faculty members within departments. Any university is the way it is, in the particulars of the people doing academic work within departments and their specializations, ultimately on the basis of the interests of administrators. Yet no one would take this to be a reason for explaining the work of individual faculty members (or even faculty members taken collectively) by referring to its economic and political goals. No historian, philosopher, biologist, or geologist does their research and works as they do to attain the political and economic goals of the university administration. Thus, it makes little sense to understand the work of a group of Chinese historians at Yale, for example, as primarily a project aimed at elevating the influence and economic power of the university in China. It still may be the case that the administrators who ultimately allowed *this* project (and not others) to develop and run are indeed concerned with this and have this goal in mind. And so certainly one aspect of the explanation of such a project will be this administrative motivation and goal. But to reduce the entire explanation to this is simply wrongheaded. The particular scholars involved are doing what they do for reasons connected to their area, intellectual discovery, etc. It just so happens that *their* project was selected, while other projects less felicitous for the achievement of the goals of the administration were not selected, because it helps contribute to their own goals. This fact does not eliminate the goals, reasons, arguments, and positions of the individual scholars engaged in the project. Part of the problem is that scholars often look for *one* overarching explanation to which everything can be reduced, instead of allowing for the overlapping of explanations, which is more true to reality. We are scared of overdetermination, perhaps because of the immense influence of the natural sciences. Of course, I think even the empirical sciences get this wrong (when they wade into philosophy), but we *certainly* have reason to reject overdetermination in terms of explanation of intellectual production. The reasons for the appearance of a book have as much to do with the author's own interests, arguments, and philosophical reasons as they do with the economic or political interests of a patron or publisher. The only reason you see one book rather than another that you do not see is because interests align—it turns out to be the same thing that accomplishes the goal of the authors and patron(s). But this neither makes the goals nor concerns the same. A cup of water may serve different goals for different people—one because they are thirsty and want to drink, another because they need something to activate their watercolors so they can paint, and another to water plants in the garden. That all three of them work together to build a well under the direction of a person who wants water because he can make money by selling it does not demonstrate that the *real* purpose of the well is to make money. None of the builders thought of it this way, even though the capitalist who directed the project used the individual motivations to profit.

ASPECTS OF THE PERSON

The connection of individual humans to nonhuman objects was understood in numerous ways. As in the early Chinese case, there were numerous aspects of the individual human explaining their personhood. The concept of *kux* can be understood as a kind of vital living energy, connected to the concept of *ch'ul* (and *itz*) discussed above,[23] that was seen as a component of the person. As we have seen, this component of the person could be seen as shared with other elements of the cosmos, allowing an individual to communicate with or otherwise manifest these elements.

The *way* of an individual is no less a part of the person. It links the individual with representative nonhuman elements outside of the body of the individual human. It is somewhat similar to the concept of the *totem* (*dodaem*) in Ojibwe culture, which has analogues in numerous other cultures in the Americas (and elsewhere). The *way* is a representative of the person in the form of an animal or other nonhuman element of the world. The glyphic representations of *way* show us the fundamental nonhuman link, with representations of a jaguar or other animal spliced with the human.

Stephen Houston and David Stuart translate *way* as "co-essence," and identify it as an aspect of the person that is not contained within the physical body or to an individual human being alone.[24] This suggests that personhood, for the ancient Maya, includes more than the physical and mental features of the single individual. The *way* resides in nonhuman objects connected to or representative of the person, and the glyph itself represents a half-human half-jaguar type figure. The suggestion here seems to be that the jaguar may be one's *way*. Many rulers or other important figures in Maya society held the name *balam* (jaguar) in their title or proper name as well, such as the well-known *Chilam Balam* (jaguar priests) of the Postclassic Period Yucatan, for example. This connection between humans and a nonhuman co-essence is based on a relationship between what is seen as the related features of the *way* in question and those of a particular person. Just as is the case for days, different nonhuman animals and elements of the world are associated with characteristic attitudes, events, and other states, such that human individuals who display characteristics mirroring these can be thought of as linked with the bearers of those states in a personhood relationship.

The *way* was not always seen as a positive aspect of the person. According to Adam Herring, the *way*, while it represented both individuals and lineages (mainly elites), was a kind of "trickster" entity. He refers to the *way* as "mischievous creatures of darkness."[25] This conception of the *way* resembles the ubiquitous trickster character of much Native American thought. When we view the *way* through the lenses of the trickster, however, it becomes much less clear that it is a "creature of darkness" at all. In many North American Native traditions, the trickster character is, although certainly mischievous and dangerous to order, a vital and even positive part of society and the operation of the cosmos. Without the trickster, there could be no properly ordered world.[26] One example of this is the *Iktomi*

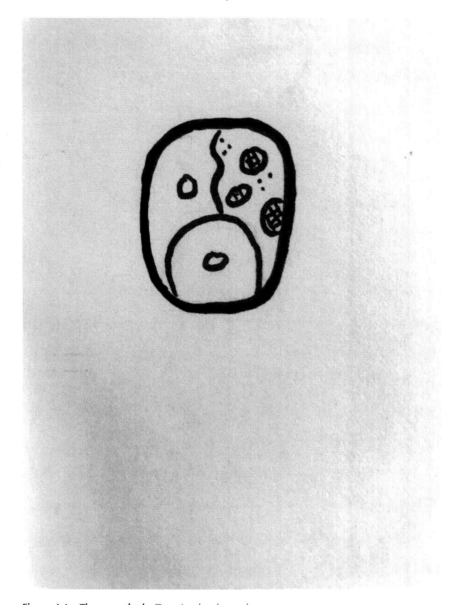

Figure 4.1   The way glyph. Drawing by the author.

character in the tradition of the Lakota people of the North American Great Plains. Iktomi, according to the Lakota, is a spider and trickster, but also a hero. He appears differently depending on the story and the context, sometimes the antagonist yet sometimes the protagonist.[27] Other trickster characters throughout Native American traditions share this feature of moral ambiguity. Many of these traditions indeed claim (plausibly) that human beings ourselves resemble the trickster in this way. None of us are wholly or always good or evil, right or wrong. Even particular stable character traits are not universally right or wrong. We can see here that moral *context* is particularly important in numerous Native American traditions. If the trickster represents anything in connection with this in particular, it is *power* and *ability* rather than particular moral traits.

The *way* in this sense seems to resemble the trickster. If the individual and the community have a trickster aspect, then they also have great power and ability. They have the mean to overcome obstacles in the world using intellect that would normally require force of a magnitude humans lack. This is likely why the *way* (like the trickster characters of other traditions) is usually represented as an animal or process, particularly a powerful one such as a jaguar, or even death itself.[28]

Friedel, Schele, and Parker advanced the view that the *way* represents groups as well as individuals. This was meant as an explanation for the fact that, while other aspects and names of kings are included on monuments and stelae, the names of the king's *way* is almost never included, thus suggesting that the king's *way* was connected to his lineage and was well-known enough not to be necessary for adding to a monument.[29] Friedel, Schele, and Parker also claimed that the Maya people were understood as transforming into their *way* when they fought battles.[30] This further bolsters the view that the *way* was understood as a single co-essence that belonged to communities or lineages. The ability of individuals to transform into the *way* also suggests that the "essence" of persons was at least in part communal. The individual human being had as part of its essence a communal entity that connected the individual to the other members of the community. This gives us a natural way of understanding the relationship between the private and the public, the life of the individual and the life of the community. The two are taken as problematic in much contemporary and Western philosophy. Philosophers have struggled to make sense of things like communal action and communal agency. Much of the reason for this struggle is that we tend to take the individual human being as the sole source of agency, and maintain that personhood does not extend beyond the individual. We see in many traditions, though, including the Confucian tradition in China (as I explain below), and even in contemporary social psychology, that agency involves far more than individual human mental states and choices.

The Maya view surrounding the *way* shows us a natural way of making sense of the connection between the individual human being and the community. The essence of the individual human being or person is made up of a number of parts, with one of these being the *way*. The *way* can be seen as the communal or social essence of the individual person—the aspect of the person through which they represent the features of a wider community. The use of the concept of "aspects" here is useful, and captures something of what is meant by the different parts of the person according to the Maya. A *way*, as a single communal entity, can also belong to individual members of the collective insofar as they are part of that collectivity. This works not only like a surname, which attaches to individual members of a family so as to mark their lineage, but such a way that a part can be representative of a whole, and the identity of the whole. The person who becomes a particular *way*, that is, becomes the *entire way*—the individual becomes a manifestation of that *way*, rather than having the *way* as a feature of the individual that might be held by a number of others along with them, similar to a surname. The ability to *become* or *transform into* one's *way* entails that one is not fully associable with their *way* at other times. This, presumably, is why it is sometimes translated as "co-essence." *Way* is best thought of as a kind of collective essence that one has in virtue of being part of a certain lineage, community, etc., and which one can sometimes more fully represent. One always *has* their *way*, but sometimes then they can become more *fully* their *way*.

This movement from individual who possesses *way* to manifestation of the *way* itself can be explained in terms of embedded identity.

The *way* is of course just one element of an intricate complex of different elements that form the person. And the Maya conception of the person, unlike those we see in some other traditions, clearly extends beyond the body and mental states of the individual human being. The person extends into additional human beings, other objects, temporal locations, and other aspects of the world. Personhood in the Maya view (as in other Native American traditions) is not simply a matter of the individual human being alone, although the human being is always *part of* or associable with a person. The parts of the world we have access to can be thought of as those that can at least potentially be linked to personhood—whether our own or that of another. Thus every object humans can interact with is a potential (or actual) part of a person.

We see some of this conception of personhood emerge in interpretation of Maya burial practices. Traci Ardren argues that the preservation of parts of the bodies of dead infants in numerous places and households (similar to the medieval practice of saintly relics), and the burial of these separate parts in the household, suggests what she calls "dividual personhood," which takes the person as a communal entity. Ardren writes:

> partible bodies reflect the existence of relationships to a variety of kin across multiple contexts, and the way lineage and familial connections can be invoked strategically. The body is used by communities to both construct and deconstruct social identities that are shared and relational.[31]

Ardren suggests that the practice of child burial in parts reflects a view in Classic Maya though of the spiritual power of young children—the view that they have a deeper connection to the unseen aspects of the world[32] than older human beings, and thus that parts of their bodies after death can impart this power to other elements of the world. She argues that infants were seen as belonging to a collective entity with intrinsic sacred significance.[33] The burial of the parts of the body of dead infants in a household, according to Ardren, was thought of as bringing life or soul to the household—or in my own terms, embedding the household into the extended (or "dividual") person represented by the dead infant.[34]

We see here that the elements of personhood for the Maya are more than simply elements of human individuals. A person can contain nonhuman elements like the *way*, as well as constructed artifacts such as memorials, stelae, households, or anything else that can be imbued with the *essence* of a person. It is difficult to get clear, however, on just what the relationship between the *way* as co-essence, the essence, and the various things that can *have* that essence amounts to. Here I attempt to construct at least one possible picture how these might fit together. To do this, I have only the tools of charity and philosophical analogy, as the Maya texts themselves do not give explanation of this.

As discussed above, the essence of a person is made up of *ch'ul*, which can be understood as a form of *itz*.[35] *Itz*, in particular, as we have seen, may have had another important meaning for the Maya, connected to its sense as an essence of persons. According to Friedel, Schele, and Parker, *itz* and *ch'ul*, while distinct concepts, are fundamentally interrelated, in that they can both be understood as the essential "life-force" found in blood. This further suggests a metaphysical picture of essences in which what differentiates them is their being aspects of a single essence as process. We can profitably speak of *the* essence of a person, which can be manifest as a number of its aspects, whether *itz*, *ch'ul*, or *way*. *Itz* and *ch'ul* appear to have a different (and closer) relationship, however, than does either with *way*.

A plausible way of understanding the connection between *itz* and *ch'ul*, as I have suggested above, is to take *ch'ul* as a specifically human form of *itz*. One way of making sense of this is to distinguish *between* the features of different kind of *itz*. If *itz* is essence, shared by everything that exists, and it also (in part) explains how things have the features they do, then *itz* must be either of different kinds or be manifest in different entities to different extents. Whichever of these is the case, the power of *ch'ul* can be taken as itself the power of *itz*, even though this power is not manifest *everywhere* we find *itz*.

We find a parallel to this in early Chinese philosophy, concerning the relationship between *qi* 氣 (vital energy) and *jingshen* 精神 (pure spirit). According to the *Huainanzi*, *jingshen* is a particularly human form of *qi*, one that explains the unique abilities humans have compared to other things in nature. All things have (or are comprised of—depending on how we read the text) *qi*, but we notice that humans appear to have distinct abilities (consciousness, etc.) that are not shared by other objects in the world. The *Huainanzi* (and other early Chinese texts) explains this by holding that *jingshen* is a more purified *qi* than the *qi* present in (or comprising) objects without consciousness or the other abilities of humans. It is the *jingshen* that allows us understanding of the cosmos, and thus *qi* plays a vital role in the *Huainanzi* as a whole. There are complicating questions in early Chinese thought (especially in texts such as *Huainanzi* and *Chunqiu Fanlu*) concerning whether *qi* is something possessed by all things or whether *qi* comprises all things, and this uncertainty seems present in Maya thought as well concerning *itz*.

Insofar as we take *ch'ul* or *itz* as the essence of a person, we see that the person can be seen as comprising something beyond the boundaries of the individual human being. *Ch'ul*, as the uniquely human form of *itz*, is not a *personal* feature. There is not Person A's *ch'ul* and Person B's *ch'ul*, there is only *ch'ul*, taken as a single pervasive force in humans, a manifestation of *itz*. We see this through the separability of the individual and *ch'ul* in Maya sources, and through the fact that *ch'ul* is never spoken of as possessed by an individual. The contemporary Zincanteco Maya, according to Vogt, hold the *ch'ulel* (equivalent to *ch'ul*) to be a pool of soul-stuff that can transmigrate from individual to individual. The Zincantecos associate *ch'ulel* with both the concepts of *ch'ul* and *itz* discussed here. Vogt writes:

> Virtually everything important and valuable to Zincantecos also possesses a *ch'ulel*: domestic animals and plants, salt, houses and household fires, crosses, the saints, musical instruments, maize, and all the other deities in the pantheon. The most important interaction in the universe is not between persons and objects, but among the innate souls of persons and material objects.[36]

Persons, for the ancient Maya, were seen as complex individuals, sometimes taken as the collective entity and sometimes as the individual, which always has the potential to manifest the collective entity, as *embedded* in this entity. The scope of "person" can thus be different, depending on its use, and depending on ritual context.

In early Confucian philosophy in China, we also see a conception of personhood that holds the person to be an entity involving more than the individual human being. In the Confucian case, however, it is primarily human communal groups and societies that play the fundamental role in personhood. While this is an aspect of Maya thought (we see this through the role of *way*), personhood extends beyond the community as such—the key to personhood is the collection of *essences*, ultimately aspects of a single essence that can belong to humans and nonhuman elements (such as artifacts) alike. The Confucians do not accept anything like the essences, but rather build a conception of personhood from the communal integration of individual humans through roles and performance of ritual connected to those roles.

While there is clearly something somewhat different going on here than the conception of personhood based on human communal features that we find in early Confucianism (as well as later Chinese thought), there are some key shared features with the early Confucian account that can help explain Maya conceptions of personhood. The key difference is that while the person for early Confucians could only be thought of in terms of the human and human interaction (Confucians are insistent that the *human* and the person are necessarily linked—there can be no nonhuman elements of the person), the Maya view of the person is more expansive and allows for the inclusion of nonhuman elements. *Way* as animal or other nonhuman co-essences, as well as artifacts imbued with aspects of a person's features, can be elements of the person. Part of the metaphysics in the background here is the correlative metaphysics discussed above. While in the early Confucian case, the correlative metaphysics develops later than the basic conception of personhood, this is less clear in the ancient Maya case. What *is* clear enough is that a correlative metaphysics grounds and makes intelligible the notion of a physically extended, discontinuous person that comprises more than the individual human being associated with a person.

EMBEDDED IDENTITY

Janaab Pakal, at his tomb at Palenque, is depicted in the Temple of the Inscriptions at the side as the maize god, signifying rebirth, and is adorned with the Chac Xib Chaak ornament, linking him to the other members of the lineage who wear the same ornament in their depictions.[37] This sign of the god Chac Xib Chaak identified Janaab Pakal with the other members of his lineage through a representation of his *essence* as the god itself. Pectoral adornment in Maya imagery generally represented the essence of the person depicted. We see the sign for death (*kimi*) worn on the chest of the god Chaak as executioner, numerous *way*, and other figures associated with Xibalba (the realm of the dead).[38] Friedel, Schele, and Parker argue that the pectoral adornment represented spiritual transformation into the being represented in the ornament, through the act of dressing and performing the role of that particular entity.[39] This act is often called *substitution* (*k'ex*)—a term that also refers to ritual sacrifice in its various forms.[40] Sacrificed humans in ancient Maya society were "substitutions" in this sense, in being sacrificed they represented or took on the essence of the original sacrifice of the Hero

Twins. Substitution was thought of as a method of one entity's taking on the essence of another, and in this *becoming* the being represented. One did not, however, lose one's individual essence in taking on or becoming part of the substituted entity. This is the sense in which we might call the identity of one being with a substitute an *embedded* identity. A ruler, such as Janaab Pakal of Palenque, can become or represent Chac Xib Chaak through substitution, while still remaining Janaab Pakal. At the time of substitution, Janaab Pakal is Janaab Pakal *and* Chac Xib Chaak.

The question then becomes how do we think of entities/persons such as Chac Xib Chaak. One way of thinking of them is as *collective* persons—a single person made up of a collectivity of essences, perhaps related to the Palenque rulership lineage (or some other group). Further features of *k'ex* (substitution) can help us here, to understand how the individual and collective essences are related. Numerous scholars have discussed the features of the concept of *k'ex* that link individuals with collective identity. James Mondloch noted that in contemporary *k'iche'* communities, *k'ex* involves naming, in the practice of naming children after their grandparents. He sees this as representing a mechanism for replacement of ancestors, and a way to attain immortality.[41] There are parallels here between this practice and one documented in ancient China, where a grandson could stand in as ceremonial representation of the grandfather.[42] Interestingly, in this case, the tradition maintained that a son cannot stand in as his father, but only for the grandfather. Presumably the generational relationship was too close between father and son for it to be plausible that a son could be a representation of his father, rather than a clearly distinct individual. While in the ancient Chinese case, this substitution was not, as far as we know, seen as a literal joining of essence of the grandson and grandfather, in the Maya case, this *does* seem to have been so.

Robert Carlsen comes closest to offering a view of *k'ex* that captures this aspect. He writes:

> it [*k'ex*] relates to a what might be best described as a form of reincarnation, an integral aspect of Mayan religion [...] *K'ex* is a process of making the new out of the old. At the same time, just as a single plant produces multiple offspring, *k'ex* is change from one into many. Together *jal* and *k'ex* form a concentric system of change within change, a single system of transformation and renewal.[43]

Stephen Houston translates *k'ex* as "cyclic replacement,"[44] tying the taking on of an entity's essence to the supposed cycles of time and creation underlying Maya thought. As I argue in chapter 2, cyclicality, although certainly an aspect of Maya thought concerning time and reality, is not central to Maya thought in any unique way, and that much of what we attribute to concern with cyclicality should be understood instead in terms of concern with embedded identity.

THE EARLY CONFUCIAN CONCEPTION OF PERSONHOOD

In this section I lay out the Confucian view of moral personhood as developed in the *Analects*, which offers us an alternative view of "collective personhood," but one in which we can see some aspects of the Maya view. Most of my argument for this view comes from Book 4, with related passages from other books of the *Analects* in support. I focus on five passages in particular, which, read together and (I argue) in the right way, present a compelling case that there is a view of moral personhood operative in the *Analects*, and that this is the main issue under consideration in 18.5–7.

In the *Analects*, it is the developed social entity whose integration (in the right way) into a community imparts on them agency, as linked to a larger communal agent, and whose moral responsibility, action, and identity are linked to the community into which they are integrated. A person, on the Confucian view, gains features of individual character as derivative from communal dispositions, where features can be thought of as manifesting wider group regularities. The person, in this sense, for the Confucian, is *not* an autonomous individual, but rather a representative of a communal agent. The character of the person, according to the Confucian view, is derivative of the character of the community, such that communal dispositions or patterns of action (understood in terms of shared collective dispositions, which I will explain below) are in part due to the contribution of the individual to the shared collective actions and abilities that underlie this disposition.

One is a person, minimally, when one plays a role in a community by contributing to shared communal activities, is responsive to communal concerns, committed to joint activity, and committed to communal support. Because of this, a person manifests characteristic patterns of action of his or her community.[45]

The concept of personhood is gained from understanding the moral properties in the text, and that the moral properties are primarily communal rather than individual properties. In the case of one of the most important (perhaps the most important) moral concepts in the *Analects*, that of ren 仁 (humanity), the view advanced in the *Analects* takes it as primarily a communal moral concept that belongs to individuals only in a derivative sense. The view of moral personhood in the *Analects* holds that all moral properties of individuals are like this. Not only is moral agency dependent on being a member of a community, but the features of one's character and dispositions are based on wider features of the community of which one is part.

In *Analects* 4.1, we see a statement of the necessity of being in a ren community for the attribution of the property:

> The master said, "Living in the midst of ren is beautiful. If one does not reside in ren, how can one therein obtain knowledge?"

The community having a certain property (in this case, *ren*) is necessary in order for the individual to have access to another property (here, knowledge). Although by itself this passage does not show that one gains the property of knowledge through being a member of a community and that ren attaches to the community primarily (because it could simply be that one has to be around a community full of *ren* individuals as it is conducive to individual virtue), read in conjunction with the passages below, it becomes more plausible that *Analects* 4.1 refers to a communal requirement for possession of moral properties. *Analects* 4.25 reads:

> The master said, "excellence (*de* 德) is not alone; it of necessity (*bi* 必) has neighbors."

It seems plausible here to read *lin* 鄰 (neighbors) as a necessary condition of *de*, similar to the way that being in a ren community is a necessary condition for gaining knowledge (in 4.1). Note here that the statement of *Analects* 4.25 is given necessity by the term *bi* (necessarily), claiming that it is not simply helpful or generally efficacious to have neighbors, but in every case, necessarily, moral excellence (*de*) does not come about without neighbors. Why might this be? If being part of a community is necessary in order to have moral properties and moral responsibility, that is, in order to be a person, then it would be necessary to not only gain virtue, but any other moral property. But what reason do we have to think that 4.25 and 4.1 show us a connection between being in community and personhood, rather than being in community and virtue?

Analects 4.7 provides part of an answer. It reads:

> The master said, "the mistakes of people (*ren* 人) are in each case (*ge* 各) attributable (*yu* 於) to their group (*dang* 黨). Observe their mistakes, and you will know whether humanity (*ren* 仁) obtains."

Here, we see a stronger connection made between personhood and community. Not only is virtue linked to the community one belongs to, but vice is also so linked. More than this, we see in *Analects* 4.7 that membership in community is a necessary condition of having negative moral properties. It is "in each case" (*ge*), according to this passage (a necessitating mark similar to *bi* in Analects 4.25) that moral mistakes are attributable to one's community. This makes community membership a necessary feature for the attribution of vice. In addition, if we look at the second part of the passage, we see a link (already hinted to above) between community membership and virtue. It is by observing one's mistakes, which are attributable to his or her group, that one can discover whether *ren* obtains. This entails that positive moral properties like *ren* are also attributable to one's group. If both positive and negative moral properties are attributable to one's community, then all moral properties are attributable to one's community. All individual activity can take a moral value only insofar as it is linked to the characteristic dispositions of the individual's community. Community membership is a necessary feature of moral agency, as we see in *Analects* 4.7.

Membership in community is a necessary feature for personhood, but there are also levels of moral quality of persons. Not all persons are ideal persons, and Confucius speaks about the sage and the *junzi* 君子 (superior person) in different ways than he speaks about the *xiao ren* 小人 (petty person). While communal membership is a threshold condition for personhood, one's moral value as person depends on one's degree of commitment to the community, the commitment to and skill with which one performs one's communal role(s), and the virtues cultivated within the social context. *Analects* 6.30 explains how a person achieves positive moral properties such as *ren*:

> As for the *ren* person, desiring to establish himself he establishes others, and desiring to achieve he helps others achieve. To be able to make oneself close (*jin* 近) to others and to identify with them can be called in the area of *ren*.

Analects 12.1 further explains the moral development of the person, again pointing us to greater integration into a community:

> Yan Yuan asked about *ren*. The master said, "Turn away from yourself (*ji* 己) and return to ritual (*fu li* 復禮)—this is *ren*. If for only one day one could turn away from oneself and return to ritual, the entire world would return (*gui* 歸) to *ren*. Becoming *ren* is caused by oneself (*ji*)—how can it be caused by others?"

Being a member of a community is a necessary condition for personhood, but the way to ideal personhood is to perfect that membership, which is a matter of lessening one's concern with individual desires and projects and integrating more deeply into communal projects and concerns, via ritual.

The Maya conception of personhood also seems to fundamentally rely on ritual. In the beginning of the *Popol Vuh*, the gods continually destroy the creatures they have created due to their inability to remember the gods through rituals, in particular through "keeping the days." Once humans are created, the primary explanation of their success is their ability to formulate and engage in the proper ritual conduct.

PERSONHOOD AND ITS COMPONENTS

In recent years, it has become popular in Maya studies to focus on the *body* as the central element of selfhood or personhood for the ancient Maya. In a number of important studies,[46] the body, as individual human organism, is taken as the locus of the person, and indeed identical with the person. This seems to me a strange situation, and to miss much about the ancient Maya conception of the person. Houston and Stuart recognize[47] that there are numerous elements of the person according to the ancient Maya conception not clearly identifiable with the body, not least of which is the *way* (co-essence, described below). The focus on the body is largely the result of trends in contemporary thought, and Houston, Stuart, and Taube admit as much in the first chapter of their 2006 book *The Memory of Bones*. But there are some key structural difficulties of the account they offer and the importance they accord to the body *for the Maya* that make analyses of the body such as the ones mentioned here problematic as a way of making headway on understanding Maya views of personhood. Houston et al. write:

> Through the medium of the body, philosophical subjects (our conscious selves) relate to objects (all that is external to those selves), an existential task of the body emphasized by both Lacan and Mead. A result of this interaction is that the body learns that it is not alone, that it coexists, not with projected phantasms of the mind, but with fellow subjects that are equally capable of thought and activity.[48]

There are a number of problems with this position as both a philosophical account of the body and as an interpretation of the ancient Maya view. First, a distinction is drawn here between the subject, the conscious self, and the body. Thus these cannot be simply the same thing. The body is not then the self. The authors here talk of using the "medium of the body" to relate to objects that are not the self. We might make sense of this even if the body is identical to the self, given self-reflexivity. The self, that is, as subject can use the self as object to distinguish itself as subject from other things in the world. This much is relatively problematic. But the body here discussed as medium is *not* identified with the "conscious self" or philosophical subject. And even if it were so identified, why then refer to this as the "body," rather than as something more clearly robust and subject marking, such as the "self"? The distinction is drawn between the two in the first sentence of the quote. The self *uses* the body to relate to objects. This has to mean more than simply "the self uses the self to relate to objects." The latter claim is trivial. How can a self relate to objects through any other means but itself and what that self has access to? But if they mean the "body" to correspond to something like the "self-as-object," then it is unclear why they should stress the physical aspects of this, or connect this with the sense of "body" most readers will understand, and which they seem to mean to use. Throughout the works on body in ancient Maya thought, the discussion surrounds various physical functions of human bodies and features of human bodies. This is the "body" they must then be discussing here, which is the subject of their work. But if that is the case, this cannot be simply the "self-as-subject," because the self-as-subject need not be associated with the body at all. As Rene Descartes showed, one can (and often does) have a self-conception as "thinking thing." Indeed, this is perhaps why we are prone to say things like "*my* body," "I want to keep going but my body gave out," etc. While it *can* be the body that plays the role of self-as-subject, this is a very unusual case, in either the Western or Mesoamerican traditions. What distinguishes *me* from others, whether things or people, is rarely ever seen as *this body*. This is likely the reason that most languages speak of the body using possessive markers, rather than identity markers. Thus "my hand hurts" rather than "the hand part of me hurts."

Presumably part of the reason humans came to think this way (though not the only reason) was the recognition that we could lose body parts and still be the *same* person. I can lose that hand, and am not now one-tenth less of the person I was before. Joyce and Meskell discuss Descartes as a ground point for their consideration of what they think is the difference of the Maya (and Egyptian) traditions, but I don't think the traditions are actually all that different from Descartes. Descartes is often misread as making the claim that the mind can and does exist independently from the body because we can conceive of it as so and because the self is fundamentally or essentially a thinking thing. This is not the case. Though he does hold that the self is essentially a thinking thing, he also holds that it can no more exist without a body than a song can exist without a musical instrument. That is, in Descartes' case, the way he *demonstrates* the existence of the body is by showing that if we did not have bodies, the mind would not have the ideas it does, concerning extension, color, etc. His position about the thinking thing is that it is *essential* to the self in a way the body is not. But to hold that something is an essential feature of a thing is not to hold that thing does not *necessarily* have other features. A particular *shape* (such that it has the ability to hold liquids) is the essential feature of a *cup*. No particular material is an essential feature of a cup—ceramic, plastic, styrofoam, etc., but no cup can exist without being made of some particular material. So even though no particular material is an essential feature of a cup, it must have some particular material. One way we can describe this is to say that the *materiality* of the cup is an essential feature. But even putting it this way does not avoid the situation that some feature of any particular cup without which that cup could not exist is not in fact an essential feature of the cup.

All this is to say that Descartes never drew the radical distinction between body and mind that Meskell and Joyce attribute to him, and likewise the Maya (I'm unsure about the Egyptians) did not radically eliminate this notion of the separable and disembodied mind (or rather spirit). There is a clear place for such in the ancient Maya tradition, and we miss much of what they were doing when we try to import a contemporary eliminativist physicalist view to ancient Maya thought, as a reaction to radical "Cartesian" dualism. The ancient Maya were not physicalists, and one needs to radically stretch the evidence to hold that they were anything like this, and explain away some very difficult things.

The ancient Maya notion of the person was clearly one that was robust and, as Houston and Stuart say, "extendable." The individual human body is a *part* of the person in the ancient Maya conception, but there are other physical and nonphysical elements of the person as well. A few of these are discussed by Houston and Stuart in their landmark paper on the concept of *baah*, which they translate as "self."[49] They argue that "*baah*" originally signifies the face or head, but came to take the meaning of "self" as well, self-reference being associated with the head. This meaning of *baah* as head translated also into the idiomatic meaning we also have in English, meaning "leader" or "chief." Thus, *baah* could signify a number of different things, applied to the self. The face, according to Houston and Stuart, represented and "realized" the aspects of personhood of the individual person (p.77). The extendibility of this face, however, should be understood in terms of the ability of objects and elements outside of the body of the individual to represent and indeed be included in the person. In the ceremony of "impersonation," for example (about which more below), one took on the identity of a god (embedded identity) through the adoption (through dance or other ceremonial activity) of the face or likeness of the god in question. Houston and Stuart argue that this was a "merger" of the identities of the individual and the god.[50]

The person or self expressed by *baah* is also something extendable through the representation of the person in artifact construction. This is part of the key to the importance of the memorials and stelae in the Classic Period. Not only did they recount the events in the lives of rulers and associate them with actual and mythic history, but they manifested and represented the person of the ruler himself.[51] Discussing the Central Mexican view of the representation of *teotl* (divine or sacred energy) in created artifacts meant to mirror the individual, Houston and Stuart write:

Evidence now suggests a Maya (and probably Mesoamerican) understanding of representation that is quite similar, making use of an extendable essence shared between images and that which is portrayed. The act of carving, modeling, or painting creates a semblant surface and transfers the vital charge conferring identity and animation to the original.[52]

Nowhere is this more apparent than in the stelae of Waxaklajuun U'baah Kawil at Copan. The stelae here are shaped into the full figure of the ruler, representing larger-than-life full forms of the ruler. The reliefs of Waxakla-juun U'baah Kawil on the stelae are so prominent that the stelae are nearly statues of the figure, including glyphic texts on the sides. The effect of these stelae gives one a sense of the immediate presence of the ruler, towering over his subjects.

In these stelae the person of the ruler is made manifest through a duplication of the complete body of the ruler, idealized and enlarged, manifesting the power and divinity of the ruler. The glyphic texts on the Copan stelae themselves hint at this purpose, making claims of hegemony over the four directions of the Maya world by Waxaklajuun U'baah Kawil. These stelae are meant not just as *representations* of the ruler, but as containing the ruler in a more intimate sense. They are part of the *person* of the ruler, in the sense of *baah*. The person is extended through these stelae. In creation of such stelae, then, the person's essence can be duplicated and extended.

One central question here then becomes: *How* does the creation of objects such as stelae extend the personhood of the individual depicted? Is it simply in the resemblance to the person that the essence is extended? Or is it in the intention of the creators of the artifacts, or their goals? Presumably the Copan stelae, though they depicted Waxaklajuun U'baah Kawil, did not look much like him. It is doubtful he was that large, or had the features depicted in the stelae. Certainly also in other stelae and memorials representing other rulers that do not depict figures at all—what is it that makes *these* bearers of the essence of the person? Not just *anything* can bear essence of the person. And physical resemblance is something we simply do not see in these artifacts. There are a few possibilities here: 1) the *intention* of the builders, including the ruler who commissions these memorials, is what creates the resemblance that extends the essence; 2) the *meaning* of the artifact, construed independently of the creators' intentions, is what creates the resemblance that extends the essence, 3) a causal connection between the states of the individual and those of the artifact create the resemblance.

Or perhaps some combination of 1–3 is sufficient for an artifact to serve as representative of a person, including the essence of that person. That is, one or more of them may be necessary but not sufficient. Perhaps the meaning of the artifact and its depiction must be representative of the person, but it must

Figure 4.2   This photo of Copan Stela 4 in 1935 gives a sense of the scale of the stelae, as well as the anthropomorphic "statue" quality of the Copan stelae. Visitor standing beside Stela 4 in the archaeological park of Copan, Honduras, March 19, 1935. © Dumbarton Oaks, Pre-Columbian Collection, Washington, DC.

also be the case that the artifact was constructed for the purpose of expressing personhood, and by the right people—ones invested with the task of "impersonating" by the person represented (generally a ruler). Houston and Stuart claim that stone and other objects themselves contain a kind of "vital essence" that can be formed to represent the person in this extendable identity:

> That stone "lives" or contains vital essence—that it contains the "body" of something else—helps explain the "animation" of Mayan hieroglyphic elements. Signs of the script frequently convey a certain vitality, ranging from basic signs with a facial profile to "full-figure" forms that interact vibrantly and kinetically with other signs around them.[53]

Houston and Stuart also link the "full figure" glyphs to the self or *baah*. There is an inconsistency in the way Houston and Stuart talk about the *baah*, as they associate it with something that can be expressed and extended in numerous ways and contexts, but then also define it narrowly as having to do with the physical body in particular, rather than the person.[54]

Given the modern predilection to materialist reductionism or eliminativism, we can see why scholars would read things this way. But why think that the ancient Maya shared these materialist views? There seems much more reason to believe that they, like the majority of civilizations everywhere in the world throughout history, rejected the kind of reductionist materialism that only developed relatively recently in human thought, and had very few adherents before the modern period.

Baah seems more likely something akin to the *ihiyotl* or *tonalli* of the Aztecs, which could move and be widely associated, rather than a physical body part such as the head, or even the body taken as a whole. How can the individual body be identical with crafted artifacts, or be represented by an individual in the ceremonies of impersonation? The embedded identity here seems to be one in which each individual thing *retains* its unique qualities, but becomes embedded in the identity of a particular person. Thus, when the ruler engages in the ceremony of impersonation, it is not that his body transubstantiates and becomes that of the god impersonated (which would have to be the case if fusion with the *baah* of the god was understood as bodily). The ruler *remains* the ruler, and his body remains as it is. The elements of the ruler's person, in this act of impersonation, become embedded in the person of the god, such that the god's person is represented in this stage *by* that of the ruler. In embedded identity objects retain their features and nature, but become part of or representatives of other personal entities. This concept is not completely foreign to us. The way we think about the identity of continuing roles is very similar, as discussed above.

According to a number of scholars[55], the Maya conception of the soul or animating spirit of the person is dual featured, similar to the Aztec conception and that of early China. The contemporary Zincanteco Maya associate one of these souls with *ch'ul* as discussed above, calling it *chu'lel*. The *chu'lel*, according to the Zincanteco, is an indestructible and eternal aspect of the person (sharing this with the *ch'ul* and *itz* of early Maya thought, as well as the *teotl* of Aztec thought). The other part of the soul is similar to the *way*, an animal guardian that the Tzotzil Maya call *chanul*.[56] The *ch'ul* part of the soul, as universal and extendable, can be connected to entities outside of the body of the individual. This is presumably how the ruler/shaman is able to communicate with entities sharing the same features and *ch'ul* through ritual.

The *baah*, as self, is composed of those same elements, and the *ch'ul* element is something that can be given through the similarity in features of a person and other objects, including representative stelae and sculptures, deities, time periods, and other elements of the world. The *baah* is extendable through *ch'ul*, which is ultimately, as discussed above, a form of *itz*.

NOTES

1. See Zagzebski, "Exemplarist Virtue Theory."
2. While Andrew Jackson is surely an exemplar of the role "President of the United States," in that his features influenced deeply the conception of what it is to perform this role, I certainly do not mean to endorse him as a *moral exemplar*. In fact, this was one of my reasons for choosing him as an example—the norms of particular roles can be "infected" by bad characters as much as they can be "broadened" by good ones. This attaches moral responsibility to later bearers of the role or office.
3. Kupperman, "Tradition and Community in the Formation of Character and Self."
4. *Analects* 11.12.
5. McLeod, "*Ren* as a Communal Property in the *Analects*."
6. *Analects* 18, McLeod "Ren as a Communal Property."
7. *Analects* 18.5–18.7, McLeod, "In the World of Persons," 450.
8. See Kupperman, "Tradition and Community."
9. Ames and Hall, *Thinking from the Han*, 43. They adapt a view they read as originating with George Herbert Mead to understand the Confucian position.
10. Harman, "Moral Philosophy Meets Social Psychology";Zimbardo, *The Lucifer Effect*.
11. Priest, *One*, 179–180. There, Priest attempts to construct a formalized version of the Huayan view.
12. The Yogacara view, on which Huayan is based, and other Buddhist views on the two truths theory, are outlined in Thakchoe, "The Two Truths."
13. This comparison is used by F. Kent Reilly in connection with the royal blood-letting ritual, which he claims creates "a portal to the supernatural ... in the same

way that, at the moment the Host is consecrated in the Mass, the veil between heaven and earth parts and the divine is made manifest here on earth." Reilly, "Olmec Iconographic Influences on the Symbols of Maya Rulership," 156.

14. See chapter 2.

15. We may see this as just the problem of the Advaita Vedanta tradition on the identity between the self (*atman*) and the universal spirit (*Brahman*).

16. Paul VI, *Mysterium Fidei*, #46.

17. Schele and Freidel, *Forest of Kings*; Stuart, "Of Gods, Glyphs, and Kings," Kovacevich, "From the Ground Up."

18. Houston, *The Life Within*, 31–32.

19. Astor-Aguilera, *Communicating Objects*.

20. Astor-Aguilera, *Communicating Objects*, 42.

21. Many anachronistic categories are often used to describe features of ancient thought, while "philosophy" tends to be left out. One example of this can be seen in Chang, *The Rise of the Chinese Empire*, 69: "it was in the final analysis the nature course of action for a great empire after long, intensive, and extensive changes in Han society in social, political, economic, ideological, military, and leadership terms." The suggestion in much historical work seems to be that "philosophy" is simply a particular kind of ideology—a suggestion most philosophers, including myself, would reject.

22. Major et al., *Huainanzi*, Vankeerberghen, *The Huainanzi and Liu An's Claim to Moral Authority*.

23. Houston, *The Life Within*, 78.

24. Houston and Stuart, "The *Way* Glyph: Evidence for 'Co-Essences' Among the Classic Maya."

25. Herring, *Art and Writing in the Maya Cities, AD 600-800*, 237. Friedel, Schele, and Parker claim that the "negative" conception of *way* may be a prejudice of later Christian interpretation, but I think (as mentioned here) there is precedent in various other systems of thought in the Americas for morally ambiguous "trickster" entities whose moral evaluation is based on situational features. Such an interpretation of the *way* makes sense of *why* the later Christians would have (wrongly) thought of them as demonic or evil.

26. Ballinger, *Living Sideways: Tricksters in American Indian Oral Traditions*, 16–18.

27. Walker, *Lakota Myth*, 108.

28. Herring, *Art and Writing in the Maya Cities*, 237.

29. Friedel, Schele, and Parker, *Maya Cosmos*, 191–192.

30. Friedel, Schele, and Parker, *Maya Cosmos*, 192.

31. Ardren, *Social Identities in the Classic Maya Northern Lowlands*, 94.

32. Ardren uses the phrase "spirit world," which I avoid here for reasons discussed in chapter 3. While I think she is right about the view that young children have a greater capacity for vision, I reject the view that what they communicate with is another *world*—rather, it is the unseen aspects of our own world.

33. Ardren, *Social Identities in the Classic Maya Northern Lowlands*, 102.

34. Ardren, *Social Identities*, 122: "fragments of buried human bone that may have been curated for many years were often redeposited in household structures, likely as an offering to ensoul or bring new life to the new architecture."

35. Friedel, Schele, and Parker (*Maya Cosmos*) understand and interpret *ch'ul* and *itz* as distinct parts of the essence of a person.

36. Vogt, *The Zinacantecos of Mexico: A Mayan Way of Life*, 18–19.

37. Fitzsimmons, *Death and the Classic Maya Kings*, 129.

38. Friedel, Schele, and Parker, *Maya Cosmos*, 217.

39. Friedel, Schele, and Parker, *Maya Cosmos*, 217.

40. Scherer, *Mortuary Landscapes of the Classic Maya*.

41. Mondlock, "K'ex: Quiché Naming," 9.

42. *Liji, Quli* 62.

43. Carlsen, *The War for the Heart and Soul of a Highland Maya Town*, 50–51.

44. Houston, *The Life Within,* 72.

45. I explain this further in McLeod, "*Ren* as a Communal Property in the *Analects*," from which the discussion in this section is taken.

46. Houston, Stuart, and Taube, *The Memory of Bones*. Meskell and Joyce, *Embodied Lives*. Houston 2014, *The Life Within*.

47. Houston and Stuart, "The *Way* Glyph."

48. Houston, Stuart, and Taube, *The Memory of Bones*, 5.

49. Houston and Stuart, "The *Way* Glyph."

50. "Textual allusions to the 'image' or 'self,' *ba(h)*, as part of this impersonation point directly to the transcendent merger or supernatural and human identity, to say nothing of further linkages with community deities..." Houston and Stuart, "The *Way* Glyph," 81.

51. Stuart, "Kings of Stone," 149.

52. Houston and Stuart, "The *Way* Glyph," 86.

53. Houston, Stuart, and Taube, *The Memory of Bones*, 76.

54. Houston, Stuart, and Taube, *The Memory of Bones*, 59. They write here that *baah* "relates less to a general meaning of 'being' or 'person' than with the material form of the person."

55. Vogt 1976, Sosa 1988, Friedel, Schele, and Parker 1993.

56. Friedel, Schele, and Parker, *Maya Cosmos*, 182.

Conclusion

Maya Philosophy and World Philosophy

THE MAYA TRADITION IN THE CONTEXT
OF MESOAMERICAN PHILOSOPHY

The concepts, views, and broader thought of the ancient Maya share a number of features with other traditions in Mesoamerica. The most prominent of these is the tradition of the Nahua (Aztecs) of Central Mexico. Aztec philosophy, as outlined by scholars such as Miguel Leon-Portilla and James Maffie, among others, exhibits a clear family resemblance to Maya thought. Indeed, there was almost certainly cross-influence between Maya groups and those peoples of central Mexico who were precursors to the Aztecs. The similarities between Maya and Aztec thought are most pronounced when we consider the thought of northern Yucatan Maya people in the Postclassic period. The emphasis in cities such as Chichen Itza on gods such as Kukulkan (Nahuatl *Quetzalcoatl*) and Itzamna shows clear influence from central Mexican groups and other non-Maya people. In recent years, there has been more focus on the exchange, cultural and economic, between the Maya and surrounding groups.[1] This comparative approach within fields such as anthropology bears some similarity to my own approach to Maya thought. The idea seems to be that we can come to a better understanding of the Maya through understanding what they held in common with their neighbors, as well as the ways they interacted with them. Through using the thought of other Mesoamerican groups as a frame very similarly to the way comparative philosophers approach different traditions, we uncover new aspects of Maya thought.

Though I have not focused on other Mesoamerican traditions such as that of the Aztec in this book, comparative investigation of the Maya tradition alongside of these traditions is certainly important. It will form an essential component of the comparative philosophical project concerning Maya thought, and I hope we see such comparative philosophical studies emerge in the future. Here, I want to briefly outline what I see as a number of fruitful points of contact between Maya philosophy and other Mesoamerican traditions.

While there are numerous people and intellectual traditions in Mesoamerica, the best known of these beside the Maya is that of the Aztecs. Part of the reason for this is that the Aztec Empire was at its height during the period in which Europeans first traveled to Mesoamerica in the sixteenth century. There are many descriptions in Western languages of Aztec culture and practices (even if many of these are negative or biased), and we also have a much larger number of texts from Aztec sources. These include of pre-Columbian texts (a very small number), and texts written during the early colonial period, in Nahuatl rendered both with Latin script and with earlier pictographic script. Because of this, the textual resources we have for the Aztec are far greater than anything we have for any of the other Mesoamerican traditions. This has made it possible to engage with Aztec philosophical thought specifically.

Future comparative studies may shed light on important parallels in the Maya and Aztec philosophical traditions. One particular issue on which I think comparative engagement of Maya and Aztec philosophy can be extremely fruitful is the nature of truth. Both Maya and Aztec traditions conceive of truth in a manner that is relatively unfamiliar to contemporary philosophers working in the "Western" tradition. It is unfamiliar, however, to the *philosophical* concern with truth in our time and place. Maffie, following Leon-Portilla,[2] offers an interpretation of the Aztec concept of *neltiliztli* as an account of truth as "well-rootedness." What an entity is rooted *in* that makes it well-rooted is *teotl*, which is ultimate reality and a continual active process. Truth is understood primarily in terms of its support of instances of knowledge (*tlamatiliztli*), where knowledge specifically has to do with skill or performance.[3]

Since the concept of truth for the Aztecs is not connected to linguistic entities such as statements or propositions primarily (Maffie discusses *cognitions* as truth bearers),[4] what it is for a thing to be well-rooted may be understood to change with the entity we are considering. What it means for a cognition to be well-rooted and for a human being to be well-rooted will necessarily be different. As in Maya and early Chinese thought, Aztec philosophy considers human beings, in addition to activities, objects, and statements, as truth bearers.[5] The Maya concept of *itz* and its relationship to the broader concepts of essence such as *ch'ul* is relatively similar to this. In further investigating the Maya and Aztec conceptions of truth alongside of one another, we might develop an adequate pluralist account of truth. This could be aided by consideration of certain early Chinese views that also suggest a pluralist approach to truth. By investigating Maya concepts in light of Aztec concepts, we can both come to a better understanding of these concepts on both sides (as well as the ways they relate to one another), and develop ultimately more adequate accounts of these fundamental concepts, like that of truth.

NON-WESTERN COMPARATIVE PHILOSOPHY AND THE DECENTERING OF THE WEST

Comparative philosophy, in its recent incarnation in the academy, has mainly focused on the engagement between non-Western and Western traditions. It is common to find studies on Confucius and Aristotle,[6] or Nyaya and Kantianism,[7] for example. This tends to be the standard—some non-Western thinker, text, or school, understood through the comparative lenses of some Western thinker, text, or school. There has been much excellent work done in this kind of comparative philosophy (including the works mentioned in the notes here). The prevalence of these non-West/West comparative studies, however, has tended to lead to the understanding of traditions such as those of the Maya and others in terms of their relationship to the Western traditions. When we understand traditions through a single frame, in this case the Western tradition, it necessarily distorts our image of it, and of the numerous traditions with regard to one another. The focus of comparative philosophy on Western thought effectively centers the West in the philosophical conversation, such that we understand traditions like the Maya or Chinese traditions primarily in terms of the extent to which they resemble Western traditions. Comparative philosophy, in order to live up to its potential to both clarify target traditions and draw out and refine positions through constructive engagement, must involve more than only West-focused comparisons. If we place Chinese thought in engagement with the West, for example, we generate the real danger of missing important features of Chinese thought that would emerge more clearly with a different comparative focus. We will overestimate the centrality of those views and concepts that take center stage when the West is used as the comparative lens through which to view the tradition.

There has been some movement in recent years within comparative philosophy to bring alternative comparative frames into use. Of particular interest has been the rise of Chinese-Indian comparative philosophy.[8] There has also been work in Chinese-Islamic comparative thought in the last few decades.[9] In general, comparative work using non-Western traditions in engagement with one another has tended to surround traditions where there is historical contact. As I have shown throughout this book, Maya thought can be usefully understood using Chinese philosophical traditions as comparative lens. This comparative structure brings out both important elements of the Maya tradition as well as less-recognized elements of the Chinese tradition, neither of which may get as much attention with a comparative project centered on the West. Indeed, the Chinese tradition in this sense is a much better lens through which to understand ancient Maya thought, as there is more overlap between the fundamental concerns of the systems than with either and much of the Western tradition.

Decentering the West in our comparative projects is necessary to make new strides in comparative philosophy. Part of the reason there have been relatively few comparative projects in which the West is decentered is the difficulty of gaining expertise in numerous traditions, including access to source languages. I would like to argue here, however, that this difficulty is overstated, and should not stop comparativists from attempting to engage with multiple non-Western traditions.

First—it is not as daunting as sometimes claimed to gain sufficient expertise in more than one philosophical tradition. One rarely hears the complaint from philosophers that we can insufficiently understand Plato and Kant both, because they are thinkers from two different traditions (ancient Greek and modern European, respectively). Nor is language ever invoked as a barrier for understanding the two of these—at one time, it would have been seen as a basic expectation to read both German and Greek, and likely Latin as well. The problem is not so much one of inherent difficulty in the languages or material involved, but rather of insufficient coverage of the relevant languages and material in departments and institutions. It is rare to find a philosophy department in the United States, for example, with even a single specialist in any non-Western tradition or in comparative philosophy,[10] and is even more rare to find courses in the languages of many non-Western traditions, such as Classical Chinese, Sanskrit, or Classic Mayan. Because of this, the would-be comparativist must be prepared to strike out on his or her own. Autodidacticism is a necessary skill for the multi-tradition comparativist. The hope is that as a result of our efforts, departments of philosophy and others will become less insular and that future generations will be able to study these traditions and languages within our institutions. The need for studying on one's own, however, is not as impenetrable a barrier as it may seem. There are many excellent materials today for studying non-Western traditions and languages, and while it may be *ideal* to have a teacher, it can be done on one's own as well. We do no favors to the advancement of our field by insisting that one cannot learn languages such as Classical Chinese, Sanskrit, or Classic Mayan without a teacher. The knowledge of teachers can be, and has been, codified in books, videos, and other sources—there is no reason learners cannot use this. I have studied languages and cultures both under teachers and on my own, and have not found my self-study to be any less effective, even if somewhat slower. It can be done—especially if it is the center of one's professional focus. Where I have seen most people give up is in cases in which learning other traditions and languages are peripheral to one's training or study. Self-study of difficult traditions and languages is demanding, but can be done if one devotes one's energy to it.

Second—there is much one can do even *without* access to the languages in which texts from non-Western traditions were originally written. There are more and more translations of non-Western philosophical material available today than ever before, and many of these translations are excellent. In some cases, as with well-known texts such as the *Analects* of Confucius, the *Upanishads* or *Bhagavad Gita*, and even the *Popol Vuh*, there are multiple translations, which can be consulted and compared. My own teacher (and predecessor at the University of Connecticut), Joel Kupperman, did excellent and insightful work on the Chinese philosophical tradition in just this way, using multiple translations of key texts like the *Analects*, *Mencius*, *Daodejing*, and *Zhuangzi*. We should not shy away from engaging in comparative philosophy because we may lack a perfect knowledge of a particular language or context. One *never* has perfect knowledge, and even the specialist who has spent their whole career studying a tradition will never have such. What is the baseline of knowledge of a tradition one must achieve to have anything useful to say about it in scholarship? I think we should be more focused on the achievement of insight into a tradition than on maximal breadth of knowledge of its cultural and linguistic context. This is not to say that there is no place for such knowledge. Specialists in Maya thought, for example, had better have a broad understanding of relevant languages, literatures, and cultures. Comparative philosophers, however, will necessarily have a different focus. Comparative philosophers are not, and should not be, area specialists. They should rely on the work of area specialists, but the nature of the comparative philosophical project is very different than that of area specialists. Part of the problem that has developed in recent years is the idea on both sides that one's own project is the one that everyone whose work overlaps with our own should be working on.[11] Comparative philosophers should strive to *understand* the traditions they work on, to be sure. But given that their aim in engaging with these traditions will most often be very different than the scholar of area studies, it is strange to think the two should train in the same way, and use the same tools. This would be like insisting that an architect become an expert in every system of the building they construct—a master plumber, electrician, welder, builder, etc. No one could ever have such expertise, and requiring the architect to have it is unnecessary. It is enough that the architect understands enough about each of these areas to know what kinds of design will and will not work on the basis of the constraints of pipes, plumbing, electric wires, etc. The architect must have wide learning, but to expect the architect to master the norms and practice of any of the other individual arts involved in constructing a building would suffocate the practice of architecture.

It is my hope that the previous chapters of this book can serve as a demonstration of the what we might gain from a comparative philosophical project with the West decentered. Maya thought in particular serves as a good example of a tradition that can best be understood through the lenses of Chinese thought, rather than Western thought. Indeed, it may be part of the reason ancient Maya thought has been understood as adopting the kind of time-reductionism I criticize in chapter 1 that it has, at least in academic scholarship, been understood mainly in engagement with Western thought.[12] The comparative project with the West decentered opens up new possibilities in each of the traditions we engage with one another. Just as I have used early Chinese philosophy to illuminate aspects of Maya philosophy, Maya philosophy can also help us to appreciate aspects of Chinese thought that are often missed or insufficiently appreciated.

With the West decentered in the comparative project, we can discover new features of a system of thought that can then be used in contemporary philosophical projects, or in a number of different contexts. The decentered West approach is particularly helpful for contemporary projects, as it helps to ensure that we locate ideas that are sufficiently different from those of the Western tradition as to be challenging and present us with viable alternatives. Eric Schwitzgebel has discussed this as a general comparative method,[13] arguing that the interpretation of a text that attributes to it the most unintuitive or seemingly bizarre view is to be privileged, as this offers us the most useful position for use in countering our own philosophical presuppositions. My problem with this method is that it seems overly focused on the usefulness of texts and traditions independently of the actual concerns of those texts and traditions. If we are primarily concerned with challenging our philosophical presuppositions, why don't we instead simply locate those presuppositions, and try taking seriously their opposites or some imagined different position? It's unclear to me that we need non-Western or other philosophical traditions to do that.

What *is* useful about other traditions, though, is that the ways these traditions diverge from (and correspond with) Western philosophical traditions. This can tell us important things about what philosophy is, how it is done throughout the world and in different ages, and suggest to us ways that we might reenvision our own philosophical projects, so as to make them more inclusive, representative of human thought, and comprehensive. My own conception of the comparative project owes much to the Han dynasty Chinese text *Huainanzi*, whose authors held that it was only through understanding the myriad traditions of human thought (which for them included those of the known realms within and around the Han empire) that we can hope to conclusively answer fundamental questions concerning humanity and the cosmos. The first chapter of *Huainanzi*, titled *Yuan Dao* (Origins in the Way), includes a statement of this:

> Now if someone spends an entire day pole-fishing along a riverbank he will not be able to fill up even a hand basket. Even though he may have hooked barbs and sharp spears, fine line and fragrant bait, and, in addition, the skills of Zhan He or Juan Xuan, he would still be unable to compete with the catch hauled in by a trawling net. Or suppose a bowman were to stretch out the famous Wuhao bow and fit it with the fine arrows from Qi and add to this the craft of Yi or Feng Mengzi. If he wanted to hunt birds in flight, he would still be unable to match the amount caught by a gauze net. Why is this? It is because what he is holding is small by comparison.[14]

Maya philosophy represents a unique and rich tradition, one that has thus far been completely neglected by philosophers (like a number of other philosophical traditions). Part of the reason for this neglect, of course, has been that Maya thought is seen as the purview of anthropologists, archaeologists, and contemporary Maya people themselves. It is my hope that in outlining Maya philosophy here, I can encourage more philosophers to engage with Maya thought, and more Mayanists to engage with philosophy. The Maya tradition has much to contribute to contemporary thinking about fundamental philosophical issues, both in the academy and beyond. My choice of early Chinese thought as the specific comparative frame here was based on what I see as the deep resonance between certain aspects of the Chinese and Maya traditions. It is my hope that the benefits of this project will draw more attention to both philosophy in Maya thought and to the kind of "south-south" comparative project that this book represents.[15]

ENGAGEMENT WITH MAYA PEOPLE

It is important that this process not simply co-opt ancient (or modern) Maya thought for the purposes of advancing projects pursued mainly by non-Maya people. Part of the process of constructing truly global philosophical outlooks is to include the *people* of the world in the project, and to take their thought and their concerns seriously. One way of proceeding in the comparative project is to begin with a host of considerations, methods, and views from one's "home tradition," in this case contemporary analytic philosophy, and simply force other systems of thought into a form in which they can be digested and taken on board by the home tradition. This is not the best way of proceeding for multiple reasons. First, it is far from clear that contemporary analytic philosophy, its methods and the questions it asks, is the most fruitful way of

thinking about philosophy. We should be open to the possibility that the age
of analytic philosophy is coming to a close, as new institutional structures,
new concerns, and new ways of thinking about the fundamental philosophical questions confronting humanity emerge. Global philosophical systems
can both help us to understand ways in which we might develop this new
philosophical project, and set its parameters. Part of this project should be,
however, engaging with and including the projects and methodologies of
people in these various traditions, outside of the Western academy. Integrating Maya thought in a new way to re-envision the contemporary philosophical project should involve engagement with Maya thinkers, dialogue with
them and others concerning how we should move forward. Ownership of the
project is important. Who is the "we" spoken of when the claim is made that
"we should re-envision the philosophical project"? Fairly often, I think, this
implicit "we" is Western academics in American or (sometimes) European
institutions. But the concerns and projects of this group will necessarily be
much different from those of other groups, and it seems plausible to think that
we cannot truly develop a global philosophy while construing the "we" who
do philosophy this narrowly.

Other fields such as anthropology have been somewhat better at this than
philosophy, but even there the narrow Western (and often white) "we" pre-
dominates. From my own place within the Western academy, of course, I am
located in this narrow "we," but I think we (in this same narrow sense, which
I imagine most, but hopefully not all, of my readers will fall into) should aim
to integrate these views into our own projects, and to engage the *people* working in these areas as equal partners in our project as well. In discussions of
comparative philosophy as a kind of mining of "Non-Western" philosophical
traditions for useful resources, some have sounded a note of caution. Michael
Levine writes:

> Is exploring another philosophical tradition's insights or arguments with the aim
> of bringing them back home count as constructive engagement? Many Native
> American philosophers would see it as expropriation and piracy.[16]

Constructive engagement, as Levine calls it, without true fusion, results in
a kind of material appropriation of other cultures for the purposes of a narrowly defined group, such as Western academics. But what does it mean to
engage in true fusion? Levine himself disparages the project referred to sometimes as "fusion philosophy" (following the terminology of Mark Siderits).[17]
Part of what is at issue here is that fusion philosophy, as he understands it, is
the use of non-Western sources to contribute to debates and concerns in current philosophy within the Western academy (and other areas influenced by
it). While I am not as unfriendly to the fusion project in this sense as Levine, I

think there are *additional* projects that we might call "fusion philosophy" and a truer sense. As far as the Siderits fusion project is concerned—I'm not sure comparison with problematic cultural appropriation is apt. What, after all, is objectionable about such appropriation? Surely not the fact that one is making use of the resources of another tradition—but rather that such use is made without concern for or regard for the people from whom the resources are taken. Thus, the seventeenth-century Spanish mine silver in Central America and send it back to Europe, to make money that will benefit the Spanish themselves, and not the natives from whose land the silver was extracted, or who suffered the most to extract it. For a more modern example—the use of white Americans throughout the twentieth century of musical forms and styles of black artists can be seen as a kind of negative appropriation. The reason for this is not that white artists took elements of black music, but rather that this use coincided with the rejection of black people as equal social partners and beneficiaries of the results of this appropriation. It seems to me that the problem here, however, was not the adoption of black music, rather the problem was racism. Cultural products such as musical style or philosophical ideas are intrinsically different from physical and natural resources, in that they are inexhaustible, require no work to produce, and do not have to be *taken away* from others. The constant development of human society has happened through cultural borrowing, without which no culture that exists today would exist. Aztecs revered Maya gods, the Maya worked with a calendar devised by the Olmec (or another Isthmian people). The Japanese use characters originally from China. Most of the products we use in the modern world (regardless of where we live) were developed by people in other places. Without cultural diffusion, human society withers and dies. And cultural diffusion never happens through agreement—one group simply uses aspects of the culture of another that it finds useful. It is unclear to me why we should see anything wrong with this. There is plenty, on the other hand, wrong with racism and systematic oppression. Thus, even the kind of "philosophical appropriation" approach to non-Western thought can be useful, and is a project worthy of pursuing. What happens when we open the toolkit of other traditions to see what we might find there to help us answer outstanding questions in our own modern philosophical project? Certainly much can be done here. It is simply another of the myriad useful and interesting projects that can be developed in comparative philosophy. We should resist any urge to collapse this methodological diversity—indeed, this diversity is what makes comparative philosophy vital and endlessly fascinating. Comparative philosophy should by all rights be the most exciting and important area in philosophy today.

A different methodology, and one I have attempted to advance here, is what we might call "true fusion" (for lack of a better phrase). Though I do not mean to advance the true fusion project as the "One True Method" to which all others must bow, there are some advantages it has over other methods on some considerations. Which method is best for us to adopt will likely depend on which project we are engaged in. True fusion will not present difficulties of appropriation in any sense. The reason for this is that true fusion not only takes aspects of traditions, but is also open to the inclusion of other people and traditions in the fusion project itself. True fusion is open to the expansion of the "we" so that it comes to include not only those who originated exchange, but also those with whom exchange happens. And in this openness, the idea is that the conception of the project itself will change as the fusion happens. The questions we begin with—those we encounter other traditions to answer—will not be the same questions with which we end. They may be closely related, or may be completely different, but the constructive engagement itself will shape the way we think about the project, and the very character of the "we" who think about the project. Still—the question arises—what does this entail for projects like those of contemporary Western academia? My own project of interpreting and developing themes in Maya philosophy, for example—is this merely philosophical appropriation, or is it true fusion? My audience is mainly comprised of academics (though I hope others engage with this work as well). I can be open to learning from the methods, arguments, and views of the ancient Maya, listening to and learning from the current-day Maya, and to allowing modern Maya people to be part of the project (how can I stop them?), but can I transform the project from one that is intrinsically a modern academic project to something else, that might be guided by Maya conceptions of the intellectual project? To what extent can I actually take on ancient Maya practices and forms, many of which are limited to their time and place—there is no way anyone could effectively be an *ahau* or do the work of an *ahau* or even a *sahal* in the modern world, for example. And as far as Maya people—the academic projects those of us in academia are involved in should always be open to and welcoming to Maya (and other) people—but the extent to which they will be included will be largely an institutional matter beyond the control of those of us engaged in comparative philosophical projects. We can insist on sufficient diversity in our places on hiring committees, etc., include Maya voices in our conferences on Maya thought, etc., engage in interdisciplinary cooperation bringing Maya people from different areas into engagement with our work, etc., but beyond this there is little we can do.

And a related difficulty arises here. Why should we assume that a modern Maya person has any greater understanding or access to the ancient Maya tradition than a non-Maya student of the ancient Maya? Does one's ethnic, racial, or cultural identity give one a privileged access to an intellectual tradition of the past? Could there not be experts of early American political philosophy in China who understood eighteenth-century American thought far better than nonspecialist Americans or even American specialists and those in related areas? That is, it is unclear what, if anything, being a member of a particular culture or ethnicity gets one as far as privileged access to ancestral cultural traditions. The ways we think about the transmission of culture, and who is a member of a particular culture, are deeply confused. Part of the reason for this is cultural essentialism—the idea we cling to that there are discrete borders between traditions, such that we can neatly divide "Western" from "Non-Western," Chinese from Indian, Maya from Aztec, etc. Much like racial distinctions, cultural distinctions are conventional and of artificial necessity. When we begin to subject them to microscopic investigation to keep closer track of them as part of a fusion project, they begin to fall apart.

In a sense, then, we are *always* doing fusion philosophy, whether we admit it or not. The key here is how widely we are willing to cast our net for ideas, methods, and ways of thinking different from those that predominate in our own circles. Part of how we can ensure this constant influx of new ideas and transformation of current projects is to include both ideas and people who are less often seen in the projects we pursue. Thus, we should engage with the thought of the ancient and contemporary Maya, and engage with the modern Maya people, in the hopes that we may have a true fusion such that one day there will no longer be Maya or Westerners (whatever that means), no longer Chinese, Indians—but a true fusion of all of these groups, such that our descendants can claim the traditions of all of these cultures as their own heritage.

WHERE DO WE GO FROM HERE?

I have sympathies with all camps involved here. Different aims may lead to different conceptions of the philosophical project to be pursued with "Non-Western" thought in general, and Maya thought in specific. That is to be expected, and should be acceptable to us. There is room enough for all of us here, and we should always be suspicious of claims to justify the hegemony of a One True Methodology. One project that seems to me to have been mainly left out of the discussion, though, is that of developing projects in "Non-Western" traditions *independently* of contemporary analytic or other forms of philosophy—that is, the development of new programs that take seriously and as central the concepts, views, and arguments of traditions like that of the Maya. Of course, one would rightly observe that there *are* people engaged in just this, Maya people advancing their own tradition, separately from the Western academy. What I propose is a bit different from this, however. It is that we (here referring to professional academics in the West and elsewhere—philosophers, anthropologists, and others) might take up as serious research programs the questions that Maya, Chinese, or Indian thinkers asked (for example), and take *their* projects as setting the foundation in which our work is defined. In such a project, one constructs systems or attempts to answer philosophical questions[18] that come from a particular tradition and set of concerns.

This kind of project is actually fairly well-known in the current philosophical community. Religious philosophers, most prominently (in American academia at least) Christian philosophers, sometimes engage in this kind of project.[19] They begin with questions, concerns, and problems drawn from a particular community, tradition, and shared doctrine. The Christian philosopher[20] asks the questions: What is the nature of God? Can we demonstrate God's existence? Is belief in God rational? What is the nature of the relationship between God and humanity? There is considerable overlap of the concern of such philosophers with those of theologians. While many contemporary philosophers might deny the claim that they too have questions, concerns, and problems based in a certain tradition and conditioned by their prerational commitments, it is no less true of them than it is of Christian philosophers or theologians. One might object here that the Christian theologian is committed to the doctrines of Christianity in a way the philosopher is not committed dogmatically. But this is an illusion. True, the non-Christian analytic philosopher is not committed to the truth of certain propositions regarding a creator or particular nature of humanity, but such a philosopher does have prerational commitments. What argument, for example, would convince a philosopher to abandon their commitment to naturalism? How much failure to bridge the "explanatory gap" in the philosophy of mind would it take to get the philosopher to accept Cartesian dualism? As much as we might dig in our heels and claim that such commitments are different than those of the Christian philosopher because they are merely contingent and subject to change based on evidence (whether empirical or rational), what reason do we have to think this is actually so, any more than the Christian philosopher? We fail to abandon physicalism even if we are presented extraordinarily difficult problems for it, such as the explanatory gap problem. We instead search for other ways to make physicalism work. How is this different from the failure of the Christian philosopher to abandon belief in God when there are problems demonstrated with the view that God exists? Neither philosopher will abandon their core commitments in the face of argument, regardless of what the philosopher might *claim* that they do. We do not, in fact, find willingness to abandon commitments.

What might such a project of taking Maya concerns as our starting point look like? One of the jobs of philosophy, as I see it, is to help us build coherent systems of thought from a few fundamental components. Doing philosophy in a specifically Maya way could happen in a number of ways. One of these ways is suggested by the project I begin with this book. That is, we can look into the ancient texts and material culture of the pre-Columbian Maya, and use these ideas to construct a coherent system making sense of the basic commitments of these early Maya systems. How, we might ask, do we determine which aspects of ancient Maya thought are fundamental, and which parts might be changed or jettisoned? Here, we simply have to make choices. Depending on what we select as fundamental, different kinds of system will be possible. We can try constructing a number of possible systems, with the test being both internal consistency and their strength against competing systems, in terms of any of the measures we might use to compare systems, including explanatory value, elegance, etc.[21] It is my hope that the project I have started in this book offers a roadmap for at least one way of both uncovering the philosophical thought of the ancient Maya, of creating systems of thought based on Maya thought, and of offering tools for both comparative synthesis and the use of Maya philosophy for the advancement and even transformation of current philosophical projects.

NOTES

1. A recent volume of papers was dedicated to this topic, Braswell, *The Maya and Their Central American Neighbors*, and the 2017 Maya Meetings at the University of Texas focused on "The Maya as Neighbors in Ancient Mesoamerica."

2. In Leon-Portilla, *Aztec Thought and Culture*.

3. Maffie, "Aztec Philosophy." This is a similar view of knowledge to that of one interpretation of early Chinese thought, offered by Roger Ames, Chad Hansen, Chris Fraser, and others. While I agree that performative or skill knowledge is one *type* of knowledge discussed by early Chinese thinkers, I reject the view that all knowledge is of this kind for early Chinese thinkers. I remain agnostic about the Aztec case.

4. In this way very similar to the thinking about truth we find in the classical Indian tradition.

5. Maffie, "Aztec Philosophy": "The Nahuas characterized persons, things, activities, and utterances equally and without equivocation in terms of *neltiliztli*."

6. Examples include Yu, *Confucius and Aristotle: Mirrors of Virtue*, Sim, *Remastering Morals With Confucius and Aristotle*, and even Bryan Van Norden, *Virtue Ethics and Consequentialism in Early Chinese Philosophy*. My own doctoral dissertation was on this topic—*Moral Personhood in Confucius and Aristotle* (2009).

7. Examples include Chakrabarti, "The End of Life: A Nyaya-Kantian Approach to the Bhagavadgita," Chadha, "Perceptual Cognition: A Nyaya-Kantian Approach."

8. Recent works in this area include Berger, *Encounters of Mind*, Ithamar and Yao, eds. *Brahman and Dao*.

9. Izutsu, *Sufism and Taoism*; Murata, *The Tao of Islam*, *Chinese Gleams of Sufi Light*.

10. Numerous philosophers have written about this problem in recent years. See Van Norden, "Problems and Prospects for the Study of Chinese Philosophy in the English-Speaking World."

11. Nylan, "Academic Silos, or, What I Wish Philosophers Knew About History."

12. Thus the focus on "linear" versus "cyclical" conceptions of time in many works, for example.

13. Schwitzgebel, "Against Charity in the History of Philosophy," http://schwitzs plinters.blogspot.com/2017/01/against-charity-in-history-of-philosophy.html.

14. *Huainanzi* 1.6. Major et al., *Huainanzi*, 54.

15. This terminology is used in recent works, derived from the phrase "global south," used to describe what used to be called the more problematic phrases "developing countries" or "third world." "South-south" makes a less unwieldy phrase than "Non-West-Non-West."

16. Levine, "Does Comparative Philosophy Have a Fusion Future?" 212.

17. In his *Personal Identity and Buddhist Philosophy: Empty Persons.*

18. The question of whether philosophy should be seen as "problem solving," as guidance, or something else, is a heated topic of discussion in a number of recent articles surrounding Michael Levine's criticisms of Mark Siderits, in the inaugural issue of the *Journal of World Philosophies* (2016).

19. it is critical to note the difference here between Christian philosophers *as such* and philosophers who are Christian. The latter group may not conduct their philosophical research in ways that are informed or constrained by their religious faith, may accept all or most of the intuitions other mainstream philosophers accept, and thus may be indistinguishable (on the basis of their philosophical work at least) from non-Christian philosophers.

20. Those who engage in Christian philosophy, doing philosophy as part of a Christian project, rather than philosophers who are Christians engaging in philosophy in the tradition of contemporary analytic philosophy or beginning from its secular presuppositions.

21. This is generally also how scientific theories are judged, with the weight on explanatory value.

Bibliography

Adjaye, Joseph. "Time, Identity, and Historical Consciousness in Akan." In Adjaye, ed. *Time in the Black Experience*. Westport, CT: Greenwood Press, 1994.

Aldana, Gerardo. *The Apotheosis of Janaab' Pakal: Science, History, and Religion at Classic Maya Palenque*. Boulder: University Press of Colorado, 2007.

Alvarado, Walburga Rupflin. *El Tzolkin es más que un calendario*. Iximulew, Guatemala: Fundacion centro de documentacion e investigacion Maya, 1999.

Anthony, David. *The Horse, the Wheel, and Language: How Bronze-Age Riders from the Eurasian Steppes Shaped the Modern World*. Princeton: Princeton University Press, 2010.

Arata, Luis. "The Testimonial of Rigoberta Menchú in a Native Tradition." In Carey-Webb and Benz, eds. *Teaching and Testimony: Rigoberta Menchu and the North American Classroom*. Albany: State University of New York Press, 1996.

Ardren, Traci. *Social Identities in the Classic Maya Northern Lowlands: Gender, Age, Memory, and Place*. Austin: University of Texas Press, 2015.

Astor-Aguilera, Miguel. *The Maya World of Communicating Objects: Quadripartite Crosses, Trees, and Stones*. Albuquerque: University of New Mexico Press. 2011.

Austin, R.W.J. *Ibn al 'Arabi: The Bezels of Wisdom*. Mahwah, NJ: Paulist Press, 1980.

Ballinger, Franchot. *Living Sideways: Tricksters in American Indian Oral Traditions*. Norman: University of Oklahoma Press, 2004.

Barrera Vásquez, Alfredo and Silvia Rendón. *El libro de los libros de Chilam Balam de Chumayel*. Ciudad de Mexico: Fondo de Cultura Económica, 1948.

Barrera Vásquez, dir. *Diccionario Maya Cordemex*. Merida: Ediciones Cordemex, 1980.

Bartha, Paul. "Analogy and Analogical Reasoning." In *Stanford Encyclopedia of Philosophy*.

Behuniak, James. *Mencius on Becoming Human*. Albany: SUNY Press, 2005.

Berger, Douglas. *Encounters of Mind: Luminosity and Personhood in Indian and Chinese Thought*. Albany, SUNY Press, 2015.

Bianchi, Ugo. "Dualism." In Eliade, ed. *The Encyclopedia of Religion*. New York: Macmillan. 1987.

Blackson, Thomas. "The Stuff of Conventionalism." *Philosophical Studies* 68 (1), 1991.

Bonnett, Alastair. *The Idea of the West: Culture, Politics, and History*. London: Palgrave, 2004.

Braswell, Gregory, ed. *The Maya and Their Central American Neighbors: Settlement Patterns, Architecture, Hieroglyphic Texts, and Ceramics*. Abdingdon: Routledge, 2014.

Carlsen, Robert. *The War for the Heart and Soul of a Highland Maya Town*. [Revised Edition]. Austin: University of Texas Press, 2011.

Carlsen, William. *Jungle of Stone: The Extraordinary Journey of John L. Stephens and Frederick Catherwood, and the Discovery of the Lost Civilization of the Maya*. New York: William Morrow, 2016.

Chadha, Monima. "Perceptual Cognition: A Nyaya-Kantian Approach." *Philosophy East and West* 51 (2), 2001.

Chakrabarti, Arindam. "The End of Life: A Nyaya-Kantian Approach to the Bhagavadgita." *Journal of Indian Philosophy* 16 (4), 1988.

Chakrabarti, Arindam and Ralph Weber, eds. *Comparative Philosophy without Borders*. London: Bloomsbury, 2015.

Chang, Chun-shu. *The Rise of the Chinese Empire: Nation, State, and Imperialism in Early China, ca. 1600 BC- AD 8*. Ann Arbor: University of Michigan Press, 2007.

Christenson, Allen. *Art and Society in a Highland Maya Community: The Altarpiece of Santiago Atitlán*. Austin: University of Texas Press, 2001.

Christenson, Allen. *Popol Vuh: The Sacred Book of the Maya*. Norman: University of Oklahoma Press, 2007.

Coe, Michael. *Breaking the Maya Code*. London: Thames and Hudson, 1992.

Coe, Michael. *Lords of the Underworld: Masterpieces of Classic Maya Ceramics*. Princeton: Princeton University Press, 1978.

Colas, Pierre. "K'inich and King: Naming Self and Person among Classic Maya Rulers." *Ancient Mesoamerica* 14 (2), 2003.

Culbert, T. Patrick. "Maya Political History and Elite Interaction: A Summary View." In Culbert, ed. *Classic Maya Political History: Hieroglyphic and Archaeological Evidence*. Cambridge: Cambridge University Press, 1996.

Culbert, T. Patrick, ed. *The Classic Maya Collapse*. Santa Fe: School for Advanced Research Press, 1973.

De la Garza, Mercedes. "Time and World in Maya and Nahuatl Thought." In Dascal, ed. *Cultural Relativism and Philosophy: North and Latin American Perspectives*. Leiden: Brill, 1991.

De Landa, Diego. *Relación de las cosas de Yucatan*. México: Miguel Angel Porrua, 1982 [1562].

DeCaro, Mario and David Macarthur, eds. *Naturalism in Question*. Cambridge, MA: Harvard University Press, 2008.

DeCaro, Mario and David Macarthur, eds. *Naturalism and Normativity*. New York: Columbia University Press, 2010.

Deloria, Vine. *Spirit and Reason: The Vine Deloria, Jr. Reader*. Golden, CO: Fulcrum, 1999.

Demarest, Arthur. "The Collapse of the Classic Maya Kingdoms of the Southwest Petén: Implications for the End of Classic Maya Civilization." In Arnauld and Breton eds. *Millenary Maya Societies: Past Crises and Resilience*. Paris: Musée de Quai Branly, 2013.

Demarest, Arthur, Prudence Rice and Don Rice, eds. *The Terminal Classic in the Maya Lowlands: Collapse, Transition, and Transformation*. Boulder: University Press of Colorado, 2005.

Descartes, Rene. *Meditations on First Philosophy*. Cress, trans. Indianapolis: Hackett, 1993 [1637].

Droit-Volet, Silvie, Sophie Fayolle, and Sandrine Gil. "Emotion and Time Perception: Effects of Film-Induced Mood." *Frontiers of Integrative Neuroscience* 5 (33), 2011.

Eberl, Markus. "To Put in Order: Classic Maya Concepts of Time and Space." In Aveni, ed. *The Measure and Meaning of Time in the Americas*. Washington, DC: Dumbarton Oaks Research Library and Collection, 2015.

Elder, Crawford. *Real Natures and Familiar Objects*. Cambridge, MA: MIT Press, 2007.

Evans, Susan and David Webster, eds. *Archaeology of Ancient Mexico and Central America: An Encyclopedia*. Abingdon: Routledge, 2000.

Fasquelle, Ricardo and David Beyl. *Copan: reino del sol*. Copan: Kingdom of the Sun. Honduras: Editoral Transamerica, 2007.

Fitzsimmons, James. *Death and the Classic Maya Kings*. Austin: University of Texas Press, 2009.

Foster, Lynn. *Handbook to Life in the Ancient Maya World*. Oxford: Oxford University Press, 2002.

Friedel, David, Reese-Taylor, and Mora-Marin. "The Origins of Maya Civilization: The Old Shell Game, Commodity, Treasure, and Kingship." In Masson and Friedel, eds. *Ancient Maya Political Economies*. New York: Altamira Press, 2002.

Girard, Rafael. *Los mayas: su historia, sus vinculaciones continentals*. Ciudad de México: Libro Mex Editores, 1966.

Goldin, Paul. *Rituals of the Way: The Philosophy of Xunzi*. Chicago: Open Court, 1999.

Gracia, Jorge and Manuel Vargas. "Latin American Philosophy." In *Stanford Encyclopedia of Philosophy*, 2013.

Graham, Angus. *Yin-Yang and the Nature of Correlative Thinking*. Singapore: Institute of East Asian Philosophies, 1986.

Grene, Marjorie. *Descartes*. Indianapolis: Hackett, 1985.

Guernsey Kappelman, Julia. "Carved in Stone: The Cosmological Narratives of Late Preclassic Izapan-Style Monuments from the Pacific Slope." In Stone, ed. *Heart of Creation: The Mesoamerican World and the Legacy of Linda Schele*. Tuscaloosa: University of Alabama Press, 2002.

Guernsey Kappelman, Julia. "Sacred Geography at Izapa and the Performance of Rulership." In Koontz, Reese-Taylor, and Headrick, eds. *Landscape and Power in Ancient America*. Boulder: Westview Press, 2001.

Guernsey, Julia. *Ritual and Power in Stone: The Performance of Rulership in Meso-american Izapan Style Art*. Austin: University of Texas Press, 2006.

Gyekye, Kwame. *An Essay on African Philosophical Thought: The Akan Conceptual Scheme*. Cambridge: Cambridge University Press, 1987.

Hall, David and Roger Ames. *Thinking from the Han: Self, Truth, and Transcendence in Chinese and Western Culture*. Albany: SUNY Press, 1998.

Harman, Gilbert. "Moral Philosophy Meets Social Psychology: Virtue Ethics and the Fundamental Attribution Error." 1999.

Harris, John and Stephen Stearns. *Understanding Maya Inscriptons: A Hieroglyph Handbook*. Philadelphia: University of Pennsylvania Museum of Archaeology and Anthropology, 1997.

Hart, Thomas. *The Ancient Spirituality of the Modern Maya*. Albuquerque: University of New Mexico Press, 2008.

Henderson, John. *The Development and Decline of Chinese Cosmology*. New York: Columbia University Press, 1984.

Herring, Adam. *Art and Writing in the Maya Cities, AD 600–800: A Poetics of Line*. Cambridge: Cambridge University Press, 2005.

Houston, Stephen, Oswalkdo Mazariegos, and David Stuart, eds. *The Decipherment of Ancient Maya Writing*. Norman: University of Oklahoma Press, 2001.

Houston, Stephen, and David Stuart. "The *Way* Glyph: Evidence for 'Co-Essences' Among the Classic Maya." 1996.

Houston, Stephen, David Stuart, and Karl Taube. *The Memory of Bones: Body, Being, and Experience among the Classic Maya*. Austin: University of Texas Press, 2013.

Houston, Stephen, John Robertson, and David Stuart. "The Language of Classic Maya Inscriptions." *Current Anthropology* 41 (3), 2000.

Houston, Stephen. *The Life Within: Classic Maya and the Matter of Permanence*. Houston, Stuart, and Taube, 1996.

Izutsu, Toshihiko. *Sufism and Taoism: A Comparative Study of Key Philosophical Concepts*. Berkeley: University of California Press, 1984.

Johnson, Scott. *Translating Maya Hieroglyphs*. Norman: University of Oklahoma Press, 2013.

Jones, Grant. *The Conquest of the Last Maya Kingdom*. Palo Alto: Stanford University Press, 1998.

Josserand, J. Kathryn. "The Narrative Structure of Hieroglyphic Texts and Palenque." In Robertson, ed. *Sixth Palenque Round Table*. Norman: University of Oklahoma Press, 1991.

Joyce, Rosemary and Lynn Meskell. *Embodied Lives: Figuring Ancient Maya and Egyptian Experience*. Abington: Routledge, 2007.

Kelley, David. *Deciphering the Maya Script*. Austin: University of Texas Press, 1976.

Kelley, David. "Mesoamerican Astronomy and the Maya Calendar Correlation Problem." In *Memorias Il Colloquio Internacional de Mayistas*. México: UNAM, 1989.

Knowlton, Timothy. *Maya Creation Myths: Words and Worlds of the Chilam Balam*. Boulder: University Press of Colorado, 2010.

Kovacevich, Brigitte. "From the Ground Up: Household Craft Specialization and Classic Maya Polity Integration." In Marken and Fitzsimmons, eds. *Maya Polities of the Southern Lowlands: Integration, Interaction, Dissolution.* Boulder: University Press of Colorado, 2015.

Kristan-Graham, Cynthia. "Structuring Identity at Tula: The Design and Symbolism of Colonnaded Halls and Sunken Spaces." In Kristan-Graham and Kowalski, eds. *Twin Tollans: Chichen Itza, Tula, and the Epiclassic to Early Postclassic Mesoamerican World.* Cambridge, MA: Harvard University Press, 2007.

Kupperman, Joel. "Tradition and Community in the Formation of Character and Self" in Shun, Kwong-loi and David Wong, eds. *Confucian Ethics: A Comparative Study of Self, Autonomy, and Community.* Cambridge: Cambridge University Press, 2004.

Lee, Janghee. *Xunzi and Early Chinese Naturalism.* Albany: SUNY Press, 2005.

Leon-Portilla, Miguel. *Tiempo y realidad en el pensamiento maya.* Ciudad de Mexico: Universidad Nacional Autónomica de México, Instituto de Investigaciones Históricas. 1968.

Leon-Portilla, Miguel. (Davis, trans.) *Aztec Thought and Culture: A Study of the Ancient Nahuatl Mind.* Norman: University of Oklahoma Press, 1963.

Levine, Michael. "Does Comparative Philosophy Have a Fusion Future?" in *Confluence* 4, 2016.

Lewis, David. *On the Plurality of Worlds.* Oxford: Blackwell, 1986.

Lima Soto, Richard. *Aproximación a la cosmovisión maya.* Guatemala: Universidad Rafael Landivar, Instituto de Investigaciones Económicas y Sociales, 1995.

Liu, Jeeloo. "Chinese Qi Naturalism and Liberal Naturalism." In *Philosophy, Theology, and the Sciences* 1 (1), 2014.

Liu, Jeeloo. "In Defense of Qi Naturalism." In Li and Perkins, eds. *Chinese Metaphysics and Its Problems.* Cambridge: Cambridge University Press, 2015.

Loewe, Michael. *Faith, Myth, and Reason in Han China.* Indianapolis: Hackett, 2005.

Looper, Matthew. *To Be Like Gods: Dance in Ancient Maya Civilization.* Austin: University of Texas Press, 2010.

López Austin, Alfredo and Leonardo López Luján. *El pasado indígena.* México: Colegio de México, Fideicomiso Historia de las Américas, 1996.

Luxton, Richard. *The Book of Chumayel: The Counsel Book of the Yucatec Maya 1539–1638.* Walnut Creek, CA: Aegean Park Press, 1995.

MacIntyre, Alasdair. *After Virtue.* South Bend: University of Notre Dame Press, 1981.

Macri, Martha, and Gabrielle Vail. *The New Catalog of Maya Hieroglyphs, Volume Two: The Codical Texts.* Norman: University of Oklahoma Press, 2009.

Maffie, James. "Aztec Philosophy" *Internet Encyclopedia of Philosophy.*

Maffie, James. *Aztec Philosophy: Understanding a World in Motion.* Boulder: University Press of Colorado, 2014.

Major, John, Sarah Queen, Andrew Meyer, and Harold Roth, trans. *Huainanzi: A Guide to the Theory and Practice of Government in Early Han China.* New York: Columbia University Press, 2010.

Major, John. *Heaven and Earth in Early Han Thought: Chapters Three, Four, and Five of the Huainanzi.* Albany: SUNY Press, 1993.

Malmström, Vincent. *Cycles of the Sun, Mysteries of the Moon: The Calendar in Mesoamerican Civilization.* Austin: University of Texas Press, 1996.

Mathews, Peter and Linda Schele. *The Code of Kings: The Language of Seven Sacred Maya Temples and Tombs.* New York: Scribner, 1999.

Matul, Daniel and Edgar Cabrera. *La cosmovisión maya.* Guatemala: Liga Maya, 2007.

Mbiti, John. *African Religions and Philosophy, 2nd Edition.* London: Heinemann, 1990 [1969].

McEvilley, Thomas. *The Shape of Ancient Thought: Comparative Studies in Greek and Indian Philosophies.* New York: Allworth Press, 2001.

McKillop, Heather. *The Ancient Maya: New Perspectives.* Santa Barbara, CA: ABC-CLIO, 2005.

McLeod, Alexus. "*Ren* as a Communal Property in the *Analects.*" *Philosophy East and West* 62 (4), 2012.

McLeod, Alexus. *Astronomy in the Ancient World: Early and Modern Views on Astronomical Events.* New York: Springer, 2016.

McLeod, Alexus. *Theories of Truth in Chinese Philosophy: A Comparative Approach.* London: Rowman and Littlefield International, 2015.

McLeod, Alexus. "The Convergence Model of Philosophical Method in the Early Han." *International Communication of Chinese Culture* 3 (2), 2016.

Meggers, Betty J. "The Transpacific Origin of Mesoamerican Civilization: A Preliminary Review of the Evidence and Its Theoretical Implications." *American Anthropologist* 77 (1), March 1975, 1–27.

Menchú, Rigoberta. *I, Rigoberta Menchu: An Indian Woman in Guatemala.* London: Verso, 1984.

Milbrath, Susan. *Star Gods of the Maya: Astronomy in Art, Folklore, and Calendars.* Austin: University of Texas Press, 2000.

Miller, Mary and Karl Taube. *The Gods and Symbols of Ancient Mexico and the Maya: An Illustrated Dictionary of Mesoamerican Religion.* London: Thames and Hudson, 1993.

Molesky-Poz, Jean. *Contemporary Maya Spirituality: The Ancient Ways Are Not Lost.* Austin: University of Texas Press, 2006.

Monaghan, John. "Of Calendars and Computers: Comparing Mesoamerica and Bali." In Aveni ed. *The Measure and Meaning of Time in Mesoamerica and the Andes.* Cambridge, MA: Harvard University Press, 2015.

Mondlock, James. "K'ex: Quiché Naming." *Journal of Mayan Linguistics* 1 (2), 1980.

Montejo, Victor. *Maya Intellectual Renaissance: Identity, Representation, and Leadership.* Austin: University of Texas Press, 2005.

Montgomery, John. *Dictionary of Maya Hieroglyphs.* New York: Hippocrene Books, 2002.

Murata, Sachiko. *Chinese Gleams of Sufi Light: Wang Tai-yu's Great Learning of the Pure and Real and Liu Chih's Displaying the Concealment of the Real Realm.* Albany: SUNY Press, 2000.

Murata, Sachiko. *The Tao of Islam: A Sourcebook on Gender Relationships in Islamic Thought.* Albany: SUNY Press, 1992.

Nagel, Ernest. *The Structure of Science: Problems in the Logic of Scientific Explanation.* San Diego: Harcourt, 1961.

Newsome, Elizabeth. *Trees of Paradise and Pillars of the World: The Serial Stelae Cycle of 18-Rabbit-God K, King of Copan.* Austin: University of Texas Press, 2001.

Nylan, Michael. "Academic Silos, or, What I Wish Philosophers Knew About History" in Tan, ed. *Bloomsbury Handbook on Chinese Philosophy Methodologies.* London: Bloomsbury, 2016.

O'Neill, Megan. "Ancient Maya Sculptures of Tikal, Seen and Unseen." *Res: Anthropology and Aesthetics* 55/56, 2009.

O'Neill, Megan. *Engaging Ancient Maya Sculpture at Piedras Negras, Guatemala.* Norman: University of Oklahoma Press, 2012.

Parmington, Alexander. *Space and Sculpture in the Classic Maya City.* Cambridge: Cambridge University Press, 2011.

Pauketat, Timothy. *Cahokia: America's Great City on the Mississippi.* New York: Penguin, 2009.

Paxton, Meredith. *The Cosmos of the Yucatec Maya: Cycles and Steps from the Madrid Codex.* Albuquerque: University of New Mexico Press, 2001.

Pedersen, Mikkel, Anthony Ruter, Charles Schweger, Harvey Friebe, Richard Staff, Kristian Kjeldsen, Marie Mendoza, Alwynne Beaudoin, Cynthia Zutter, Nicolaj Larsen, Ben Potter, Rasmus Nielsen, Rebecca Rainville, Ludovic Orlando, David Meltzer, Kurt Hjaer, and Eske Willerslev. "Postglacial Viability and Colonization in North America's Ice-Free Corridor." *Nature* 537, September 2016. 45–49.

Pellicer, Sergio. *Maya Achi Marimba Music in Guatemala.* Philadelphia: Temple University Press, 2005.

Perkins, Franklin. "What is a Thing (*wu*)?" in Li and Perkins, eds. *Chinese Metaphysics and its Problems.* Cambridge: Cambridge University Press, 2015.

Perkins, Franklin. SEP Metaphysics article. 2015.

Perrett, Roy. *An Introduction to Indian Philosophy.* Cambridge: Cambridge University Press, 2016.

Peterson, Marshall, ed. *The Highland Maya in Fact and Legend: Francisco Ximénez, Fernando Alva de Ixtlilxóchitl, and Other Commentators on Indian Origins and Deeds.* Lancaster, CA: Labyrinthos, 1999.

Pharo, Lars. *The Ritual Practice of Time: Philosophy and Sociopolitics of Mesoamerican Calendars.* Leiden: Brill, 2014.

Phillips, Stephen. *Yoga, Karma, and Rebirth: A Brief History and Philosophy.* New York: Columbia University Press, 2009.

Pope Paul VI. *Mysterium Fidei.* Vatican City, 1965.

Prager, Christian, Beniamino Volta and Geoffrey Braswell. "The Dynastic History and Archaeology of Pusilha, Belize." In Braswell, ed. *The Maya and Their Central American Neighbors.* Abingdon: Routledge, 2014.

Proskouriakoff, Tatiana. *Maya History.* Austin: University of Texas Press, 1993.

Puett, Michael. *The Ambivalence of Creation: Debates Concerning Innovation and Artifice in Early China.* Palo Alto: Stanford University Press, 2001.

Queen, Sarah and John Major, trans. *Luxuriant Gems of the Spring and Autumn.* New York: Columbia University Press, 2016.

Radhakrishnan, Sarvepalli and Charles Moore, eds. *A Sourcebook in Indian Philosophy*. Princeton: Princeton University Press, 1957.

Reilly, F. Kent. "Olmec Iconographic Influences on the Symbols of Maya Rulership: An Examination of Possible Sources" in Fields, ed. *Sixth Palenque Round Table, 1986*. Norman: University of Oklahoma Press, 1991.

Rice, Prudence. *Maya Calendar Origins: Monuments, Mythistory, and the Materialization of Time*. Austin: University of Texas Press, 2009.

Rice, Prudence. *Maya Political Science: Time, Astronomy, and the Cosmos*. Austin: University of Texas Press, 2007.

Roys, Ralph, trans. *Rituals of the Bacabs*. Norman: University of Oklahoma Press, 1965.

Ruppert, Karl and John Denison. *Archaeological Reconnaissance in Campeche, Quintana Roo, and Petén*. Washington, DC: Carnegie Institution of Washington, 1943.

Sabloff, Jeremy and E. Wyllys Andrews. *Late Lowland Maya Civilization: Classic to Postclassic*. Santa Fe: School for Advanced Research Press, 1986.

Schaffner, "Approaches to Reduction." *Philosophy of Science* 34, 1967.

Schele, Linda and David Friedel. *A Forest of Kings: The Untold Story of the Ancient Maya*. New York: William Morrow, 1990.

Schele, Linda, David Friedel, and Joy Parker. *Maya Cosmos: Three Thousand Years on the Shaman's Path*. New York: William Morrow, 1993.

Schele, Linda. *Maya Glyphs: The Verbs*. Austin: University of Texas Press. 1982.

Scherer, Andrew. *Mortuary Landscapes of the Classic Maya: Rituals of Body and Soul*. Austin: University of Texas Press, 2015.

Schlesinger, Victoria. *Animals and Plants of the Ancient Maya: A Guide*. Austin: University of Texas Press, 2002.

Schwitzgebel, Eric. "Against Charity in the History of Philosophy." http://schwitzplinters.blogspot.com/2017/01/against-charity-in-history-of-philosophy.html.

Seler, Eduard. *Commentarios al Códice Borgia*. México: Fondo de Cultura Economica, 1988.

Sharer, Robert. *Daily Life in Maya Civilization*, 2nd ed. Westport, CT: Greenwood, 2009.

Sharer, Robert. *The Ancient Maya*, 6th ed. Redwood City: Stanford University Press, 2005.

Sidelle, Alan. "A Sweater Unraveled: Following One Thread of Thought for Avoiding Coincident Entities." *Nous* 32 (4), 1998.

Siderits, Mark. *Personal Identity and Buddhist Philosophy: Empty Persons*. Farnham: Ashgate, 2003.

Sim, May. *Remastering Morals With Aristotle and Confucius*. Cambridge: Cambridge University Press, 2007.

Solari, Amara. *Maya Spatial Biographies in Communal Memory and Cosmic Time: The Franciscan Evangelical Campaign of Itzman, Yukatan*. Ph.D. Dissertation, University of California, Santa Barbara. 2007.

Stephens, John Lloyd. *Incidents of Travel in Central America, Chiapas, and Yucatan*. London: J. Murray, 1842.

Stuart, David. "Kings of Stone: A Consideration of Stelae in Ancient Maya Ritual and Representation." *Res: Anthropology and Aesthetics* 29/30, 1996a.

Stuart, David. "Of Gods, Glyphs, and Kings: Divinity and Rulership Among the Classic Maya." *Antiquity* 70 (268), 1996b.

Stuart, David. "The Hieroglyphic Name of Altar U." Copan Note 4, 1986.

Tate, Carolyn. "The Poetics and Power of Knowledge at La Venta." in Koontz, Reese-Taylor, and Headrick eds. *Landscape and Power in Ancient Mesoamerica*. Boulder: Westview Press, 2001.

Tate, Carolyn. *Yaxchilan: The Design of a Maya Ceremonial City*. Austin: University of Texas Press, 1992.

Taube, Karl. "A Representation of the Principal Bird Deity in the Paris Codex." In *Research Reports on Ancient Maya Writing* 6. Washington, DC: Center for Maya Research, 1987.

Taube, Karl. "The Olmec Maize God: The Face of Corn in Formative Mesoamerica." *Res: Anthropology and Aesthetics* 29–30, 1996.

Tedlock, Barbara. *Time and the Highland Maya*. Albuquerque: University of New Mexico Press, 1985.

Tedlock, Barbara and Dennis Tedlock. *Teachings from the American Earth: Indian Religion and Philosophy*. New York: W.W. Norton, 1975.

Tedlock, Dennis. *Popol Vuh: The Definitive Edition of the Mayan Book of the Dawn of Life*. New York: Touchstone, 1996.

Thakchoe, Sonam. "The Theory of Two Truths in India." *Stanford Encyclopedia of Philosophy...* 2011.

Theodor, Ithamar and Zhihua Yao, eds. *Brahman and Dao: Comparative Studies of Indian and Chinese Philosophy*. Lanham, MD: Lexington Books, 2013.

Thompson, J. Eric. *Maya History and Religion*. Norman: University of Oklahoma Press, 1970.

Vail, Gabrielle and Christine Hernandez. *Re-Creating Primodial Time: Foundation Rituals and Mythology in the Postclassic Maya Codices*. Boulder: University Press of Colorado, 2013.

Van Norden, Bryan. "Problems and Prospects for the Study of Chinese Philosophy in the English-Speaking World." *APA Newsletter on Asian and Asian-American Philosophers and Philosophies* 15 (2), 2016.

Vankeerberghen, Griet. *The Huainanzi and Liu An's Claim to Moral Authority*. Albany: SUNY Press, 2001.

Vila Selma, José. *La mentalidad maya: textos literarios*. Madrid: Editora Nacional, 1981.

Villa Rojas, Alfonso. *Estudios etnológicos: los mayas*. México: UNAM, 1985.

Vogt, Evon. *The Zinacantecos of Mexico: A Modern Mayan Way of Life*. New York: Holt, Rinehart and Winston, 1970.

Walker, James (Jahner, ed.). *Lakota Myth*. Lincoln: University of Nebraska Press, 1983.

Witschey, Walter, ed. *Encyclopedia of the Ancient Maya*. Lanham, MD: Rowman and Littlefield, 2015.

Yu, Jiyuan. *The Ethics of Confucius and Aristotle: Mirrors of Virtue*. Abingdon: Routledge, 2007.

Zagzebski, Linda. "Exemplarist Virtue Theory." *Metaphilosophy* 41 (1), 2010.

Zimbardo, Philip. *The Lucifer Effect: Understanding How Good People Turn Evil*. New York: Random House, 2007.

Index

185

About the Author

Alexus McLeod is an associate professor of philosophy and Asian/Asian-American studies at the University of Connecticut. He is a specialist in Chinese and Comparative philosophy, as well as in Mesoamerican philosophy. He is the author of a number of books, including *Theories of Truth in Chinese Philosophy: A Comparative Approach* (Rowman and Littlefield International, 2015), and *Understanding Asian Philosophy: Ethics in the Analects, Zhuangzi, Dhammapada, and Bhagavad Gita* (Bloomsbury, 2014).